Japanese Portraits

Other Books by Donald Richie

ON FILM

The Japanese Film: Art and Industry, with Joseph L. Anderson, 1959
Japanese Movies, 1961
The Japanese Movie: An Illustrated History, 1965
The Films of Akira Kurosawa, 1965
Japanese Cinema, 1971
Ozu, 1976
Viewing Film, 1986
Japanese Cinema: An Introduction, 1990
A Hundred Years of Japanese Cinema, 2001

ON JAPAN

This Scorching Earth, 1956
Companions of the Holiday, 1968
The Inland Sea, 1971
A Lateral View, Essays, 1987
Tokyo Nights, 1988
Zen Inklings, 1992
The Honorable Visitors, 1994
Partial Views, Essays, 1995
The Temples of Kyoto, 1995
Lafcadio Hearn's Japan, 1997
Tokyo: A View of the City, 1999
The Memoirs of the Warrior Kumagai, 1999
The Donald Richie Reader (Ed. Arturo Silva)
Japanese Literature Reviewed, 2003
The Image Factory, 2003
A View from the Chuo Line: Stories, 2004
Japan Journals (1947-2004) (Ed. Leza Lowitz)

DONALD RICHIE

Japanese Portraits

Pictures of Different People

A series of intensely personal portraits of unforgettable
Japanese characters

TUTTLE PUBLISHING
Tokyo • Rutland, Vermont • Singapore

The original, unexpanded edition of this book was published by Kodansha International in 1987 in hardcover under the title *Different People*, and in paperback in 1991 as *Geisha, Gangster, Neighbor, Nun*.

First Edition, *Different People: Pictures of Some Japanese*, 1987
Second Edition, *Geisha, Gangster, Neighbor, Nun: Scenes from Japanese Lives*, 1991
Third Edition, augmented and enlarged, *Public People, Private People: Portraits of Some Japanese*, 1996
Fourth Edition, *Japanese Portraits: Pictures of Different People* 2005

Published by Tuttle Publishing, an imprint of Periplus Editions (HK) Ltd, with editorial offices at 364 Innovation Drive, North Clarendon, Vermont 05759 and 130 Joo Seng Road #06-01, Singapore 368357

ISBN 0-8048-3772-4
ISBN 978-0-8048-3772-9
ISBN 4-8053-0861-3 (for sale in Japan only)

Printed in Singapore

Distributed by:

Japan
Tuttle Publishing
Yaekari Building, 3F, 5-4-12 Osaki; Shinagawa-ku, Tokyo 141-0032
Tel: (813) 5437 0171; Fax: (813) 5437 0755
Email: tuttle-sales@gol.com

North America, Latin America & Europe
Tuttle Publishing
364 Innovation Drive; North Clarendon, VT 05759-9436
Tel: (802) 773 8930; Fax: (802) 773 6993
Email: info@tuttlepublishing.com
www.tuttlepublishing.com

Asia Pacific
Berkeley Books Pte Ltd
130 Joo Seng Road #06-01; Singapore 368357
Tel: (65) 6280 1330; Fax: (65) 6280 6290
Email: inquiries@periplus.com.sg
www.periplus.com

10 09 08 07 06
5 4 3 2 1

TUTTLE PUBLISHING® is a registered trademark of Tuttle Publishing.

For James Merrill

Contents

Foreword

The idea for this work came after much of it was written. From journal entries, diary jottings, failed stories and novels, I had accumulated a number of pages that appeared to be interesting, but I did not know how to use them. There seemed to be no form that would hold together pieces this various.

Then, as I was reading Marguerite Yourcenar's book on Mishima, I came across this passage: "A chain is formed of people different from one another, who are united, incomprehensibly, because we have chosen them." And I knew what this collection of mine was about and what form it should take.

I had for some time wanted to write of my years in Japan, more than half my life, but I did not want to write a memoir; those I had read seemed so explanatory, so self-serving. But here, by assembling a group of stray people who had lived on in memory, I saw a way of recording some of my own experiences without "exploiting" them. The deeper experiences might be excluded, but what perhaps counts most—the dappled surface of life itself—would be visible. And I would be there among the crowd.

I had no model for this book, though I much admired the collected character studies of the nineteenth-century Japanese writer Doppo Kunikida and his talent for what he called "sketching from life." But I did have a number of anti-models. These were those books on Japan which are written entirely in generalities. It is all them-and-us, and "the Japanese" who emerge from these works bear little resemblance to any Japanese I have ever known. I had become impatient reading about such all-explaining qualities as *giri* and *ninjo*, *hone* and *tatemae*, *ura* and *omote*, and all the rest of these abstractions. Such hypothetical opposites do exist in Japan, but they exist everywhere else as well. The terms describe theories, not people. In this collection, I wanted to draw particular likenesses undisturbed by theoretical considerations.

My methods vary. There are views from the outside, views from the inside; there are monologues and dialogues; interviews and impressionistic descriptions. If the techniques of fiction are used, they are employed only so that the likeness may the more clearly emerge. I am writing about people, not "a people"; a series of portraits of certain Japanese I have known personally, each of whom, being human, is unique.

Donald Richie

Hajimé Saisho

I awoke early that midsummer morning in 1946. The sun was not yet up and the eastern sky over the sleeping sea was dark. Walking toward the still surf over the cold sand, where I had walked the afternoon before, I suddenly stopped.

Something had changed. It had not been like this yesterday. Then there had been fishing boats and drying nets and people from the village. Now it was deserted and the beach was filled with mounds of sand, pocked with the large holes from which it came.

There were a number of them, these strange holes. I peered in the faint light, the eastern horizon now a hazy gray. There were perhaps twenty in all, as though a small army had dug in during the night.

Then, in the growing light, I saw that each of the holes seemed to be occupied. Something was lying in each. I ceased thinking about war and began to think about an invasion of creatures from the sea. It must be a migration of sea turtles, I decided, come to lay eggs.

Slowly I walked over the sand to the nearest and looked down. There, lying like a chick in its shell, was a small boy. In the next one too another was curled, and in the next. The beach was pitted with holes and in each was a sleeping child.

As the darkness drained from the sky, I stood in the middle of this foreign sandscape and wondered what had happened. It resembled a battlefield. The end of the Pacific war was just a year behind—thoughts of battles, bodies, came easily.

Then one of the small bodies stirred. A hand was thrown across the eyes. Overhead the sky was that dim, translucent gray which precedes dawn.

Another of the bodies, one further away, moved, and I saw a small knee shift. At the same time I was aware of the whisper of the surf, as though it too had just awakened, stirred by the growing day.

As the horizon warmed to a faint yellow, I moved across the still cold sand and looked into the holes. The children were all quite young. The eldest, in the largest hole, could have been no more than twelve or so. The youngest, in the mousehole he had dug himself, seemed only five or six. All were sleeping curled in their sand nests, all were alive, all now waking in the early light like the newly hatched.

The surf began to splash as though the unseen sun was working on it, and with a yawn a head appeared over the rim of sand, looked toward the east, then with a sigh disappeared. When I reached his burrow the child was again asleep, knees drawn up.

What were they doing, why were they here, I wondered, standing over this small, sleeping army. I was curious but not surprised. It was, after all, a magical land, as I had learned, a place where the mysterious often occurred. Just the day before, on arrival from Tokyo, we had walked along this beach—Kujukurihama, in Chiba—and I had stopped in surprise at the sight of the fishermen.

Young and old alike, they were utterly naked as they worked at their nets, helped by half-clad wives and sisters. Each of the men wore only a headband and, as I soon noticed, a narrow red ribbon around his penis.

They saw us there and smiled, nodded. Not at all self-conscious, they went on with their work.

– It's something to do with not offending the sea goddess, said one of us.

– Going naked like that?

– No, wearing the ribbon.

– I wonder if she's Benten, I said.

– But just look, it's like the Garden of Eden . . .

And now, on the next day, prepared for innocent magic, I stood above these sleeping children in the clear dawn of a midsummer morning.

All sign of the adults of the day before had gone, all the boats, all the racks for drying nets. It was as though the set had been dismantled, leaving only these inhabited sand castles as the scene of some strange nocturnal play.

A wave slapped and a child sat up, dark against the brilliant yellow east. Then another, and another, as if responding to a signal I could not see, some hidden sign. Soon all were awake, looking eastward, waiting.

I knew what they were waiting for. The sky shone in expectation, for there, in the wings of the ocean, was the sun itself, ready to make its due appearance.

As the sea swayed and lapped, each child, I saw, was now sitting formally, his legs beneath him. And as I gazed out across their ranks, it seemed as if those tiny figures had all been cut off at the waist and planted there, to face the sun.

Then, slowly, each half-child turned a solid black as—first a narrow, piercing sliver, then a growing, blinding wedge of light—the sun rose.

The boys, kneeling, looked ahead. I had perhaps expected them to bow or chant some prayer, but nothing happened. They knelt and watched the slow sun appear.

Overhead the plovers dipped and cried, as if also in answer to some summons. Then, when the sun, like some great radiant balloon, left its perch upon the sea and miraculously began to soar, the mysterious children stood up and, yawning, shaking off the sand, became themselves again.

One of them turned and saw me standing there. He stared without surprise, as if I were expected, then pulled on his baseball cap.

– What were you doing? I asked, as best I could.

And, unselfconsciously, as though he met white, round-eyed creatures every day on the beach, he explained as best he could. But my Japanese was primitive and he spoke with the ripest of country dialects. All the same, some understanding did pass between us, and now, knowing more, I can reconstruct what was said.

– We've been waiting for the dead, he would have answered: They come at dawn in big boats we can't see, and they're happy when they find us here, asleep. Then we take them back with us to our houses. That's where we're going now. You see, today is the first day of *Obon*.

Obon is the feast of the dead, a Buddhist rite held in the middle of summer, when the spirits are welcomed on their annual return to the land of the living and, three days later, bade farewell. There are round dances, the altars hold flowers, dumplings, fruit, and at the end there are lanterns to light the departing spirits on their way.

This was why the parents had moved their boats and taken down their racks and left nothing behind. They had swept the beach clean for the

3

arrival of these ancestors, the older generations, to be greeted by the new.

– Did you see them?

– No, but they see us. We sit and wait and they come and then we take them home.

– Where are they?

He smiled, a small boy's smile, proud of an accomplishment. Here, he said, indicating perhaps himself, perhaps the brilliant sky, the shining sand, the glittering sea—or nothing in particular.

Now all the little boys had gathered in a quiet ring, filled with their own importance. It was suddenly full morning and the surf slapped and the happy dead were all around us.

And that was forty years ago, that morning on the Chiba beach. Even the youngest of those children is now nearly half a century old. There are few boats left, fewer nets as well now that fish are to be caught only in the deep sea beyond, with heavy metal nets hauled in by motors. The fishermen wear jogging shorts or cut-off jeans; and there are no longer nests of small boys asleep in the sand as the sky slowly lightens and the silent surf brings in the barges of the dead.

But back then the now grown men were the new generation, each escorting an ancestor home for three days of dancing and music, food and company. And I was not that far distant in time from these children—only ten years older than the eldest, still young enough to feel the wonder of the daily rising sun, of the ceaseless ocean, of the notion that the dead return.

The boy, a plain country child, bowed and smiled—this country boy I never saw again, whose name I never knew (and for whom I have made one up), this child who remains for me, not a person since I never knew him, but a messenger.

Then he turned to the others and, like a flock of plovers, all instant accord, they flew off down the beach, weaving through the dunes, along the shouting sea, back to family, back to home.

And I, my shadow black behind me in the morning sun, turned to look at their sandy nests. Already the approaching tide was filling them in, one by one.

Yasunari Kawabata

The Sumida River, silver in the winter sun, glistened beneath us. We were on the roof of the Asakusa subway terminal tower, looking out over downtown Tokyo, still in ruins, still showing the conflagration of two years earlier, scorched concrete black against the lemon yellow of new wood.

This had been the amusement quarter of Tokyo. Around the great temple of Kannon, now a blackened, empty square, had once been a warren of bars, theaters, archery stalls, circus tents, peep shows, places I had read about where the all-girl opera sang and kicked, where the tattooed gamblers met and bet, where trained dogs walked on hind legs and Japan's fattest lady sat in state.

Now, two years after all of this had gone up in flames, after so many of those who worked and played here had burned in the streets or boiled in the canals as the incendiary bombs fell and the B-29s thundered over—now the empty squares were again turning into lanes as tents, reed lean-tos, and a few frame buildings began appearing. Girls in wedgies sat in front of new tea-rooms, but I could see no sign of the Fat Lady. Perhaps she had bubbled away in the fire.

What was he thinking, I wondered, looking at the avian profile of the middle-aged man standing beside me, outlined against the pale sky. I had no way of knowing. He spoke no English and I spoke no Japanese. I did not know that Yasunari Kawabata was already famous and would become more famous still. But I did know he was a writer who had written about Asakusa, and it was the place itself that interested me.

– Yumiko, I said. This was the name of the heroine of the novel *Asakusa Kurenaidan*, which Kawabata had written when—twenty years before, at about the same age as I was now, and just as enraptured with the place—he had walked the labyrinth and seen the jazz reviews, the kiss-dances, the White Russian girls parading, and the passing Japanese

5

flappers with their rolled stockings. It was here on this roof where we were standing that Yumiko had confronted the gangster, crushed an arsenic pill between her teeth, then kissed him full on the lips.

Perhaps he was thinking of his lost heroine—tough, muscled, beautiful. Or, as he gazed at that blackened landscape under this huge white winter sky, perhaps he was feeling a great sorrow. All those lives lost.

I looked at that birdlike profile. It did not seem sad. In fact, he smiled, peering over the parapet and pointing at the river.

This was where Yumiko, having given the man the kiss of death, slipped through the porthole of a waiting boat and sped away just as the river police arrived. I knew this without knowing any Japanese because as a member of the Allied Occupation forces I had translators at my command and had asked for an English précis of the novel. Now, looking at the author leaning over the railing, as Left-Handed Hiko had done when he saw Yumiko making her escape, I thought about Kawabata's love for Asakusa.

He had begun his book with the intention of writing "a long and curious story set in Asakusa . . . in which vulgar women predominate." It had perhaps been for him, as it was for me, a place that allowed anonymity, freedom, where life flowed on no matter what, where pleasure could casually be found, and where small rooms with paper flowers were rented by the hour.

Did he, I wondered, find freedom in flesh, as I had learned to? It was here, on the roof of the terminal, that Oharu had permitted herself to be kissed—and more—by members of the gang and had thus earned the title of the Bride of the Eiffel Tower. It was here that the Akaobikan, that group of red-sashed girls who in the daytime worked in respectable department stores, boasted about the bad things they did at night. Here that Umekichi disclosed that he had been raped at the age of six by a forty-year-old woman.

I wondered about all of this but had no way of asking. And soon, chilled by that great sky, we went down the steep stairs, companionable but inarticulate. I had given him an outing, he had given me his bird's-eye view of Asakusa.

I did not see Kawabata again for over ten years, and then, at a P.E.N.

conference, with the sun reflecting off the Sukiyabashi Canal just outside the big French windows, I was introduced to the white-haired man
who had been presiding.

– Oh, but we know each other, he said: We spent a very cold afternoon together ten years or so ago. I caught a cold. Was in bed for a
week.

He looked at me, kindly, inquisitively, and released my hand: I imagine he doesn't even remember me.

– But I do, I said.

– He speaks, said the writer in surprise. Then, to the others: There
we were, stuck up there, the old subway tower in Asakusa, and I didn't
know what to do about him. He was so enthusiastic and kept pointing
things out. And we couldn't talk.

– Tell me, I said, a decade-old curiosity surfacing: What were you
thinking of that day up on the roof ?

– I don't remember.

– But how did you feel about Asakusa's being burned to the ground?
You were seeing it for the first time since the end of the war.

– I'm not sure. Surprise maybe. Sadness probably."

He had gotten over it. I wasn't over it, even yet, and doubted I ever
would be. For me Asakusa had spread over the entire city, the country,
maybe even the whole world.

– And you, did you ever try translating *Asakusa Kurenaidan*? he asked.

– I never learned to read.

– Well, at least you learned to speak. We can talk, finally.

And he smiled, his white head birdlike against the light of the slow
canal and the distant clamor of Tokyo traffic.

But we did not continue the conversation. People were now pushing,
wanting to have a word with the famous novelist. We had already had
our talk. And whenever we met thereafter, Kawabata would cock his
head on one side and look at me quizzically, humorously, as though
we had something in common.

Ten years later, the translation of *House of the Sleeping Beauties*
appeared and I saw that Kawabata had been as true to his vision of
Asakusa as I had been to mine. Yumiko, or her daughter, was now in

7

this strange house in Kamakura where old men found their youth again in sleeping girls, in firm, dormant flesh.

And, later still, one day in 1972, a quarter of a century after we had stood on the tower and thought of Yumiko, I saw his face flash onto the television screen. Noted author dead, a suicide.

I could not believe it. Dead, yes, but not a suicide. How could anyone who so loved life, and sex, and Asakusa, kill himself? No, it was an accident. The body had been found in the bathroom, the water running. He had been going to take a bath. He had used the gas hose as a support, pulled it loose, was overcome. This I wanted to believe. I could hear the water running, and I remembered the silver of the Sumida, the muddy bronze of the Sukiyabashi Canal.

But in time I too came to believe that his was a suicide. The kiss of death—not arsenic but gas—had been chosen. Naked, Kawabata had stepped into the water just as Yumiko had slipped into the boat and got away.

Shozo Kuroda

Old Mr. Kuroda—Shozo his nicely old-fashioned given name, a neighbor—blinks. Old men blink like babies, as though not yet used to their eyes. His eyes widen, contract, then blink, each sight as though astonishing. He stares at me, stunned.

I stare back. Old people are faintly disreputable. We may feel sorry for them but at the same time we condemn, as if being this old, lasting this long, were somehow a social fault, a breach of etiquette.

His daughter sighs and wipes his chin, as she would that of a small child. And what is it now? she asks, turning, hearing his yammering: Oh, I see. That's nice. Then she looks away. She is speaking to him as he must have spoken to her when she was very young.

Later, while he is lying down, taking his childlike afternoon nap, she says that he has no *darashi*. Strong words: *darashi ga nai*. I know perfectly well what it means, but am not sure what it specifies.

Let me look it up in the dictionary. There. Slovenly, untidy, sloppy, disheveled, unkempt, slipshod, etc.—a list of attributes ending with, oddly: a loose fish. What could that be? One always learns something about one's own language from the Japanese–English dictionary.

And we have no comparable phrase in the West, where sloppiness is considered less of a sin and can even be seen as attractive, a sign, in young people, of naturalness, spontaneity, freedom from conservative restraint.

No virtue here, however, even—or particularly—among the young. No, certainly *not* attractive, here where everyone must pull his own weight, where nothing too different is tolerated for too long, where appearances are so much more important than truths.

Strong words, but she smiled as she said them, as one might when speaking of a child, someone you understand, forgive, love. And—she continued—he wet his bed the other night again. Talk about *darashi ga nai koto*. And who had to get up and change the bedding so that he

9

wouldn't be lying in it the whole night long? Another sigh—a fat forty, hopes blasted.

A situation reminiscent of an Ozu film—*Late Spring*, perhaps. But there the daughter still has her life before her. And there he is still a fine figure of a man. Ozu, being an artist, knew where to stop. No point in showing Setsuko Hara blowsy; no point in revealing Chishu Ryu drooling and incontinent. We already know. We sense the years ahead. Ozu need show us nothing more.

With Shozo, however, the disaster has already occurred. He has become disreputable, the way that accident victims appear. I remember an ex-landlady idly turning over the pages of a photography book and discovering a picture of survivors from the *Hindenburg*, dazed, clothes burned away. How horrid, she said, then, peering more closely: And what a way to appear in public!

A snort, a gurgle from the next room. Miss Kuroda knows all these signs as though they were a language. Oh, dear, she says: He's woken up. And here I was hoping he would sleep for an hour.

A shuffling sound. Then he reappears, kimono disheveled, sash dragging. A loose fish. Is surprised to see me. Blinks. Thinks I come every day. Is told it is the same day. Oh.

– Not long for this world. (This she says in front of him, and his trembling makes it seem that he is nodding in shocked agreement. Actually, he appears not to hear.)

I look at him and think of the brave days of Meiji when he was probably a fine figure of a man.

– Now, Father, do sit down. Don't just stand there. You'll tire yourself. See? Mr. Donald has brought us these nice pears. I'll peel you one.

She sets to work, her strong, manly fingers expert, the peel unwinding in one long strip. He waits, the corners of his mouth moist.

Of what does he remind me? A baby watching candy being unwrapped? A dog watching its dinner being made? Me, under the Christmas tree, watching tissue paper being removed—or me at a later age watching clothes being taken off?

– There now, isn't that nice?

Prettily quartered, the pear is set before him. His hand hesitates, then conveys a chunk to his mouth. His eyes close. He seems to smile.

- Juicy, she says, wiping his lips with her handkerchief. Then she straightens his kimono, reties his sash, makes him presentable.

He blinks, gums the fruit, smiles at me. Thanking me—with his mouth, not his eyes. They are far away, looking at things long past, the blank eyes of someone who has seen everything and still continues to look.

The view is suitably autumnal, with a bright blue sky, the red of the ripe persimmon, and the light yellow of bleached grass. The pears are the very last of the season. And I remember the view half a year ago, the pale sky of summer and the deep green of the grass.

She had sat there, on the same cushion. We had been gossiping about a younger woman in the neighborhood who had lost her patron— apoplexy. She laughed lightly, then suddenly frowned.

- And what will happen to me once he goes? she wondered.

I misunderstood, thinking she might be referring to too little money, too much freedom. But this wasn't what she meant.

- What shall I do? *Nani o shimashoka?* (Precisely—and she could as well have asked: Who shall I be?)

Old Mr. Kuroda slowly swallows, staring at 1900. His daughter looks at her hands, spreads her fat fingers. And I gaze at them both, caught for an instant in the sunshine of a late autumn.

Mono no aware, the pathos of things. You accept it, you even in a small way celebrate it, this evanescence. You are to observe what is happening, and be content that things are proceeding as they must, and therefore should. Very traditional this, and quite a nice idea. I wonder if it was ever anything more.

Old Shozo Kuroda looks into the sun, his eyes blinking, his lips still working, his mouth curved as though in a smile. There is no simple cut to "The End," no surge of music to indicate a final cadence. Life, not being art, knows no such conventions.

Yasujiro Ozu

Though I had met Ozu several times before, at Shochiku parties mostly, I had never watched him work. Very few had—Ozu did not like visitors. But with a kind friend's help, the director was prevailed upon to let the foreign critic visit the set.

One of the Ofuna studios was filled with a full-scale Japanese inn: two eight-mat rooms, beyond them a courtyard, and on the far side the full three floors of a wing of the inn. Here Ozu was making *Late Autumn*.

I knew a bit about the film. Its structure was similar to *Late Spring*, made eleven years before: a daughter gets married and leaves her single parent behind alone. In the earlier film (played by Setsuko Hara), she left her father on his own (Chishu Ryu). Now, the mother (Setsuko Hara) would be left behind by her daughter (Yoko Tsukasa).

Just as Ozu's themes were always much the same, so his methods had become consistent: an almost unvarying camera position, a single means of punctuation—the straight cut. And just as fades in and out and dissolves were spurned, so in these later films the camera was not allowed to turn (pan) or to move about (dolly). Out of these restrictions would come a film that was free and filled with life. I wanted to see how it was done.

When I was brought in, the actors had just completed the first part of the scene slated for that day. Chishu Ryu (this time playing Setsuko's brother-in-law, owner of the inn) had finished his lines and was sitting on one side, watching, as I had heard he often did.

After a cigarette, Ozu was ready to continue. The next episode had Setsuko and Yoko, mother and daughter, sitting opposite each other at a low table. The camera was about three feet off the floor (its habitual position—eye level when you sit down), facing one of the actresses.

Ozu's method was to do one side of the conversation and then the other. Since the alternative approach would have been to turn the camera around for each cut, the method was logical—but Ozu's way of doing it was quite his own. Each line of dialogue was considered a unit in its own right and was to be shot with reference only to itself. This is quite different from the way such scenes are shot elsewhere. While it is common enough for the two sides of a conversation to be filmed separately, the director usually does not stop the camera after each line. The camera records the dialogue, both the feed-lines and the replies, and the whole is edited for the finished picture.

Ozu recorded each line. He started the camera, then stopped it. His script lay open before him and he used it like a blueprint, constantly referring to it and to the sketches he had made in the margins, one drawing for each line of dialogue.

The camera was turned toward Setsuko Hara. Ozu nodded at Yoko Tsukasa, sitting to one side, and she delivered her line of dialogue. Start, said Ozu, and his camera, Yuharu Atsuta, squatting behind his machine, began filming. The director nodded at Setsuko, who said her line. Cut, said Ozu, and Atsuta stopped filming.

The director was apparently satisfied with the delivery and went on to the next line. Not always, however; several times during these afternoon hours of shooting he would make one or the other of the actresses repeat her line.

One cut finished, one line of dialogue completed, Ozu began getting ready for the next. The conditions seemed in all respects identical but Ozu would nonetheless reframe each cut. Hara had not moved, yet Ozu, looking through the viewfinder, insisted on a shift of half a millimeter to the right. When I saw the finished film I noticed that in some cuts Yoko's hand towel at the bottom of the screen was more visible than in others, but generally the effect would be visible to the director alone.

Reframing completed to his satisfaction, Ozu was ready to go on to the next line of dialogue. Cut. The camera was fiddled with. In reply to a nod from the director, Yoko made weeping sounds. Start.

– What a nice trip we've had, said Setsuko and then wiped her eyes.

That was the end of her side of the conversation. After a break for tea, the camera was reversed, Setsuko sat to one side and delivered her lines again, and all of Yoko's lines were filmed. This took the rest of the day.

Everyone was exhausted. What a way to make a film! There were no congratulations, such as are commonly given to an actor after pulling off a difficult bit of dialogue, none of the air of celebration or dejection that greets the completion of a sequence. There was no exhilaration, no despair—no visible emotion at all. It was carpentry. Yet, when I later saw this sequence in the preview room, I marveled.

Here was an assemblage of small segments made over several days at a speed so slow that any idea of pace or even performance was virtually impossible. Here were scenes of two women talking to no one, reacting to nothing. And yet, up there on the screen, one saw life itself, life with its own rhythm, its own rarefied reality. Ozu's calculations as to camera angle, camera distance, delivery, timing—everything was there, but it was no longer apparent. It had been transformed. What had been a blueprint was now a completed dwelling, lived in.

I thought of a pointillist painting—a Seurat I had seen at an exhibition a few days earlier. When you viewed it up close, it was all dots of different colors. Only when you stepped back did the dots merge and the illusion of life appear. And that is what you do in an Ozu film. You step back. And paradoxically it brings you closer. Through the maintenance of distance, intimacy is achieved. Perhaps consequently, the fewer the means, the greater the effect.

Two women, mother and daughter, sitting together in 1960 in an inn at a Japanese hot-spring resort. A three-minute conversation during which nothing much gets said. But through it one comprehends filial affection as though for the first time, and gazes at the deep, hidden pattern that has been made visible.

– Don't even think of crying, I remember him telling Yoko: Just suddenly put your face in your hands—that's quite enough.

Setsuko Hara

She must be in her sixties, Japan's "eternal virgin"—so billed, even now, in the continuing references to her in magazines, newspapers; even now, more than twenty years after her disappearance.

That 1963 disappearance was a scandal. She had been the most beloved of film stars, her handsome face, accepting smile, known to all. And then, suddenly, rudely, without a word of apology, she was going to disappear—to retire.

Here, where the stars hang on, voluntary retirement is unknown, particularly for one the caliber of Setsuko Hara. She had become an ideal: men wanted to marry someone like her; women wanted to be someone like her.

This was because on the screen she reconciled her life as real people cannot. Whatever her role in films—daughter, wife, or mother—she played a woman who at the same time, somehow, was herself. Her social roles did not eclipse that individual self, our Setsuko.

In Ozu's *Late Spring* she wanted to remain a daughter, did not want to become a wife. Staying on with her father was enough. But eventually she married and through it all she showed her real self. In *Late Autumn*, a 1960 version of the 1949 film, she played the parent rather than the daughter. She was now a mother, a widow, who realizes that it is best that her daughter get married, though it means that she herself will be lonely. And through it all she showed her real self.

This she did by transcending the limitations imposed on her. She won her freedom by realizing that it is only within limitations that the concept of freedom is relevant. She accepted.

At the conclusion of *Tokyo Story* she is talking with the younger daughter, who has been upset by her elder sister's behavior at the funeral. She would never want to be like that, she says: That would be just too cruel.

The daughter-in-law, Setsuko Hara, agrees, then says: It is, but children get that way . . . gradually.

– Then . . . you too? says the daughter.

– I may become like that. In spite of myself.

The daughter is surprised, then disturbed as she realizes the implications:

– But then . . . isn't life disappointing?

And Setsuko smiles, a full, warm, accepting smile:

– Yes, it is.

She welcomed life, accepted its terms. In the same way she welcomed her role, absorbed it into herself, left the precious social fabric intact. No matter that her words were written and her actions directed by Yasujiro Ozu. This screen persona became hers and, in any event, Ozu would not have created his character this way had it not been Setsuko Hara for whom he was writing.

Thus, on the screen, she did not disturb harmony, she created it. And in this harmony she found herself. It was for this that she was so loved.

Even her being an "eternal virgin" (never marrying, never having children in a country where fertile wedlock is almost mandatory) was never held against her. She was not, after all, an old maid. No, she was that positive thing, an eternal virgin.

And then this sudden retirement. And the way she did it. She simply announced it. This was no way for an Ozu character to behave.

Great was the outcry. Her studio, for which she was the major box-office attraction, tried every blandishment. She stood firm against them all. The critics, who had formerly adored her, were hurt, insulted—there was talk of her being *onna rashikunai*, un-womanlike. Them she ignored.

And then there was what she said, the reasons she gave. She implied that she had never enjoyed making films, that she had done so merely to make enough money to support her large family, that she hadn't thought well of anything she had done in the films, and now that the family was provided for she saw no reason to continue in something she didn't care for.

This was conveyed in the Setsuko Hara style, to be sure, with some show of hesitation, sudden smiles shining through the doubt, but this was one Hara performance, the only one, that was not appreciated.

For the first time since her 1935 debut she was severely criticized, not so much for wanting to retire as for the manner in which this desire was presented. There was no polite fiction about the cares of age—she was only forty-three—or about bad health or about a burning desire to take up charitable work, or a spiritual imperative that she enter a nunnery. Nothing of the sort—only a statement that sounded like the blunt truth.

She was never forgiven. But press and public were allowed no further opportunity to display their disappointment, for she never again appeared.

Where had she gone? It was as though she had walked from that final press conference straight into oblivion. But of course there is no such thing as oblivion in Japan. She was shortly discovered living by herself, under her own name—not the stage one chosen by studio officials—in a small house in Kamakura, where many of her films had been set. And there she remains, remote but still the most publicized of recluses, with readers of the daily or weekly press knowing what she buys when she shops, how often her laundry is visible each week, and which of her old school friends she sees.

Occasionally a photo is attempted, but her past experience has made her quick to sense intruders, and the picture is always taken from so far away and the high-speed film is so grainy that it could be one of any elderly woman airing the bedding or hanging out the wash.

Over the years since her retirement, public anger, pique, and disappointment have all faded. Only a hard-core curiosity has remained. This, and a new admiration.

It now seems, particularly to younger women, that this actress truly reconciled her life. Truly, in that though she played all the social roles—daughter, wife, and mother—she only played them in her films. They were inventions, these roles. They did not eclipse that individual self, our Setsuko. And in this way she exposed them for the fictions that they are.

She did not allow them to define her; rather, she defined herself. And she did this by setting up her own limitations, not those of her fictitious roles. Her real limitations are the self-determined ones of the little Kamakura house, the daily round, the visits with her women friends. Only within such chosen limits is the concept of any real self at all relevant.

And so Setsuko Hara/Masaé Aida continues as legend—to those of her own time and to the young women who came later. And a legend exerts a compulsive attraction for others, whether it wants to or not.

Thus, many times have photos been sought, many times have parts on screen or tube been offered, and only too often has the little house in Kamakura been approached. The answer is always the same—the door of the little house has been slammed in the intruders' faces.

Even when a group of former friends and co-workers appeared. A documentary was being made about the life and films of Yasujiro Ozu, Hara's mentor and the director who perhaps best captured, or created, this persona. Wouldn't she please appear in it? For the sake of her dead *sensei*? No door was slammed this time. It was politely closed. But the answer was still no.

Fumio Mizushima

We were in Ueno, in a small *nomiya*, a traditional place serving saké and *shochu*, run by an old woman originally from the country, years in the city. Drinking places like hers were now rare.

- And how much longer? she wondered: Land prices what they are nowadays. It's all tall buildings and cocktail bars and, what do they call them, "snacks"?

Fumio nodded, agreeing. Though he was only twenty he liked old things—did not read *manga* comic books or play *pachinko* pinball; rather, read historical romances and could play *shogi* chess. I had once taken him to the No, which wasn't a success; but *Seven Samurai* was.

He was, I thought, much like the dissidents of the Meiji era, over a hundred years ago. They had seen the destruction of their civilization. They attempted to keep at least some old things. They saw what was happening.

I was well into my fourth bottle of saké. Blinking, I turned to look at him, his profile as clean against the *shoji* as the face on a Meiji medal: young, lean, innocent—yes, noble, a newly civilized savage. And here we were, drinking in Ueno but still part of Meiji, and it was all so beautiful that—I upset the saké bottle.

- *Ma, ma*, said the old woman, mopping. She then refilled my cup and his glass—straight *shochu*—and recalled a story, as she often did, remembering that I liked tales from the past.

- Did I tell you about this man? Well, he had no religion or anything. And one night on his way home from Ueno he took the path across Shinobazu Pond, and he stopped because he had to take a leak, you see. Well, he'd been drinking and he didn't watch what he's doing and he pissed straight onto a big stone, the one that's shaped like a priest, hood and all, when you look at it from the front. Well, that stone is right off to the side of the island that Benten protects and you know what a powerful goddess she is. And this stone, why, it belongs to Bishamon, or one of them at any rate. So he was emptying his bladder like that, and he suddenly felt funny. And then all at once it was bright morning, and he was miles away in Ikebukuro standing there in front of everyone with this thing in his hand. Well, he was truly shocked, he was. But he got back home on the Yamanote Line and everybody marveled. And after that he stopped drinking and turned religious.

I laughed loudly at the story but Fumio marveled, shaking his head, turning to smile, enjoying himself, finishing his *shochu*—strong as vodka—and holding up his glass for more.

Just as I was beginning what must have been my sixth bottle, and was trying to tell the patient old woman why she reminded me of my mother, I noticed that the stool next to mine was empty, that Fumio was gone. Must have gone to the toilet, I remember thinking. But when I went to look he wasn't there. He had vanished.

I became worried—drunk and worried, a terrible combination. Where could my friend have gone? Having paid the old woman I wandered out into the street, all neon and chrome and traffic.

Then I climbed the stairs to the park. Where could he be? He had vanished as suddenly, as completely, as had the man in the story. I gazed hopelessly down the deserted avenues, lined with trees, disappearing into darkness.

A temple loomed. This was where the Ueno War had been fought, where many young Meiji men had been shot. Bullets were still in the temple gates. Their blood was still part of the soil over which I was now walking—staggering. And where was Fumio with his smile, his profile, his respect for the past?

A long flight of stairs down which I carefully picked my way, then, before me, a larger expanse of darkness, Shinobazu Pond. The withered lotus stalks whispered in the light breeze. In the distance a clock was striking midnight.

I was lost, alone, would never find him, would wander the dark park forever. Dead drunk, near tears, wondering at the hopelessness of life, I staggered to the shrine.

There he was, illuminated by a distant streetlight, legs apart, pissing on a large rock.

I stood, watching, unwilling to interrupt.

He finished, seemed to be waiting.

Then, slowly, his shoulders slumped.

I called his name.

We stood there in front of the Benten shrine, clinging to each other. Then he began to cry and so, therefore, did I.

– I just wanted to know, he said between sobs: I just wanted to find out. I just wanted there to be something.

I held him, patted his back, felt like a father.

– I wanted there to be something. Anything. Just anything.

Again I patted his back. Then the back heaved and Fumio squatted and was very sick.

I stood and looked at the stars over the black roof of the shrine and thought of many things: of gods and goddesses and sacred rocks, of young men with no fathers, of the consuming thirst for authenticity, and of being lost in a world in which only the body seems to have any reality.

Tadashi Nakajima

Slowly, as the summer light faded, they came, singly, in pairs, in groups, the young men of Fuchu. They came from the lanes and country roads leading into town, joined others at streets and avenues, then marched abreast, past the high school and the town hall. Like rivulets trickling into creeks, then merging to form a river, the young men of Fuchu streamed into the center of the town, where the shrine was.

The setting sun cast their shadows far ahead. The men were barefoot, wore only loincloths and sometimes a towel twisted around the head to keep the sweat from falling in their eyes. For this was a Shinto ritual toward which they were moving, a ritual that purified, and here one must be naked.

This was the famous Yami Matsuri of Fuchu, the Festival of Darkness, and it occurred once a year late in the summer. All the young men from this town outside Tokyo and the surrounding countryside came walking through the dying light, making for the central shrine where the great *kami*, deity of darkness, waited.

I too had wanted to join in, curious—had read about it, asked around, and now, having parked the jeep just outside town, was following the naked men, their numbers growing as street turned into avenue. Soon we were too many for the sidewalks, were walking down the middle of the asphalt toward the shrine, somewhere ahead of us.

The shops, the homes were already lit and people stood and stared at all these men and me, the only one in clothes, while we paraded past. As our numbers swelled, they retreated to watch from open doorways, windows. And I, among the crowd, became aware of the odor of those around me: a clean smell—of rice, and skin.

They in turn were aware of me, a foreign object in their midst. But they were also busy, intent upon the coming rite, and so a glance or two was all I received—no words at all, no questions as to what I was doing there.

I was there because I wanted to see, to experience, for myself. This was why I had driven far into the countryside and found the place, and why I was now one of them, walking through the dusk as though I knew where I was going.

But I did not need to know. The press was now so great that I was going wherever it went. There was no stepping aside, much less turning back. I was caught in this flowing river, surrounded by men who knew where they were going. Our shoulders touched as we walked, our hands collided as we swung our arms.

The sky had deepened, and all at once it was completely dark. Nine o'clock, and someone had pulled the main switch at the power station. This was the signal, the ritual had begun.

Even with eyes closed I would have known. With the instant black there was a sudden tension, like the stopped-short intake of a breath. No sooner had this jolted, body to body, throughout these hundreds than the march became a jostle.

Pushed, I lurched to one side, then the other. Those behind pressed with their hands to move me faster, and I found my palms against the bare flesh of those in front. The walk turned into a ragged trot and from blindness I returned to sight—a partial night sight, with the white of loincloths in front and, farther off, glimpsed through black trotting bodies, others as though phosphorescent in the night, and above and beyond them the summer stars.

All else was sound and smell. I saw nothing of the sudden hand that struck my side, the bare foot that heedless trod on mine. I felt flesh now close, and smelled it and heard its slap as all of us ran forward, blind, into the night. My shod foot came down, hard if innocent, and I heard the jerk of breath, the exclamation choked, cut off.

There was then a sudden tightening of all these limbs, as torsos crushed together like cattle roaring through a gorge, and I looked up and saw against the sky the great black beam passing overhead. It was a *torii*, a shrine gateway we were passing through. Then, a blacker darkness, overhanging on either side like cliffs—perhaps rows of cypress, cedar, the outskirts of the shrine.

And now a sound was growing. Jostled, hands before me, palms out, fearing collision, fearing falling, I heard it as a growling coming nearer as we raced along. But I was wrong—it was us.

It was the festival chant, heard when pulling the great wheeled float or shouldering the *omikoshi*, but now—no longer redolent of effort—it was pure sound, like surf, like wind in the pines. *Yu-sha, yu-sha, yu-sha*—repeated endlessly, a chain of sound on which we moved, our steps running to its beat. It was all around, filling my eyes and nose as well as ears. And then I heard it deep inside me. It was coming from myself as well.

Possession. We were all possessed by this deity toward whom we were rushing. Chanting, I recalled what I had heard. A Shinto deity and thus without features, name, or disposition—simply a *kami* like the myriad others—this one, however, retained a quality. He—the gender seemed inevitable—liked darkness. Just as the sequestered *kami* in the carried *omikoshi* loved to be jostled and jerked about, tossed and turned, so this god adored the dark and all that happened there.

Abruptly, there was a sharp wrench, a fracture in our chant as though a windpipe had been seized, and the crush was suddenly so great that I was lifted off my feet. We were passing through a narrower gate, I guessed, and into the compound of the shrine itself.

Then there were cries from up ahead and the sound of scuffles, and the chant was broken off; the bodies about me pressed hard into mine, and our whole enormous mass rolled to a halt.

We were in the shrine and from its other gates had pushed in gangs as large as ours; we had collided as we had for generations past, and those left outside were still pushing, pushing their way inside.

I had, I now realized, lost both shoes. My shirt was open, buttons torn away, and I was so flattened against someone's back that we seemed fused together.

At the same time I suddenly heard the silence. It was as startling as any noise. Utter darkness; complete silence. I moved my head away from it as one moves back from a too bright light. But it was not the silence of solitude, though just as complete. It was vastly peopled, and in it I was slowly being crushed by all these bodies. And the pressure became greater and greater as those outside forced their way in, fighting to join the swarm, to become one with it.

While I could still see in the phosphorescent dark, while I too could chant and run with the rest, then I had been exhilarated. But now in the sudden grip of alien skin and muscle, beginning to feel the sweat seeping out of me, sensing the seams of my clothing pulling, then giving with the strain, I became afraid.

What was I doing here in the midst of all these strangers?—a different race, animated by different thoughts and different feelings. Perhaps they could tolerate such barbarous ceremonies as this, but not I. I must escape. There must be some way out of this solid multitude. I thought of Tokyo, of the jeep. And in a few hours I was thinking of home, America.

For in these hours there had been no movement, none was possible. The only sensation was the gradually steadying pressure which now made even breathing hard. That and the few small shifts that occur when water freezes, when a plant expands. The body next to mine had suddenly found a way to turn, a movement as sudden and as meaningless as a bubble of trapped air rising swiftly to the surface.

My imprisoned hands were now a part of someone else. Moving my fingers, I felt warm, damp flesh—someone's back perhaps. Behind me a thigh shifted. Then a weight on my shoulder, the quick fall of a head—the man beside me—as though it had been severed, or as though the man had died, crushed to death, upright.

There we stood, rooted like trees. And I was terrified, seeing myself trapped here forever. There was no pushing my way free, no climbing over heads and shoulders or crawling between legs to find a way out. To sink to the ground could only mean a final, hopeless fall.

Thus my imagination gripped me. But since there was truly no escape, I just stood there and, with the other trees, endured. Then, as the hours passed, I felt rather than heard a new chant—low, soft, rhythmic, a measured breathing. With it came, at first almost indiscernibly, a gentle movement, as though this packed and standing forest was being swayed by a distant breeze.

As the chant gained, the swaying grew. Damp, hard limbs, a hip perhaps or a shoulder, rubbed me like a branch. And as the night deepened, we chanted—*yu-sha, yu-sha, yu-sha.*

I felt my fear depart. It lifted slowly and I thought no more about our differences. We were now a single mass crammed into this narrow vessel, and there was no telling us apart.

Cradled, we were slowly merging. This I knew, looking up at the dusty stars, losing all feeling in arms, in legs, smelling the hot rice odor which was now mine as well. I, the man I thought I knew, was gone, become a thousand others. I let my head drop.

It fell across a shoulder or a neck and I realized that I was floating. My feet were no longer on the ground. The pressure had pushed me up, and I was being held aloft by this tight network of bodies, swaying but supporting.

There was no more fear of falling. For the first time I no longer fought for my inch of earth. I lay back and with this came support as more and more of those swaying bodies accepted more and more of me. Or so I felt. But at the same time I knew, an ear suddenly against my cheek, that I was in turn supporting them. And then . . .

And then, I suppose, I must have slept. The deity had had his way with us. His darkness had made us one. Perhaps we all slept, slung in the air, soles off the ground—whole thousands levitating.

I remember only, after a long, long time, raising my head and seeing that pale glow which is earliest morning. Seeing also the breathing profile of the boy asleep beside me, turning and looking deep into his armpit, for his arm was flung about my neck. And I shut my eyes again, not wanting to move, to wake up. I shut my eyes as one pulls the covers over one's head, unwilling to rise.

What had terrified me now consoled me. How secure, how safe, how warm, those bodies molding mine, those several near, those hundreds farther off. This was as it should have been. Like cells we were within a single form, all breathing, all feeling together. And now it was being alone I dreaded—once more, exposed.

Yet, one by one, all of us were waking up. And those at the farthest ends, whole miles away it seemed, were now stumbling off; slowly the pressure was growing less. I was standing on the ground, the earth strange against my soles, and shortly I could turn and even stoop to retrieve parts of my trampled clothing, the jeep keys still there in the pocket, safe.

The man in front whose back I knew so well stirred and turned. The man behind released me, his flesh becoming separate. The boy whose armpit I had studied was now a plain farmhand who gave a sleepy smile, turned to look for his lost loincloth, searched, gave up.

Then, completely naked, or with dirty loincloths newly tied, or, in my case, the rags of a shirt and most of a pair of trousers, we moved slowly away from each other and out into the brightening day.

We walked, stumbled, streaked with sweat, with dirt, as though new-born and unsure on our feet, as though our eyes, blinded by the dark so long, were not fully open. There was no smell—except for that of urine, pungent, but not unclean. And now I could see, revealed in the gaps in the thinning crowd, that we were making for the font, the great stone urn in front of every shrine, where we could drink.

When my turn came I pushed my whole head into that cold, holy water, taking great gulps as though I were breathing it. I came up dripping and the farmboy led me off to a veranda.

There, on the edge of this large but ordinary shrine, we sat, uncovered in the morning light, and watched the others, our comrades, ourselves, vanish into the empty streets, each alone, silent, surrounded now only by space.

I felt lost, as though my family were deserting me, as though the world were ending, and when an old priest in his high lacquered hat came by, saw the white foreigner, stopped, surprised, then smiled, I asked: And is the *kami* happy?

He nodded, affirmed. The *kami* was happy.

It did not occur to me to ask, as it certainly would have twelve hours before, just what this ceremony was all about anyway and why we should stand there all night and why nothing had happened, or had it?

And so we sat there, recovering, and the priest with his little acolytes, either up early or up all night, brought us small cups of milky ceremonial saké; and the farmer's son, whose raw young body I knew as well as I knew my own, turned with a smile, not at all surprised that I spoke, and asked me my name.

I told him, then asked his. He told me. What was it? Tadao . . . Tadashi? Nakajima . . . Nakamura?

But before long the sun was up, the streets were emptying. Cleansed, tired, staggering, satisfied young men were going off by the hundred, their shadows long behind them. And I found the jeep just as I had left it, and was surprised that the engine turned over—that the gasoline had not evaporated during my century asleep—and drove back to Tokyo, disheveled, content, at peace.

Over the following year I often thought of this experience. And of the single person it had somehow become: Tadashi Nakajima . . . was that his name? Somehow it now seemed to belong to the whole experience, it was the name of everything, of everybody.

And a year later I went back, not because of young Tadashi, whose face I had quite forgotten, whose very name was blurred. No, because of this experience and what it had meant to me.

But now it was 1947, and already the local authorities were cleaning things up. Such relics as the Yami Matsuri did not look right in this new and modern age. Barbaric they seemed, and it couldn't have been good for the health of those poor boys jammed together in the shrine all night long.

So hundreds of years of history were brought to an end, the chain of generations severed. The Festival of Darkness was stopped—I had attended, become a part of, the very last.

Oh, Fuchu still has a Yami Matsuri of sorts—even now, forty years later—but it is not the real one and the *kami* is not, I believe, happy. This god is happy only when people return to their real state, when humans again become human, when we are as we truly are. And this can occur only in darkness and in trust.

Yukio Mishima

We often met during the summer before his death. All of Mishima's friends saw more of him during that 1970 summer. He phoned more, wrote more letters, paid more attention to us. He was going away and would not see us again, but that we did not know then.

One late summer day he called again and asked me to join him at the Tokyo Hilton, a hotel he liked. Here he could, apparently unrecognized, book a room for writing or for other purposes.

He was not alone. With him was a young man whom I did not know but whose type I recognized. Limp, callow, probably literary—the kind of youth who resembled the young Mishima himself, the sort to whom the author now extended part of his patronage.

We sat in the mirrored bar and talked, and it became clear that the youth, a literary major (French), was a present for me. I was to continue, to take over, the patronage. Mishima told me this while the young man looked modestly down at his folded hands.

I laughed and said: Yukio, this will not do. You know me better than that. If you want to give me a present it should be someone from the other half of those you patronize.

But he did not know me better than that, though we had known each other for almost twenty years. The reason was that he rarely took one's character into account, scarcely even noticed it. It was not important. What was important was the role one was to play in his life. Mishima himself decided what this was to be. Who one actually was, how one really felt, had little to do with it.

Kawabata was to be the older protector, looking after the young author's interests, and was not to be hurt in the slightest when that relationship was falsified in *Forbidden Colors*. Donald Keene was to be major foreign critic, interested only in the work and allowed not a single glimpse, assuming he would have wanted one, into the private life. I, on the other hand, along with a few others, was to be of service only in the private life, and whatever opinions I might have of the work and the writer were not to be taken seriously.

My refusal upset him. He frowned at himself in the mirror. I was not playing my assigned role, that of confidant to the hero. He is a very serious boy, he said seriously. I laughed, but there was no answering smile. Mishima, though he could be amusingly malicious, had no feeling for humor. Unlike many Japanese he also had little sense of the ridiculous. His great barking laugh was not infectious; it was a statement of amusement, not amusement itself.

This conversation was carried on in front of its subject, but this embarrassed neither of us. For one thing, such is common in Japan; for another, we were speaking English, a language presumably not understood by the young man. That I had declined the gift, however, embarrassed Mishima, who had apparently been talking up my qualifications.

The awkwardness was resolved by sending the youth away after he had enjoyed a glass of fresh orange juice, and then settling for a talk. I remember this talk in particular because it was literary, and Mishima and I almost never spoke of literature since that was not included in the province he allotted me.

Sometimes we had strayed into the literary marshes surrounding our subject: his lifelong admiration for Huysmans; his monograph on Saint Sebastian and his translation of the drama about him by D'Annunzio; his favorite modern novel, *Hadrian's Memoirs*; and of course his own *Confessions of a Mask*, a work I thought his best, indeed—though I never told him this—his only successful work.

Today, however, he talked about Hemingway. This rather surprised me. He was a writer whom Mishima had disliked to a marked degree, either because of, or in spite of, similarities: both of them conscious stylists, both romantics given to *macho* posturings, both subscribers to obsolete codes. As it turned out, however, it was the American's suicide that interested the Japanese. He might still dislike him as a writer, he said, but he had come to admire the man. He now found him consistent, he said, "all of a piece"—and this he found admirable.

As indeed he might. Mishima himself, ever since I had known him, had been engaged in creating a person called Mishima who would be all of a piece. This new person was to be predicated on everything that the old person was not. The stutterer would become fluent in languages; the introverted adolescent, a Kendo champ; the ninety-seven-pound weakling, a body-builder and father of two children. It was a most impressive achievement. But death was needed, finally, to make a man all of a piece.

And this was what we were talking of, though at the time I did not know it. From Hemingway he moved the conversation to Takamori Saigo, the nineteenth-century military hero who had sought to reestablish ancient virtues by reinstating the emperor, who saw the new government handed over to accommodating bureaucrats, and who had come to understand that, for him, the revolution had failed. He spoke of his admiration for Saigo, of his final act, ritual suicide, of the faithful friend who dispatched him before committing suicide himself. He spoke of the beauty of Saigo's act, of that one superb gesture.

Lest I miss the point—one I was to comprehend only several months hence—he then spoke of how he, like Saigo, hated the rationalizing, pragmatic, conciliatory ways that had become those of Japan in our time.

– Japan, he said, has gone, vanished, disappeared.

– But, surely, the real Japan must still be around if you look for it? He shook his head sternly.

– Is there no way to save it then? I asked, probably smiling.

He looked past me into the mirror: No, there is nothing more to save.

Then, like the playwright who artfully anticipates the climax in the first, casual-seeming allusion, like the novelist who skillfully introduces an oblique reference to the revelation to come, he said: He was the last true samurai.

I was to consider this only in the most literal sense: Saigo was the last samurai. Later, however, I was to realize with much fuller comprehension that this had been told me by the last true samurai himself.

With another person, even another writer, one would not be so certain of this. One might have called this early reference unconscious or something of that kind. Not with Mishima. Just as he chose the cast in the drama of his life according to his wishes, he also arranged its form according to his liking. I was to be astonished on that coming day in

November—in fact, my exclamation of surprise was to be the final line of my role in his life.

Later, friends of Mishima's gathered and spoke of the noted suicide. We had all, it transpired, been given similar hints. The earliest dated from two years before the event. Together we comprised the chorus—flabbergasted, as at the denouement of a Euripidean tragedy.

But, back then in the Hilton bar, I was not supposed to guess and so I didn't. Rather, somewhat mistrustful of the stern turn our talk had taken, certain that he would next begin on "purity," a subject I had heard enough about from him to want to avoid, I attempted to introduce some levity into the conversation and told him that I quite envied him his toy army.

This was a mistake. He glared at his reflection. I was absolutely wrong, I was told. Nothing of the sort at all and I could keep my suspicions to myself because I was completely in error.

So I was, and ought to have known it. Given the final role of the toy army and its members, Mishima, so careful a casting director, would certainly not have confused parts to the extent I was suggesting. Its role was to be deadly serious.

Then, smiling his humorless smile, Mishima himself attempted to lighten our talk. He had been reading a book about Elagabulus, whom he rather admired—or, frankly, envied. Leaning toward me he told me some of the more salacious gossip recorded in the book. He was going to write about the ruler, as Camus had written about Caligula, as he himself had written about Sade and Hitler. Astonishing, he said, the power that man had had.

Later, when it was all over, when the coup de théâtre had had its desired effect and the curtain been rung down, I was at one of the memorial services, and up came the young literary student.

It was *sensei*'s last wish that we be friends, I was told.

– I know, I said: But sometimes last wishes can't be granted.

I did not say that the only parts we had really played were those of stage properties in *sensei*'s last housecleaning.

– Nevertheless, he added (*keredomo*, a non sequitur quite built into the Japanese language itself): *Sensei* was a truly extraordinary man.

And I couldn't but agree.

Sada Abé

After the war, released from prison, she got herself a job in Inari-cho, in downtown Tokyo: at the Hoshi-Kiku-Sui—the Star-Chrysanthemum-Water—a pub.

There, every night, workers of the neighborhood—for it was a *taishu-sakaba*, a workingman's pub—would gather to drink saké and *shochu* and nibble grilled squid and pickled radish. And every night around ten, Sada Abé would make her entrance.

It was grand. She descended the staircase—itself a large affair which ended right in the middle of the customers. Always in bright kimono, one redolent of the time of her crime, early Showa, 1936, Sada Abé would appear at the head of the stairs, stop, survey the crowd below, and then slowly descend.

From where, one never knew. Some said that her lair was up there on the second floor, full of old photographs and overstuffed furniture. Others said that the staircase went nowhere at all, that she had to clamber up it from the back before she could arrive in public. In any event, the descent was dramatic, with many pauses as she stared at her guests below, turning a brief gaze on this one and that. And as she did so, progressing slowly, indignation was expressed.

It always appeared. It was part of the show, the entrance. Ostensibly it was provoked by the actions of the men below. They invariably placed their hands over their privates. Fingers squeezed tight, they would then turn and snicker. Above, the descending Sada Abé would mime fury, casting burning glances at those below who squeezed and giggled the more. She slapped the banister in her wrath, and merriment rippled.

This pantomime was occasioned by the nature of Sada Abé's crime. Twenty years before, she had cut off her lover's penis. This was after he was dead, of course. And he was dead because the two had discovered that if she squeezed his neck hard enough his weary member achieved new life, but one day she squeezed too hard and killed him.

It was these events to which her customers now, two decades later, referred by hiding their own penises and snickering. And it was these that she also acknowledged by pretending wrath.

At the bottom of the stairs she would stop and rake the room with her blazing gaze. There, in the growing hush, she would stand and glare.

The giggling stopped. Some of the men hunched lower, as though truly frightened. Perhaps they were, for this woman was a creature already legendary. She was a murderess. She had served a prison sentence. She had written a book about her exploits. And she might, they perhaps thought, be capable of doing the whole thing all over again.

Like a basilisk she stood. The last snicker died away. Silence, utter. Then, and only then, as though she had received the homage she desired, did Sada Abé smile. It was a cordial, welcoming smile and it accompanied her as she went about pouring drinks and slapping backs.

Like many a pub woman she became manly, just one of the boys. Unlike many, however, she had actually choked a man to death and then cut off his member. There was a consequent frisson when Sada Abé slapped your back.

– Hello there, you back again? You like this place here, eh? she asked, looking down at me and adding: Nothing but the best here, boys. Let's all drink up now.

She then moved off to another table, glancing back at me from time to time. It was an interested glance. She seemed to be thinking about something, perhaps wondering if I too knew her story.

I did, and I also wondered about her and the turn her story had taken. To have unintentionally killed a lover in a moment of passion, to have rescued from the catastrophe, in a moment of panic, an object which one, childlike, had loved—that was one thing. It was quite another, however, to connive with the crowd, to present oneself as a figure of vulgar terror and then as one of common fun.

She had certainly damaged the man initially but now she seemed to wound him doubly. And she was mutilating herself as well, making a travesty of an event of such importance to her, one that had so shaped her life. She was, I felt, precisely, faithless.

The laughter had now started up again. A few of the more daring yelled out that they were afraid to go and pee. Others shouted to hide the knives while she was around. She smiled, patted, poured, moving about in her striped Showa kimono like a teacher among unruly pupils.

Occasionally, however, the big smile faded. She seemed to be thinking. She stood there, saké bottle in one hand, abstracted. Of what, oh, of what was she thinking, I wondered, now half-drunk myself. It could have been that night twenty years before or it could have been present unpaid bills.

Whatever it was, she soon collected herself and went about among the tables grinning. Only for a time, however. Her nightly visits never lasted long. After an hour she was suddenly no longer there. No one saw her go back upstairs and no one in the drunken throng below missed her.

Perhaps she could no longer stand the travesty that her life had become. Or perhaps she had gone up to do the day's accounts.

Eiko Matsuda

– Oh, no, I really much prefer Europe, she said, dark in the summer heat, turning to watch the sun slide behind Saint Peter's.

I did not have to guess why. Many Japanese find freedom abroad but few had her reasons.

– It's so interesting. And, of course, I have friends here.

Originally an actress in Shuji Terayama's troupe, she was discovered by Nagisa Oshima and appeared in *The Realm of the Senses*, playing Sada Abé, strangling Tatsuya Fuji, cutting off his penis. Even though this scene, and many others, was missing when the film was shown in Japan, there was enough visible for newspapers and magazines to criticize.

It was shameless. It wasn't the way for a true actress to behave. And— perhaps the main motivation for the criticism—she seemed to be doing it all for foreigners, since it was they alone who were permitted fully to view the act. And yet it was a purely Japanese story. It was about, no matter what she might have done, one of our own. Why then was this cheap so-called actress exhibiting our shame abroad?

Why was *she* behaving this way, was the question. The man was never criticized. He, Tatsuya Fuji, then a minor actor, found his career enormously assisted locally by the film. Thanks to it he went on to be a star, to appear in cigarette commercials, and he never again had to appear nude.

Not so, however, in her case. She was a good actress, as she had proved, but no starring roles came her way. Only porno parts. She was also offered nude-dancer contracts. And more was suggested, amounts of money that would allow Japan to experience in the full flesh what had been denied it on the screen.

– Oh, no, that's not the reason at all, she said, her skin brown in the failing light, Saint Peter, black: I don't care what the press writes. If I did, well, I wouldn't last very long. No, really. I like Europe. I have this little place of my own in Paris now. And I do like coming to Rome.

She sat there in the twilight—black dress cut low in the back, necklace of ebony and amber, good black leather shoes, good black leather bag. And I knew what was under all this elegance. For I too had seen the film and so her naked flesh was more real to me than the poised elegance now sitting beside me on a Roman balcony.

– It certainly wasn't because of what they wrote. Actually, many women who've done less have had it worse. There were even some compliments—*Nippon Sports* called me brave. Did you know that? Well, they did.

She was very different from Sada Abé in the film. There, a housemaid, open, innocent, earthy, playing childlike games with the master. Now, black and elegant, chilled martini held between lacquer-nailed fingers, turning to speak in French to someone else, turning back to me to answer an earlier question.

– Every day? Oh, I shop. I see films. Friends—go to cafés, things like that.

She was brittle, sitting on the edge of the chair as though she did not belong there, as though she had only lighted, bird-like, on her flight to somewhere else, as though she might break if touched—and yet she was the same woman I remembered as all muscles, juice, and open thighs.

Every lineament now stated a firm, polite request—do not touch me, her body said, each line an unmistakable refusal. She was as though immured in a sexless chic.

And the real Sada Abé, had she too done this to herself? After she left the Inari-cho pub, she disappeared. The Nikkatsu film company had made a soft-core porn film out of her story and this had brought no complaints. Then Oshima had wanted to make his version and thought that he perhaps needed permission. She was discovered, after a long search apparently, in a Kansai nunnery—shorn, devout, and making no objections.

– It's easy to make out that I'm some kind of martyr, run out of my own country, Eiko Matsuda said, smiling: But, believe me, it wasn't like that at all.

One need not have one's hair shorn to expiate, one could also have

37

it newly coiffed. Her Paris dress was black as a nun's habit. She had, in her own way, become Sada Abé; had paid something of the same price for doing so. There are various kinds of nunneries.

Kazuko Morinaga

One Sunday morning when I was walking by Otsuka Station, near where I used to live, a young woman suddenly stopped directly in front of me.

She was looking at me, mouth half-open, eyes half-shut. It was the face of someone determined to do something she did not want to do.

– Excuse me. I'm very sorry to bother you. Do you speak Japanese and are you by any chance an American?

I closed my face. It was Sunday—fanatic Christians were about. Nevertheless I said: Yes.

– I'm so glad, she replied, then hurried on: Really, I'm very sorry, but do you know anyone at the American Embassy? You see, my mother here and I are so worried we don't know what to do.

Behind her, I now saw, was a middle-aged woman, her mouth also half-open. She bobbed when she was mentioned and attempted a smile, but she too was obviously upset.

So I asked what I could do to help and they exchanged a glance of relief. The daughter then explained.

Her name was Kazuko Morinaga and she had been going to this club in Roppongi, a disco really, and her friend Midori had introduced her to this American and they had danced a lot. Really, that was all. Just danced.

She paused and her mother nodded fiercely, as though she had been contradicted.

And then Michael has started coming early to the discotheque and wanting to take her home after, wanting to hold her hand, wanting to dance close, that sort of thing. She hadn't been too concerned about this. She'd just wanted to dance and he was a very good dancer. And she wanted to keep her relationship with him the way it was. And he didn't.

She stopped, looked down at her hands. She was a beautiful young woman. Then I noticed that her knuckles were white—her hands were clasped that tightly. It was difficult for her to talk like this, to a stranger, in front of a crowded station.

– Anyway, Midori gave him my address and telephone number. I don't suppose she meant any harm. I never asked her to. And I don't see her any more. I stopped going there.

And then, she continued, the trouble began. Michael had started to call. This was awkward because he knew no Japanese and she knew very little English. So, after a time, she just took to hanging up.

Then he started calling at odd times, like in the middle of the night. And though she didn't understand very well what he was saying, it seemed to be that he wanted to take her back to America, wanted to marry her, that he loved her.

– I don't know what to do. He found the house somehow and came late last night. He knocked on the door for hours, it seemed like. My mother and I—my father's dead, we live together—hid in the bathroom till finally he went away. Then the phone began again. We ran out of the house, the two of us. We came here and then I saw you.

She stopped, her story told.

Her mother continued. They couldn't call the Japanese police, you see. It was none of their concern. And they would simply say that the girl here had got what she'd asked for.

And she felt sorry for this poor American, too. Until he'd fallen in love he had probably been nice enough. And so, wouldn't I do something, please? After all, we were fellow Americans, weren't we, he and I?

After a pause during which I tried to find something to say, I asked: Do you know anything about Michael—where he lives, for example?

– Oh, some camp or other, said the daughter.

– He's a soldier?

– Yes, and he comes to Roppongi on Saturdays. So it isn't as bad as it could be, you see. He can only get out then. So we only need worry on Saturday nights. But, of course, he can phone whenever he wants.

I considered, standing there in front of the station, wondering what I could do. At that point Kazuko's mother suddenly remembered her manners.

– Isn't his Japanese good, though? He must have studied for years.

Very intelligent, probably. Why, he speaks better than we do, doesn't he, Kazuko?

And while the beautiful Kazuko nodded in agreement I felt very sorry for these two women, innocently victimized by American Love, yet still mindful of Japanese Good Manners.

– If he's a soldier then the army ought to make him stop, I said.

– But I wouldn't want to get him into any trouble.

I looked at her. Why not? I asked: He's certainly made trouble enough for you.

– Yes, but he couldn't help it. He's had a difficult life, you see. He just misunderstood. I was being nice because I felt sorry for him.

I wondered how she had come to know about his difficult life, and she, as though guessing this, began to rummage in her purse.

– I've got a picture of him, one of those machine-made things. After we danced one night.

She handed me a small square photograph—face down, which is the way one is handed things in Japan. Across the back I saw, penciled in a Western hand: Michael White.

Then I turned it over. Michael White was black. A pleasant-looking young GI in civvies, mouth half-open, eyes smiling, having a good time. I now understood.

– What should I do? she asked.

What, indeed? And what should I do?—someone picked out of the crowd for my presumed nationality, suddenly linked with this young lovelorn soldier I had never met and, with any luck, never would.

I was on her side. Michael ought not to go around forcing his problems on other people. Then I remembered that she had originally mentioned the embassy. So I suggested that she call and talk to the proper authorities, whoever they were, and ask for help.

And, since I am the kind of person I am, I had the number of the U.S. Embassy written down in my date book. This I copied out for her.

Mother and daughter were grateful—not, perhaps, for what I'd done, since I had done nothing, but rather for having been able to talk about this with someone, to tell of their concern.

We stood there, the three of us. People passed around us and we felt awkward. They seemed to think the crisis was over—they had actually stopped an American and received some advice. I was aware that I had not really helped them at all.

Then Kazuko's mother, smiling for the first time, asked if they might not know the name, address, and telephone number of their benefactor so that they could send a little token of appreciation.

And, standing there, I sensed a future in which Kazuko's mother and Kazuko herself, and Michael White too for all I knew, played a part. I imagined late-night telephone calls from the mother and polite raps on the door as Kazuko called with cakes. I found myself thinking that these people really could not go around forcing their problems on others.

So I shook my head, smiled, said I'd been of little use, that I wished them luck, that I must be on my way. And I left them there, Kazuko smiling in a puzzled fashion, her mother bowing.

For they had frightened me, just as Michael had frightened them. And neither Kazuko's beauty nor their need, nor my own curiosity, was sufficient to overcome this sudden trepidation, this glimpse into life as it is when the patterned surface cracks and we look beneath.

The two, mother and daughter, forced into the street to ask help from strangers, did not insist. They bowed. I smiled and turned away.

Saburo Sasaki

A youth of eighteen or so, he was was being bullied in the public bath by two grown men with tattoos. They made him scrub their backs, called him *shombenkozo* and *kuso*, pushed him into the cold pool. The other bathers, all from the neighborhood, ignored this. So did I, sunk in the hot water.

We ignored it because it was serious. This much even I knew—from the language. The first term meant bed-wetter and the second meant shit.

After they had gone, abusing him all the way, and I was drying myself, I heard the chicken man arguing with the bath lady. He was saying that of course they were gangsters, what with their tattoos and all, and she was saying that, tattoos or not, they weren't gangsters, they all worked at the local sushi shop. The big ones were the new staff from downtown and the little one was the *kozo*.

So he really was a *kozo* after all, an apprentice, someone who washes the dishes, sweeps the floor. It is not unusual for the youngest member to be mistreated by his elders, but this amount of abuse was uncommon. I was curious.

Consequently, several days later I went to the Fuji sushi shop around the corner from the bathhouse. It was early evening and there were a number of other customers, all sitting on the stools facing the counter, all watching what was going on behind it.

– Little shit, can't even fill a teacup proper, said the larger of the two, tattoo showing just beneath his crisp white sleeve.

The *kozo* was standing, head bowed, holding his hand in front of him. His fingers were bright red. He had apparently scalded himself on the tea.

– The little shit can't do anything proper, said the other, hands busy, slicing manfully.

The other customers, interested, stared at the young man with the scalded fingers. It is not uncommon for a crowd to enjoy the spectacle of someone ganged up on like this. There was some murmuring, most of it satisfied. The man next to me spoke of the low caliber of youngsters these days.

I did not enjoy my sushi, watching this and further humiliations, but then I had not come to enjoy sushi. I was there to satisfy my curiosity.

My curiosity unsatisfied, I called up the Fuji several days later and ordered some sushi to be brought to my house.

Sure enough, it was delivered by the *kozo*. One finger was bandaged, either caused by the scalding or some later enormity.

– Why do they bully you like that? I asked.

– Me? Bullied? I'm not bullied.

– I see, I said. And so, indeed, I did. Loyalty to the shop would prevent him from criticizing it, particularly to a stranger.

The next time we met, however, he apparently thought differently. This was again in the bathhouse. It was early and he was alone. I looked at his black eye and said nothing. He glanced at me several times, then joined me in the hot water.

– It's a tough life, he said after a while, now wanting to talk: And it gets worse all the time. I just don't know what to do.

After that it all came out. The two new *sushi-ya* from Asakusa, from the tough and manly downtown of Tokyo, had only recently moved to the Fuji. He himself, Saburo Sasaki by name, now just nineteen years old, had come up from the country. The two had been pleasant enough at first but then had changed. He pointed to his black eye.

The reason then appeared. If he wanted to stay and work with them and make his way up and become a *sushi-ya* himself, which he thought he did, then he ought to get tattooed, as they were. He had demurred, then refused—hence the present mistreatment. What did I think he ought to do, since I had earlier expressed an interest in his case?

Our conversation was interrupted by the arrival of the brutal pair. One of them had Fudo, guardian of hell, fanged and clawed on his back, which seemed appropriate. The other, I now saw, had, incongruously, Kannon, goddess of mercy.

– Hey, shit, yelled Kannon, get your ass out of the hot tub and start scrubbing.

44

– Yes, piss-pants, shouted Fudo, and on the double or we'll black the other eye for you.

The others in the bath joined in the genial laughter that greeted these sallies and I left, not wanting to see any more. That evening, very late, Saburo knocked softly at my front door.

Over cocoa we talked. Getting a tattoo would provide an entrance into the small world of the sushi shop, but it would slam forever the door to the great wide world. No one would hire a man with a tattoo, some uptown bathhouses would not admit him—why, he couldn't even go to the beach.

Yes, he knew all that, but if he lost this job he would have to leave Tokyo and go back to Ibaraki. No, he didn't think he could get another job this good. And did tattooing hurt?

Saburo was, I saw, a person caught in an archetypal situation; but he was already predisposed. The pain of being excluded was greater than the pain of having his skin needled.

– At least it wouldn't cost much. They said they'd pay half and the other half could come out of my wages. It's expensive, you know, tattooing.

It was not only the pressures he was thinking of. He was also thinking of the joys of conforming. And after all, he added, smiling, *shikataganai de sho*, it can't be helped, I suppose.

No, it can't be helped. Not even when it can. So he finished his cocoa and stood up, smiled, and thanked me for this opportunity to discuss his problem, to *sodan suru*, to help him make up his mind.

I did not see Saburo again until several weeks later. It was again at the bathhouse. This time he was seated on a low stool, and Fudo and Kannon were crouched on either side of him. Fudo was drawing hot water and testing it with his finger. Kannon with a soapy rag was carefully washing Saburo's back on which were the deep blue lines of Koi-Taro, a popular and husky little boy riding a carp up a waterfall.

– It's just bound to hurt a little bit at first, said Fudo solicitously: And the hot water is going to hurt a little more. But you just put up with it, you *gamman suru*, like a man, *otoko rashiku*.

Kannon smiled in a motherly fashion and said: It's the red hurts the most. But Taro doesn't have much red in him so that's okay.

– He ought to lie down after, said Fudo, worried: Yes, you do that. We can cover for you easy at the shop. No, sir. You got to take care of yourself now that you're one of us.

Up to my ears in the hot water, I looked at the two of them as they soaped and rinsed the boy. He turned and saw me there.

And he smiled—a wide, secure, contented smile.

Kishio Kitakawa

Though in his final year at university, just about to go out and make a living, he—unlike many—retained much of his childhood: liked stag beetles, would turn and watch moths or butterflies, stop to listen to the cicadas of late summer, loved trees.

Born in Kyoto, going to school in Osaka, he seemed in the midst of the concrete city to remember those bamboo groves and foothill forests left behind in the old capital.

On Sundays, after breakfast, he would sometimes want to go to Sumiyoshi Shrine and wander through the park.

– Why do you want to do that? Let's go to the movies, I would say.

– We can go to the movies later, he would answer in that reasoned, boyish way of his: But we can go to Sumiyoshi now.

Once there we never did much. He would walk about and admire the trees, sometimes running his hand over the bark. Though quite tall, on the basketball team, getting ready to leave school, he still looked very young.

But then he graduated and the next time I saw him he was wearing that expression one sees on young men just out of university, just into the real world. It is not exactly shock, but there is something dazed about it. It is the look of someone to whom something incomprehensible has happened.

The incomprehensible had been the sudden revelation of the world as it is, not as school and a sheltered life had indicated. Like most graduates, Kitakawa was unprepared.

In his own way, particularly so. He had wanted to study natural history but his parents had insisted on something practical—business management. What he had learned in such a discipline I never knew. He did not talk about it, did not seem interested in it. And now, suddenly, he was to make his living by it.

– Everyone goes through this, I said, unhelpfully.

We were not in leafy Sumiyoshi but in concrete Dotombori, having been to a movie about a sports champ who makes good.

– I didn't know it would be like this, though. Anyway, I passed the company exam. I go to work next week.

– What kind of company?

– A paint company.

A paint company—could anything have been further from his interests, I wondered.

A few months later he came to Tokyo, to visit the home office, as he put it. I suggested we meet at Hibiya.

As the sun went down and we were walking through the park, he said: It's so good to get outside like this again.

– You don't much in Osaka?

– Oh, no, they work you all the time . . . You know, they paint just about everything in this company I'm with now.

– Well, that's their business.

– But even the most beautiful pieces of wood. Like the pillars in the house—the *tokonoma*. They've started to paint those now. Did you know that?

– No, I didn't. They must look rather strange.

– Awful, he said softly.

Then he looked up at the branches outlined against the evening sky, and I wondered how long this gentle person would last with his paint company.

Later I thought of him, back in Osaka, in cap and apron, stirring up batches of paint; saw him practicing brushstrokes, making sure the bright colors went on smoothly; envisioned him, now all dressed up—matching tie and breast-pocket hankie—going from door to door with his color charts.

As always happens to new employees, he was kept very busy. Coming in at the bottom, as one invariably did, there were many jobs to be learned before the business-management level was attained.

He could not come to Tokyo and I did not go to Osaka, so an entire year passed without our seeing each other. Then one weekend I went down. We arranged to meet in the lobby of a hotel near his office.

It wasn't that I didn't recognize him. Of course I did, but the change was there too, the subtle difference. The tall basketball player's body now seemed heavier, less supple. And the triangular face, usually that of someone younger, had matured, turned squarish, less mobile. We shook hands and his grip was firm.

– They really keep me busy, he said over dinner.

– Doing what?

– Well, I'm the only one in my section who majored in business management and so they need me for my skills.

– For your skills? I asked, surprised.

The surprise must have shown.

– Yes, he said, for an instant shy, then more nearly belligerent than I had ever seen him: That was my major, after all.

Then, as though apologizing, he smiled. This was something I remembered. But once it had been a boy's smile; now it was merely boyish.

– They really run your ass off in that company of mine, he continued: Would you believe it—I don't get home till ten or eleven every night?

– Door-to-door the whole time?

– No, no. I didn't have to do that for long. I told you. Business management. You see, it's a growing concern, so we all have to pull together.

After dinner I asked where he wanted to go.

– I don't know. Dotombori? But I can't stay late. Got to get up early. Conference tomorrow morning with the boss.

– On Sunday?

– On Sunday.

– Well, let's see then. How about a walk in Sumiyoshi?

– Sumiyoshi? It's dark ... Oh—you remember we used to go there. It was nice, wasn't it? But that was in the daytime when we could see things, right? They've got this new film on downtown. *The Bridge on the River Kwai.*

There was a silence, each of us thinking of different things. Then: I wonder if trees sleep, I asked. It was indeed something I had sometimes wondered about. Fish slept with their eyes open. Perhaps trees slept too.

He looked at the gilded ceiling of the restaurant for a second, as though thinking, or as though looking through it to the sky above.

– Maybe, he said, then: No, I don't think so. They're asleep all the time.

– Or awake, I said.

He smiled, then looked up again, the movement I remembered, the mouth half-open, as though in wonder at the firmament.

– Just look at that, he said, gazing at the ceiling: I wonder who got that contract.

Hiro Obayashi

Short, youngish, eyes already ringed with fatigue and heavy smoking, he was a successful businessman—a publisher. His was a small company but, as he often said in his excellent English, "quite vital, actually."

It was "vital" in the field of children's books, and every year the Frankfurt Book Fair was brightened by stacks of his illustrated English versions of *Little Red Riding Hood* and *Hansel and Gretel* and other works in the public domain.

They were inexpensively made, the unit cost far below that of the competition, and they sold well—particularly to countries like Kenya—but Obayashi wanted more. More precisely, he wanted prestige. That was where I came in.

A published author, I had recently returned from a post at a famous American museum and was now presumably in search of a position. He believed that if he hired me I could help him attain prestige. He would publish books on art and literature and sell to countries other than those in Africa.

So he began to woo me. Having a friend in common made it easy for him to invite me for a friendly drink and then a friendly dinner. And since he wanted to impress me, the drink was at the old bar of the Imperial Hotel, and the dinner was at Kicho with its Kyoto food, electronic nightingales, and high prices. Afterward, there was this little place he knew, the notoriously expensive hostess club L'Espoir where the beautiful women, knowing at once who to make a fuss over, admired my tie, snuggled closer, and put a hand on my thigh, while Mr. Obayashi—no, you must call me Hiro, you're a friend—lit up yet another Hope.

After a number of such evenings, I finally agreed to work for this ambitious man and his vital company because I needed the salary—high—and the sponsorship—seemingly secure. Dom Pérignon was opened, a gentleman's agreement was shaken on, and the hostesses applauded.

When I reported to work, however, I found a new desk and an electric pencil sharpener but no duties. I had been acquired but as yet my employer had not decided what to do with me. Perhaps he thought I would simply generate my own work.

– You are to do as you want to. We are proud to have a person like yourself on our staff. As you know, we are having a modest success with our children's line but we would like to expand into something more prestigious—even if it's less lucrative. Here, my dear Mr. Richie, is where you play your part.

Being a gentleman publisher was appealing (though in real life I never actually met one), and I began a series of memos to the president which were as prestigious as anything he could have hoped for. I remember recommending an illustrated edition of the *Kojiki*, a publication which would have had all the sales potential of an illustrated edition of *Beowulf*; a multi-volume history of Buddhist art; and the first English translation of Paul Claudel's Japan diaries.

To each of these ideas Hiro paid what appeared to be close attention. He seemed to be considering their merits in a manner which did justice to my cultural acumen. And it was with what appeared to be actual regret that he found reasons for not adopting them. Never, however, because they would make no money, for he had already told me that prestige was something he could afford to pay for. In the meantime I was to consider his office as my own and to come to see him whenever I wished— he always had time for someone as prestigious as myself.

His house was also to be considered mine as well, and I was often invited to a dinner of Kobé steak and Mouton-Rothschild and asked to admire the majolica plates off which we were eating and the real Bernard Buffet lithograph on the wall.

His wife would sit with us (none of this old-fashioned keeping the spouse in the kitchen) after serving us. She was a vivacious woman, inclined to be talkative, but kept on a short leash. Hiro often interrupted her, never laughed at her social sallies, and when she mentioned Marie Laurencin told her she didn't know what she was talking about.

It was here that I saw his other side. He had been a kamikaze pilot during World War II, I knew—one of the few who either got back or were never sent—and he believed in discipline. Telling his wife to shut up and go and open another bottle was part of this.

So was browbeating poor Mr. Yago, his production manager, whom I would sometimes hear him shouting at—usually about getting the price down and not caving in to those rapacious paper dealers, those thieving bindery people.

With me, however, he was wise father and benevolent older brother. I was given no glimpse of the do-or-die kamikaze cadet, and it seemed I could do no wrong. At the same time, nothing I proposed ever got accomplished. I lowered my aim a bit and suggested the *Kojiki* as a children's book, maybe with a seven-headed dragon pop-up.

What a good idea, he said, but that pop-up would have to be all handwork and the people who did that were notorious robbers and he really didn't want to throw money away on them. So he smiled ruefully, reached for another Hope, and told me I was always welcome to come and talk with him; and if I had nothing to do, well, I had that new typewriter now and there were probably books of my own I wanted to write.

Thus encouraged, I did my own work on his time, trying meanwhile to guess what he wanted me there for. A large paycheck arrived every month and my sponsorship was assured—I had a three-year visa. And so, thinking I ought to do *something*, I often wandered into his office to outline large, impractical plans as he smoked one Hope after another, and I would leave ringing with reassurances of regard.

Knowing that he, a Zero fighter pilot, was fond of model airplanes, I suggested a cut-out plane or battleship series. Yes, he had thought of that but he wanted only the best and Janes would not sublicense. Guessing he liked gimmicks, I told him about a new 3-D process which might work in kiddy books. Yes, he knew about it—it was German, not perfected yet. I even descended to scratch-and-smell, where you apply the infant fingernail and inhale the apple. Yes, how clever of me to know about that, but of course I couldn't know that the Ministry of Health would never approve it for a children's book.

Unwilling to believe I was merely an expensive but useless decoration—like one of the ladies at L'Espoir—I decided that he really needed me to advise him on his own ideas, steer him away from errors of judgment. One of these ideas was to go with a photographer to Majorca and do a series of tasteful female nudes to be sold as 3-D pictures. I came down heavily against it. If it was really prestige he wanted, this was the way to lose, not gain it. He didn't want to become a pornographer now, did he?

He seemed to take all this in, nodded thoughtfully, said that it deserved some consideration, and sent me back to my desk feeling pleased that I had found a way to earn my keep. I would be an ombudsman, fearlessly telling the truth, guarding his integrity.

From then on I often went into his office with suggestions. He had earlier had a company devoted to art publications. It had gone bankrupt. This, I explained, was because he paid none of the foreign authors whose work he published and he had been consequently afraid to advertise. If he had paid them, he could have advertised the books; they would have sold, and the company would still be solvent.

Betraying his first irritation, he stubbed out his cigarette and told me that the company had been a tax shelter, designed to go under when its period of usefulness was over. Then, to lighten a suddenly heavy atmosphere, he smiled and took from his desk drawer a 3-D photo. It moved as you shifted it in your hand, and a naked lady alternately hid and revealed her charms, winking the while.

When he announced that we were going to dinner together that night to talk about this idea, I told him that I couldn't, that I was busy. For one thing, he already knew what I thought of the notion. For another, the expensive evenings out were cutting into my own time.

My idea of working hours was still very Western—nine to five and an hour off for lunch. During these hours the company could make its due demands on you, but not outside them. How different the Japanese reality was. Five o'clock came and went and not one of the secretaries hooded her typewriter. Poor Mr. Yago would not even look at the clock but sat on with his calculator till long afterward.

As resident foreigner I could leave early, but by doing so I was removing myself from that warm family spirit which pervaded a Japanese company when the "working day" was over and everyone was still there, nobody daring to make the first move out of the door. It was around then that the boss appeared, feeling expansive, telling a few jokes, inviting the chosen few out for a few beers. And even for those not chosen, the day's work was often not over. They went and got their own beer and bad-mouthed the boss.

Mr. Yago, probably feeling it diplomatic to do so, took me out one evening and told me what a tyrant the man was. Hadn't I noticed that he never began his own work until late in the afternoon to make sure everyone was still there after dark? Yago-san seemed to be trying to warn me. Warn me about my boss's character, I initially thought, but now I believe it was about my own, in the hope of making me conform a bit more, stay late once in a while, try not to break taboos—like telling the boss how to run his business. I had already all but said that the boss cheated his authors, and of course he really was cheating on his taxes. More seriously, I had disapproved of so many of his pet plans (those naughty nudes, for example). I was only an employee, even though I happened to be a privileged one.

This, I now think, the harried Mr. Yago was trying to tell me over warm beer in Roppongi. But in my idleness I was by then convinced that I had been appointed my friend Hiro's conscience, that I would somehow make him a better person, that in fact he was paying me, as he would an analyst, to do so. Not only did I heap scorn on the winking nudes and ridicule Bernard Buffet, but I proceeded to find ways to make his fairytale books more artistic, insisting we go back to the original Perrault text for the new *Sleeping Beauty*, and then suggesting we commission the expensive Maurice Sendak to do *Momotaro*. Told that Sendak was not cute enough for his market, I said that that was the problem and that was why only Africans bought the products.

I now see the man's patience as monumental, though at the time I thought him stubborn. Nor did I detect his deep disappointment in me—an investment which had turned out to be worthless. So I persevered. Became even more personal.

Really, he was smoking too much. And he worked too hard. Every hour not asleep he was in the office. All thoughts were about the publishing house and how to make it more profitable—as well as more prestigious. He took no vacations and resented any of us taking ours. This was not good for him, I said—now Dr. Richie in everything but white coat and stethoscope—just listen to that cough, just look at those black bags under his eyes.

In the meantime, as I went about my medical duties, things were changing, but so slowly that at first I did not notice. I was still attending editorial meetings, and it took some time for me to see that when I talked no one made pencil marks on their yellow-lined, legal-sized tablets. When an important meeting occurred and I was not included, I just assumed that what was being discussed had nothing to do with my department, and took the afternoon off. The boss still treated me with indulgence, even though I was told more often than before that he was rather busy at the moment; and if those awful evenings at his home had ceased, I was glad. I thought a kind of equilibrium had been reached.

The first real indication that something was wrong was that my electric pencil sharpener disappeared. One day it wasn't there, just the screw holes where it had been. I asked around, no one knew. I jokingly suggested a burglar, no one laughed.

I also noticed a coolness among the rest of the staff. Poor Mr. Yago never really had time for me now. The secretaries turned a bit curt. The cleaning lady slopped a bit around my desk and that was all.

Even then, it may not have been too late. The boss reassured me that his door was still open. Maybe it was, but in a state of pique, I left it shut. I who was being slowly ostracized—like strangulation by degrees—decided to ostracize him, to deprive him of my care and company. If he had no use for me, then I had no use for him.

After all those years in Japan, I still didn't have a clue. I may have known all about *mura hachibu* (ostracization in the village, where all they'll do is douse the roof if it's on fire), but I could not recognize it off the page. And I decided not to make the customary—indeed, obligatory—New Year's call on my superior. That would let him know of my displeasure with him.

Instead, after the holiday came word of his displeasure with me, a formal letter expressing his complaints: that I was not doing my work, that I was taking days off, that I was doing other things on company time, that I was missing company meetings. He therefore had no recourse but to fire me.

One does not fire people in Japan. But then the Japanese do not behave as I had done. From my point of view, he had read everything wrong; but, from his point of view, I had done everything wrong.

My friends—my American ones—said I should sue. But suing takes time and money, and besides I am not one of that generation of Americans that regards suing as an immediate recourse. Instead, I wrote him a letter, upholding his right to do what he did, but deploring the way in which he had done it. And, rather like a wife served with divorce papers, I wondered what had gone wrong. What had he expected me to do? What had he really wanted?

He replied announcing the terms of my severance pay—quite generous, he was a gentleman till the last—and giving me instructions on how to get unemployment compensation from the government. Perhaps he knew that if I applied I automatically lost my sponsorship, and then perhaps he didn't.

Since I never saw him again I could not ask. He continued to overwork and to oversmoke and before long he was in the Cancer Institute and in another six months he was dead. I went to the funeral, where I saw his vivacious wife and, uninterrupted, we spoke of Marie Laurencin.

I also learned for the first time that Hiro had been a Catholic. As I sat in the dark church and thought about what had happened, I still couldn't decide how much of a sinner Hiro was, how much of one I was myself.

Masako Tanaka

Masako worked in the barbershop, third chair, the one in the back, the one few customers sat in since Japanese men do not like to entrust to a woman something as important as having their hair cut. The waiting bench would be full, all the comic magazines open, and Masako would be idle.

A plain girl in an apron, she would make tea, sweep the floor, see to the hot towels. Occasionally she was allowed to wash a head, a lesser occupation. After that the male barbers would again take over. Masako was paid, I would imagine, half of what the men were.

I ask for her. This pleases her: she flushes a deep and beautiful pink. The male barbers, the other customers, all swivel, then, having stared their full, decide that there is nothing unusual in a *gaijin* asking for a girl. We have both found our level since neither of us belongs to this barbershop *nakama*, this just-us-Japanese-males-together.

I have my reasons. I need not wait since her chair is forever free and I do not have to make the barber's life interesting by acknowledging his chatter, and—since women barbers always take a very long time—I can read a large chunk of whatever book I am carrying. Finally, Masako is a good barber.

She looks at my head, thinking. She has beautiful, soft, brown eyes. Her gaze is contemplative, inward. She seems to be assessing the work at hand, deciding how best to complete it. She is tentative, combs the mop this way and that, then with that small nod which signifies decision, she picks up the shears and begins to snip. I open my book.

One day, engrossed, I was surprised to hear Masako addressing me. What was I reading, she wondered. And was it English?

– No, it's French. A French novel by a woman called Colette.

She paused, scissors raised. She knew that name. Where could she have heard it? Oh, yes, in a former neighborhood, back in the country, the man down the street had had a small dog. It was called Koretto. Was my book about a dog?

– No, it's about an actress.

She shook her head and, for the first time, smiled. It was a smile that indicated that this was all beyond her, that she knew nothing of such things but that she marveled nonetheless.

I outlined the story and Masako listened, then asked: And did she really have the courage to go out into the world, just like that, all on her very own, knowing no one, having no friends, and then just get up there on the stage and do her best?

It was a very long sentence. She stood back once it had appeared, as though surprised. Then, with a small smile, a shake of the head—such dreams were not for her—she lowered her gaze and went on with my haircut.

The next time I went to the barbershop—more than a month later, since Masako cuts hair short—I carried a small paper-wrapped volume. As I had hoped, Masako remembered Colette. Had she found true happiness, she wanted to know. Well, she found this man, I began.

– No, not things like that, said Masako.

Here, for the first time, I saw impatience, willfulness—in short, character.

– I mean, she said, was she happy leading her own life on the stage?

– Well, she seemed to find it interesting.

The scissors ceased. Masako was thinking.

– I think, she said, it must have been very interesting.

When I left I gave her the book I had been carrying. In a secondhand bookshop in Kanda I had found a Japanese translation of *Mes apprentissages*. She accepted it and looked at me. The other barbers looked as well. One of them smirked and asked, as I was going out the door, who Masako's new boyfriend was. That is how I first learned her name.

She responded, as Japanese girls often do, obliquely. After New Year's I found in my mailbox, unstamped, a small parcel. It was decorated with colored ribbon and had a Snoopy card attached with her full name on it. Inside were six rice cakes brought all the way back from the northern province where she was born.

Other girls might have responded in kind, another book. But some

Japanese proceed through analogy—I had given her a product of my civilization and so she now gave me one of hers.

When next I went to the barbershop I smiled to indicate both my gratitude and the fact that I was not going to embarrass her by thanking her. Neither Colette nor rice cakes were mentioned. Yet a difference had been made. She was no longer looking at my nape, my brow: she was looking at me. And her gaze was plainly thoughtful. When she had finished I, for the first time, tipped her.

I had my reasons. Money restores equilibrium. Any male foreigner in Japan soon learns that he can be attractive to a dissatisfied girl. It is his foreignness, not his maleness, that attracts. She wants a mentor, not a friend; a confidant, not a lover. The foreign male, this one at any rate, is wise to avoid complications. Plain Masako with her touching ambitions was not, I decided, going to complicate my life. Hence the tip. Money is a conservative, even reactionary commodity. It always restores the status quo.

Snipping away, Masako was thereafter silent. No talk of Colette, no mention of rice cakes and the far north. I looked at her reflection in the mirror as, sober, serious, she cut my hair. And I wondered why I had been afraid of her. That she would touch something in me? In me, who had already touched her?

Then, one day, I went to the barbershop and at the back chair stood an acned youth.

– Notice anything different? asked the head barber with a smirk: Your girl friend's gone. (This was said with a laugh.) Just upped and left. Not a word to anyone. Never saw anything like it. Why, she doesn't know a soul in Tokyo but I called her folks back in the country and they haven't heard anything. The young people these days. No idea of what a woman should be (*onna rashikunai*).

– Aren't you worried, though? Something might have happened to her.

– Well, she moved all her stuff out of the room we'd put her in. All this without a word of thanks, not an ounce of gratitude. Just upped and left. Oh, she had us fooled, she did. She was a sly one.

I thought of quiet Masako and her brown eyes. Whatever else she may have been, she was not a sly one. She might have been a desperate one. She might yet be a brave one.

And now she was out in the city, out there somewhere, alone. She had done what few girls did. And I wondered, too, if I had helped her. Colette and I.

Thereafter as the months passed I always asked after her while the acned youth snipped inexpertly and left my mane fashionably shaggy. But no one had ever heard anything at all. It was their opinion that she had shortly come to no good. Was probably making more than they were by doing something indecent.

And I came in time to regret my cowardice. I would very much like to know what happened to Masako, out on her own in the cold world— she, who had so much more courage than I did.

Akira Kurosawa

One day in winter, 1948, when I was twenty-four, my friend, the late composer Fumio Hayasaka, took me to the Toho studios to watch the shooting of a film for which he was doing the score.

On an elaborate open set of postwar streets, ruins, shops—so detailed it looked hardly different from the neighborhood outside the studio—a good-looking young man in a white suit and slicked-back hair was being directed by a tall, middle-aged man wearing a floppy hat.

During a break Hayasaka introduced me. After our halting conversation they went back to work. I spoke no Japanese then, and they, except for Hayasaka, no English. I watched and wondered who they were and what the film was about.

The young man in the white suit was Toshiro Mifuné, the tall man in the hat was Kurosawa, directing the young actor for the first time, and the film was *Drunken Angel*.

Then there was a spring day in 1954, and I had just emerged from the first screening of the full *Seven Samurai*. Never had I seen a film like it—my ears were still ringing, my eyes still watering. People gathered, talking, as they do when the film is a success. Several clustered around a tall man in a floppy hat, the same man I had met six years before. I did not think I would be remembered (Hayasaka was nowhere around). So, though I could now speak some Japanese, I did not go and congratulate him as the others were doing. Instead, I stared, admired.

In late autumn, 1956, Joseph Anderson and I were in Izu, at one of the open sets for *Throne of Blood*, Kurosawa's adaptation of *Macbeth*. It was known that we were doing a book on the Japanese film and would probably be writing this picture up for the press. Toho was most cooperative.

Work was running far behind schedule, Kurosawa having refused to use a completed set because it had been constructed with nails and the long-distance lenses he was using might show the anachronistic nailheads. Both Joe and I were thrilled by this unwillingness to compromise.

The present set represented the provincial palace of Lord Washizu, the Macbeth character, and Duncan's approach was being filmed: soldiers, banners, horses, a stuffed boar slung from poles—an entire procession. When an assistant gave the signal it moved forward under the late autumn afternoon sun.

Above us, on a platform, were Kurosawa and his cameraman. We had spoken with the director earlier and he had told us his plans for this scene. Now we were watching him do it. The entire afternoon was spent stopping and starting this distant procession. Sections of it were being filmed with the long-distance lenses, then refilmed, then filmed once again.

Half a year later when we saw the finished picture in the screening room, not one of these shots was in it. I asked him why. The scenes were nice enough, he said, but not really necessary. Besides, they interrupted the flow of the picture. Both Joe and I marveled.

Then again, in late summer, 1958, I was at one of the open sets for *The Hidden Fortress*, near Mt. Fuji. After a long day's shooting Mifuné was in the bath. I was sharing it with him. It had been a difficult day, the same scene shot over and over again.

I had noticed that, during this scene, Kurosawa's ballpoint pen stopped working. Instead of throwing it away and getting another, he had spent all that afternoon, between takes, trying to make this particular pen work.

Mifuné was sunk up to his neck in the hot water. He had been in the offending scene. I mentioned the ballpoint pen. Yes, he said: I know what you mean. I felt just like that pen . . . But did you notice? He finally got it to work.

It was a cold winter day in 1964, on the studio set for *Red Beard*. The picture was over budget and long over production schedule. Not a happy time, and Mifuné, with other contractual obligations, was still in full beard and unable to fulfill any of them.

By now it was known that I was writing a book on Kurosawa. This being so, I could approach him whenever he was free. He was sitting in a canvas chair, wearing a white cap and dark glasses, now that his eyes were giving him trouble. He looked dejected.

In order to have something to say, I told him that he didn't really look so different from the first time I had met him. Yes, he remembered the occasion, way back in the days of *Throne of Blood*, with Mr. Anderson.

– No, I said: Back in the days of *Drunken Angel*, with the now long-dead Mr. Hayasaka.

He looked at me and frowned. On the Kurosawa set a mistake gets first a frown.

– I don't remember that.

I observed that there was no reason he should but that it had happened. He then set to work remembering. Nothing came of it, but *I* remembered the nails in the abandoned castle, the ballpoint pen that would not work, the unhappily bearded Mifuné. We were problems—all of us—problems to be solved.

In 1978, a summer day, I was at the Toho studios at Seijo. No film was being made but Kurosawa was there because that was where he had an office. He was now in the office, working.

The work consisted in drawing and painting. He had no money for his film—notorious as he was for going over budget, over schedule, over the wishes, the commands, of producers and production companies—all so that he could create the perfect, uncompromised film.

In order to keep firmly in mind the film he next wanted to make, he was now doing it by hand. There was picture after picture of samurai, of battles, of horses. His large craftsman's hands were painting one scene after another, the movements swift and sure. He always knew just what he was going to do. The entire film was in his head, emerging through his fingers. Since he had no money, he would make the picture on paper. What other director, I wondered, would do this, would care this much, and would be this immune to despair?

What was the name of this impossible film, I wondered aloud. Well, I was told, they were thinking of calling it *Kagemusha*.

It was two years later, March 23, 1980—Kurosawa's seventieth birthday, and a party at a Chinese restaurant near Seijo: his family, his children, grandchildren, staff, a few friends. And presents, lots of presents. But the best present of all was that the money had been found. Thanks to profits from *Star Wars*, *Kagemusha* would become a reality.

Watching him, I thought back to the thirty-eight-year-old director on

64

the set of *Drunken Angel*. The intervening years had not made much difference. Now he wore caps instead of floppy hats, now he wore dark glasses.

Those big, strong hands were delicately opening birthday presents, the fingers precise but very firm with unwilling knots. I thought of the will that had created those films. Kurosawa turned, smiled, and with one large hand carefully smoothed the hair of a favorite grandson.

I thought too of that now long-gone ballpoint pen, coaxed until it forgot it was broken, until it began again to write.

Toshiro Mifuné

I look again at Mifuné. He is sixty-five now. Yet he remains much as he was at twenty-five. The face has changed but the person is the same.

His laugh, for example. The lips curve but the eyes remain serious. It is a polite laugh, one intended to bridge silences. It is also a social laugh, one intended to prevent misunderstandings. In addition it expresses agreement, concern, unease—all qualities other than humor.

Mifuné's humor consists of belittlement—of himself. He learned early on, perhaps, that making light of himself, or seeming to, was a way of earning regard. When speaking of himself he adopts that reasoned, fair, but guarded tone that some men use when speaking of their sons. He will spread his fingers and raise his eyebrows when he mentions his career, then sigh—as though it were not his own. This is charming— something he perhaps discovered long ago.

The laugh is part of the charm: it indicates that he is not taken in by himself, that he is not vain, not proud, regards his accomplishments (whatever they are, he seems to suggest) seriously but not too seriously, and is quite willing to consider himself as just another person, someone on the same level as—well, you and me.

His manner has its uses. When a famous man, and Mifuné is now world-famous, projects what is called a low profile, then the result is likability. If the actor is also a businessman, as Mifuné is, owning his own production company, the result is also productive—he is a man to be trusted.

Yet one should not consider this a veneer, a front, something he deliberately uses. The self we present is no less real because we choose to present it; it is something we come to embody. Mifuné is an actor, but in this sense we are all actors. And the qualities he embodies—hard-working, scrupulous, trustworthy, *nesshin* (doing his very best)—are real enough.

But sometimes these fall sort. Just when he is being his most reasonable and straightforward, the gaze will withdraw, the laugh will sound empty. One guesses that these distractions are personal. One feels that they are permanent.

Mifuné has had his problems: his company and its ups and downs; his divorce proceedings, messy ones; his friend—twenty-five years younger—and the child she bore him; the uproar when he took her to a 1974 state dinner attended by Gerald Ford and the emperor, and the actor was accused in the press of an act of *lèse majesté*, of flaunting his mistress in the imperial presence. All this and then the break with Kurosawa.

Yet, since he has not changed in the last forty years, since the withdrawn eyes and the empty laugh were there when he was twenty-five, the problems—if that is what they are—must be deeper, more complicated.

One of Mifuné's problems is that he wants to do the right thing in a world that is plainly wrong. I know nothing about the reasons for the divorce but I think it possible he might have infuriated his wife by trying to be good, by trying to do right, by being so eternally such a nice guy.

The world does not like nice guys. Not really. They always come in last, says Western wisdom. And Eastern wisdom acts as if they do. They are charming, fun to be with, absolutely trustworthy, and so what? So says the world.

Mifuné has been cheated in his business dealings, has been victim of fraud and misrepresentation, and, finally, has been misunderstood in the most important emotional relationship he ever had—that with Kurosawa.

In Mifuné Kurosawa found his ideal actor, one so open and so intelligent that he understood at once, instantly embodied the director's intentions. Kurosawa in his autobiography mentions this: If I say one thing to him, he understands ten. I decided to turn him loose.

And he may have thought he did. But it was always Kurosawa himself who was molding the performance.

Mifuné has appeared in almost a hundred and twenty movies by now and yet only in the sixteen Kurosawa films is he a fine actor. It was unpleasant Kurosawa who drew from pleasant Mifuné these performances— Kikuchiyo in *Seven Samurai*, Nakajima in *Record of a Living Being*,

Sutekichi in *The Lower Depths*, Sanjuro in *Yojimbo* and *Sanjuro*. If we do not recognize the Mifuné before us in these shadows on the screen it is because he does not either—and Kurosawa did.

Perhaps only a man as self-effacing, as thoroughly nice, as Mifuné could have put up for so long with all that it takes to be an object of attention to Kurosawa. The object is, naturally, never seen for what it is, only for what it is capable of. Like any good director Kurosawa sees people in terms of how they can be useful to his project—his current film.

The break between director and actor is commonly thought to have begun with *Red Beard*. Mifuné, in his own beard for over two years, was unable to take on any other work—yet unable to work on this film because Kurosawa kept delaying—in debt, worried, yet, with all of this, behaving well.

There were, however, words. And when Kurosawa, like many directors, senses defection of any kind, he will then push until an open break is achieved. In this he was successful. The last time I spoke to him about using Mifuné again—now that the director was making *Ran* and Mifuné was the right age for the part—Kurosawa said brusquely that he wouldn't have anything to do with actors who appeared in the likes of *Shogun*.

That Mifuné more and more appears in the likes of *Shogun* is because he needs the money. Also, he needs to be working, like any actor. And he knows this feudal warrior role so well that he can do it easily. Moreover, he is a very nice man who finds it very difficult to say no.

Perhaps that is the permanent worry behind the absent gaze and the empty laugh. It is the look of a person who is doing his best to be good in a world that is not. Mifuné has no drive for perfection, he has a drive for virtue.

How otherwise transparent the man is. His office has plaques on the walls, trophies. It is the room of any Japanese business executive. One expects golf clubs or racing-car pictures. His living room has lots of beaded lampshades, an onyx coffee table on gilt legs, an overstuffed chair like a throne, embossed wallpaper, diamond-patterned carpet, ludicrous crystal chandelier. It is all in the ordinary taste (or lack of it) of the newly rich in Japan, but there is nothing in it of Mifuné.

He is not concerned with office and house. Someone else designed, chose, bought for him. He is interested only in how well he does, how true he is, how understanding he can be.

The devotion to virtue is a terrible thing. It also accounts for Mifuné's being no different from what he once was. Being good is the ambition of a certain kind of child—the child who graduated from being bad but who never went on to being both, the usual definition of maturity.

His distracted gaze, his laugh, his concern that the conversation continue on its meaningless way, his acquiescence, his understanding, distant but there. Being all good seems to be as difficult as being all bad.

Being all anything is hard. As I look at him and again he laughs, briefly, looking down at the table, I seem to hear his parents saying what a good boy Toshi-bo is. And I can see Kurosawa, that bad parent, turning away from this good son who loved him.

Then Mifuné suddenly smiles. Not laughs. Smiles. The smile is something else. His face lights up, his gaze returns. He looks at you as though he sees you and is amused—by you, by himself, by life. The smile is many things—it is also a sign that for a short time Mifuné has forgotten about Mifuné.

Ruriko Otani

– May I help you?

She was smiling, holding the menu with both hands in front of her. She knew me. That is what the smile said. It both welcomed and presumed.

And I knew her but could not remember from where. She was a tall woman, just middle-aged, large brown eyes, a mole between them over the bridge of her nose, and wearing a pink sari. The menu was held by large, capable hands.

Then I began to remember. Whenever she saw me she looked up with the same smile, but she was always wearing white.

– I thought it was you when I saw you come in. And I said to myself: Well, he'll really be surprised to see me here. This is the last place he'd expect to see me.

And I associated an odor with her as well—a clean, fresh odor . . . something medicinal.

Medicinal . . . medical . . . hospital . . . and I had placed her. Every other month for some years I had seen her, been greeted with: Hello there, Mr. Richie. Let's see, yes, here's your file. Are you in a hurry today? I could phone down and have them get your medication ready now. That way you wouldn't have to wait.

Head nurse at the eye clinic, an important position. Nurse Otani, that is what I had heard her called. She assisted the doctors, told the other nurses what to do, ran the place, and yet always had time to smile and ask how you were and if she could help.

And here she stood in a pink sari, wearing copper bracelets, her nails crimson. She was telling me about the tandoori chicken special just as a year before she had told me about my new glaucoma drops.

– And *lhasi* comes with it—that's yoghurt with cucumber in it—and *nan*.

She knew as much now about Indian food as she had known about medicine, and she spoke of it in the same neutral and nurse-like way.

The tables were filling up. It was lunchtime and Indian food has become popular in Japan. Nothing else Indian is popular; Japan has otherwise as little interest in that country as it has in the rest of Asia. Perhaps it is because the food is cheap. Perhaps it is because of the rice.

She glanced at the other waiting customers as she had glanced at patients in the waiting room at the hospital. She seemed to be calculating just how much time each would take. I ordered quickly, aware that at the clinic I always signed my slips in a hurry. She smiled—a professional smile but a wide one.

Later, dawdling over my canned mango, I looked up to find her standing by the table and asking if there was anything else she could do, just as at the hospital she always asked if she could help. The customers were thinning out, her duties were over for the moment, and so I asked her what had happened.

She looked down at her pink sari, pulled at one transparent corner, and said: Yes, it is quite a difference. You must remember me only in my nurse's uniform. Well, I don't have any now. Gave them all away.

In small doses, I was told what had happened. I remembered old Dr. Igarashi, didn't I? Yes, he was head of the eye clinic there at the hospital. Well, he was quite old, actually. And so he finally retired.

Head Nurse Otani, over fifteen years on the job, hard-working, cheerful, popular, was called in by the administrative head. She had thought it was for notice of transfer. It wasn't. It was for notice of dismissal.

– But that wasn't fair, I said: You worked there for years and you were so good at your job.

She looked at her strong hands with their bright red nails, looked at them as she might have looked at the hands of a stranger. Well, yes, she said, and smiled: But, you know, that isn't the way it is. That isn't what counts.

Yes, I knew that. What one does, even who one consequently is, is not what counts. What counts is who you are connected with, who you work for.

– And the new eye doctor, well, he had his own staff, his own head nurse. And the old doctor, he had no more use for me. The other girls, the other nurses, they got transferred, but I'd belonged to Dr. Igarashi, because I was his head nurse, you see. So I was associated with him. When they saw me, they thought of him. And he had retired, so naturally I ought to retire too. Otherwise, it would be as though he hadn't retired at all. Well, I could understand all that.

I couldn't, sitting there in front of my canned mangoes and looking at this capable person in her silly pink sari and her stupid red nails. I knew things like this happened, even knew why, but I did not understand them. To understand would seem to accept.

Then I saw whom she resembled, standing there in her Indian dress, her Indian bangles. She looked like an Indian widow. Husband dead. On her way to suttee. A stupid sacrifice. Her fine brown eyes suddenly seemed bovine.

– You ought to sue, I said in my Western way.

She smiled, almost fondly: Can you see me doing that?

No, I couldn't. I could only imagine her successfully relieved of the position she had filled so ably, the work she had done so well. And all because of a strange tribal custom which removed all members of the court once the master was dead.

She looked at me, still smiling, not at all ashamed of her calamity, for it had not, after all, been her fault. I noticed her mole.

– The mole is in just the right place for an Indian, I said: It looks like a caste mark.

– High class, I hope, she added. Then: Working in this costume I get to feel that I'm almost a foreigner.

I knew what she meant and what, whether she knew it or not, she was implying. But I did not want to dwell on her loss, so I said: I know what you must be feeling.

She blushed, a delicate pink which matched her sari.

– Oh, I didn't mean you, she said.

– I understand, I replied, and smiled to show that indeed I did: You know, being a foreigner, or feeling like one, you can understand a lot more.

– Can you? she asked doubtfully.

– With a little practice.

She removed the empty mango dish.

– Well, in that case, she said, I have plenty of time.

Then, reverting to herself as she was, her head-nurse manner again visible, she told me: Our lunch menu changes every day, you know. Tomorrow is *sag* mutton. Very nutritious, and quite cheap as well. If you came every day, each day would be different. And it would be good for you too.

Kunio Kubo

After he had been bantam-weight champion (and, oh, that had been the life: picture in the papers, carried shoulder-high by the crowd, different girl every night), they asked him to take over the organization. It was small, just a group really, not a proper gang, couldn't be compared with any of the really big *kumi*, but he'd been friends with old Sunada who had, after all, been one of his earliest sponsors and so he did have some obligation now, didn't he?

This was how Kubo entered the underworld. In his boxing days, admittedly, he had had a good view of it. Sporting circles are just as involved in this world as are construction companies and political factions of the extreme right. Also, he had known many people in it because a boxing champion attracts gambling money. But he had never formally entered. Now he did so.

– I thought I knew all about the *yakuza*, he said: But I didn't. I expected them to act like in the movies. You know, code among men, sincere, kind to the poor, violent but polite. Maybe once it was like that but not now. A gang organization is like any other company these days. I don't know why I agreed to take charge of this little group. I just never had a business head. If I had I'd never have become a boxer.

Those who chose Kubo, however, knew what they were doing. They needed someone popular, a good figurehead, and they wanted someone expendable, that is, someone not from the ranks of the gangs. The ex-boxer would attract new recruits and at the same time would not interfere with ancient ties. And, as for his motivation, well, a has-been boxer can open up a gym if he has a backer or he can take his chances if he hasn't.

The small group that Kubo was now nominally heading was composed of young men who wanted to get on in the underworld. The way this is done is to encroach on the territory of other small gangs, provoke a confrontation, fight, and then take over. The men of the beaten gangs always come over peacefully and so your group gets twice as big and has twice as much territory. And you do this, gang by gang, district by district. That's how really big outfits—like the Wada-gumi and Shimizu-gumi in Shinjuku, or the Kyokuto-gumi in Ikebukuro—got started after the war.

– Like samurai, I said: Changing sides all the time.

Kubo smiled: Yes. I think that's why these *chimpira* punks like to talk about the old-time *yakuza*, about loyalty, and why they go see old action movies when they can. If you come from nowhere it's good to find a home and a history.

I wanted to know if it was true about little fingers, that one was cut off as atonement, that you cut it off yourself to show your sincerity.

– Maybe. I never saw it done. Maybe that's movie-talk too. For a while one of the punishments was to hold the guy down and then rip the nail off one of his big toes with a pliers. It didn't show, you see, if you had your shoes on. A missing little finger is pretty visible, right? Then there's the candle.

– What's that?

This was also used for punishment or intimidation. The culprit was put in the middle of a circle of members and all his clothes were taken off; then a candle was lighted. It was moved toward him and when he backed away he was pushed back into the middle and got burned. He'd turn around to escape, and get pushed back and burned again. They burned him just anywhere. Under the arms when he held up his hands to plead. Or under his behind, or his balls, when he bowed for forgiveness. Not on the face, though. Burns on the face would show.

– The strange thing was that it was so quiet. Just his whimpering. Then he'd try to break out of the circle and he'd be pushed back and this little candle would be waiting. I never held the candle but I was once one of those who did the pushing. And in about five minutes the poor guy was crying, tears running down his face, but they didn't stop. They burned him till he just lay there and didn't move. It hurts all right, but it's only skin. It heals and doesn't leave much of a scar. Discipline was important, you see, because without it you had a loose organization and loose organizations don't make money.

Money. You made it in a number of ways. Protection, intimidation, blackmail, or you got a franchise on something—peanuts or lemons, say—and made all the bars in the territory buy from you at stiff prices. But the main way was expansion. You got concessions from neighboring gangs. You forced them, for example, to hand over their bars, or their laundries and dry cleaners.

He had had some experience of this. A bigger gang had wanted some concessions from his area and tried to frighten him into giving them.

– I was alone. I'd come in good faith, you see. Maybe I'd seen too many *yakuza* pictures. But once I was there they held this pistol at my back. But before that they made me take off my trousers and shorts. I wondered why, I remember. Then they made me kneel, and with the gun still there at my back, they tried to make me agree. I wouldn't.

So then the leader of the other group lost his temper. He signaled to two men standing on either side. They took out their knives—*katana*, they called them, though they weren't swords. And they slowly shoved those two six-inch blades into him as he knelt there, half-naked.

One on each side, they pushed them into his buttocks, pushing slowly until the handles met the skin.

– I didn't move. It felt cold more than it hurt. It didn't hurt till later. If I'd moved they might have shot me too. When the knives were in they asked again and I didn't answer. Then they took out the blades and pulled me up, put bandages over the cuts, got me into my trousers, and shoved me out the door.

They hadn't got their concessions and he had saved his own gang from a possible takeover. As for the wounds, the one on the right side was clean and healed well enough. The other guy, though, had twisted the blade and made a hole.

– Here. Look.

Kubo stood up and lowered his trousers and shorts. There on his left buttock was a large scar.

– I'm just lucky it didn't get infected. Some of those *katana* can be pretty dirty.

This was in 1960, a summer afternoon, Kubo standing there, half smiling at the stories he had been telling me, that faintly apologetic smile which people have when they have been talking about themselves, looking at me with the simplicity you find in people who have worked their bodies to make a living.

He pulled up his shorts, zipped his trousers. The body was still a boxing champion's but it was failing him. That was why he was in the dangerous-sounding business that he was.

– I'm going to get out, as soon as I can put a bit more away.

He was going to go straight and wash his hands (feet, in Japan) of it all, but I wondered if he could get out that easily. I recalled a recent newspaper report of a case in Kamata where a young thug was beaten to death with boards, inside a circle of former friends, for trying to quit.

– No, I've got influence. I've got this guy. He'll protect me. I'll wait a bit longer and then I'll get out.

– Well, be careful of your big toenails, I said.

Then, later, big business really took charge of Japan. There were many mergers, many takeovers, and the present giants of industry appeared. These became household names throughout the world.

The underworld too shaped up. Smaller gangs were eliminated. There was a massive amalgamation as money was poured into the organization. The present giants of the underworld put the profession back on its economic feet, and the *yakuza* wore white shirts and ties and had name cards with Ginza office addresses. Peanuts and lemons were forgotten, as outfits now with respectable names ending with Ltd., or Inc., or K.K. expanded their market to include other really profitable companies.

It was almost eight years before I saw Kubo again. But one summer afternoon he appeared. At first I did not recognize him. He had a moustache, his hair was cut short. Also, he had no left hand.

– Yes, he said, smiling his apologetic smile: It's been a long time. No, no. I didn't want anything. It's just that we hadn't met. And you were interested in me once.

A lot had happened. He'd got married, for example. Nice girl. And he'd found a new job. A salesman, kind of. And he would have had a kid too but there'd been a miscarriage. Here was his card. He produced it. No Ginza address for him. He lived in the industrial north.

Looking down at himself as though at a stranger, he said: You know, you're the only person I'm still in touch with who knew me as I was back then. Back when I was a champion. Maybe you're the only one who remembers. Imagine that.

And he shook his head, good-naturedly overwhelmed by fate. His body seemed smaller now, turned in on itself, and his hand lay in his lap.

– Oh, that? No, no, no—it isn't what you think. I had this construction job and I didn't get my hand away from the pile driver in time. Really. That's the truth.

And he picked up his drink with his right hand and smiled. The smile alone had not changed.

– It's good now. Oh, it's hard sometimes but at least I don't have anyone following me around any more. There was a period there when it was sort of bad.

And then nothing more for another five years until, one day, the telephone rang. It was a woman. She sounded worried and apologetic. We hadn't met but . . . she'd been going through a few of his things and had found my name card, and she thought she would just call and find out, and really, she was very sorry, but could I tell her where Kunio Kubo was? This was his wife, you see. Had I seen him or heard from him in the last year or so? Could I help her?

Minoru Sakai

In school, out of pocket, Minoru answered the advertisement. You too can make enough to live a modern life, it said. Easy hours. Tips. And, said the smooth young man who interviewed him, if you work it right, perks.

Minoru was to present himself every evening at the Empire Club. There he was to assist until his trial period was over and he became one of the regulars, like Hiroshi and Saburo and Ichiro.

Assisting meant running out to buy a pack of Kents for the company president's wife, or peeling an expensive papaya in the tiny kitchen, or sitting with the others at one of the tables, looking bright and laughing at the jokes.

But assistance extended only so far. Minoru had taken pity on a widow sitting lonely in the corner. No sooner had he asked her to dance than Ichiro was onto him, furious, pulling him off to the kitchen where he hissed that one trick more like that and he was out on his ear, that she was his, he was warming her up and that if Minoru thought he could just come in and make off like that he had another think coming. Acting like that and him only a helper!

From then on Minoru no longer took pity. He admired rings and hairstyles, exclaimed over polaroids of fat children, sat with impatient guests while the regular was elsewhere occupied; and, at the end, brought in the large bill on its doilied tray.

The regulars got most of the money. They were popular. Minoru looked at the slick and vacuous Ichiro and wondered why. Because, he was informed, when new customers appeared they always asked who was popular. Told that Ichiro was, they asked for him. Consequently, he became all the more so.

As for the helpers, they got the tips, the thousand-yen notes left behind on the table or roguishly stuffed into their breast pocket by the departing guest. It was not much. Minoru began to wonder how he could make enough to lead a proper modern life on such leavings as these.

But he lasted. He needed the money, these tiny tips. So he sat at the corners of tables, laughing when he judged it appropriate, avoiding the fingers of a certain Mrs. Watanabé every Thursday. Soon the right patron would appear. Soon he too would be popular.

In the afternoon, instead of going to classes, he was told to scout. This was what the others did. This was how Ichiro had got his start.

One was supposed to loiter in Shibuya or Ginza and pick out someone likely. One began by saying: I was drawn to you. I know I shouldn't ask, but you do seem to be a woman who would understand. Though I'm only a student, and I've everything to learn, I wonder if you'd care to have some tea with me.

This direct approach was not often successful, but all the boys were convinced that an initial, dishonest display of honesty was best. Women often accepted adventure only if it was offered with modesty and complete untruth.

Coffee and cakes were the first and final things for which the youngsters paid. The next step was to say: Interesting place I work in part-time. A kind of snack bar we students help to run.

And then the executive's wife, the widow, the older, unmarried woman sometimes actually appeared. If not discouraged by the bill, she was considered hooked. She was also considered the patron of the young man who had done the initial legwork. For a good deal more she might avail herself of further services. These, boasted Ichiro, led from cuff links and three-piece London suits all the way to Porsches.

Ichiro was something of an expert. He had three patrons—Mondays, Wednesdays, Fridays—and he was so skillful they had never once collided. He enjoyed talking about the business after hours, leaning forward, hands folded, imparting his knowledge to the trainees.

– You got to go slow, you see. You got to gauge your clientele. With some it's you who's got to be seduced. With others, though, you have to pant and press. Others still you got to rape. Why? Because that's what the customer wants.

– What if you rape someone you ought to be seduced by? asked Minoru, who thought he might be able to be seduced but was certain he could never rape.

Ichiro tapped his smooth forehead: Inspiration! It's all up here. Either you have it or you don't. That's business, boy.

He held up a manicured hand, then looked at Minoru: Now you, you haven't got it. Never will. Probably fall in love. Probably give it away free.

Minoru nodded. He probably would. Then, thinking, he asked: But what about love? I've never been in love but I hear it's common. It's what men and women feel together and after that comes the sex.

Ichiro appeared scandalized. Look, he said sternly: This is business. We're a company here like any other. We do our job, we stick together, we push the product.

Then he softened, smiled, shot a cuff, and said: But it's an art too, you know. It's serious. And slow, that's the secret. Dedicated, like a crafts-man. And done with class. Lots of little things a person like you would never think of. A little stroking here, a little licking there.

Minoru shook his head in wonder. He had never thought of things like that.

– You get them where you want, and then you keep them there, kind of hovering. It's like a game but serious. They're paying all this dough. You just got to make certain they keep on paying.

Saburo smiled, scratched his head: I'd come, he said, and laughed.

In practice, these outside excursions brought in few patrons. Mostly the customers were bar hostesses or the mamas who ran the bars. Weary of being nightly pawed, they came themselves to paw. There was one who wore a wig and had sharp canines from whom the boys used to hide, crowding into the tiny kitchen and leaving Hiroshi to cope.

Most of the time, however, the customers were well behaved. And most of those from other bars, Minoru noticed, seemed much more in-terested in each other than in the boys. Except that the interest was not friendly. What's that older person having at that table over there? Oh, fruit? Apples, oranges? Well, boy, you bring us some real fruit. Yes, kiwi, papaya, mango.

– So what? said Ichiro: So long as they have a good time and keep coming back. And if Madame Kazu wants to drag you into the toilet, then you get dragged into the toilet.

Madame Kazu was the one with the sharp teeth.

After hours the boys would gather around Ichiro and talk about hidden assets. Saburo exposed a pair of cuff links, with the comment: Sapphires, she said. Glass, if you ask me.

Snickers, giggles from the others. Then Hiroshi scuffed a gleaming pump: Cordovan, all the way from Spain, she said. More likely horse, all the way from Gumma.

More chuckles, then Ichiro removed a diamond from his finger and peered at it suspiciously: South African yellow, she said. More like piss yellow, if you ask me.

Everyone laughed hard at this because the joke was Ichiro's. Then Minoru, emboldened, looked at the ring on his finger: Silver, she said, ha-ha—more like tin, if you ask me!

No one laughed and Ichiro turned in sudden fury: Where did you get that ring? Which one gave it to you? Listen, boy, if you get into my territory you are dead. Come on. Which one?

And Minoru had to admit that he had found it in front of Isetan Department Store, and everyone laughed immoderately.

Night after night Minoru watched the other boys as they chattered away, turning their heads, waving their hands. This, he thought, is the way the bar hostesses on TV behave when they are alone together. They are always talking about the patrons and their presents.

Maybe men and women are not, after all, that different, he thought. He looked about him, at Hiroshi in his velvet jacket, his close-cut perm. Maybe it was only what they had learned, been taught, men and women, that made them different. Maybe when they did the same work—host or hostess—they became the same again.

He turned this novel thought over in his head as he watched. The buzzer sounded. Customers? As late as this? At once the boys went into action. Ichiro swirled to face the mirror. Hiroshi emptied ashtrays and trotted to the kitchen. Saburo straightened the chairs and smoothed the doilies.

Then, with a quick, housewifely glance around, Ichiro tested his smile before unlocking the door and swinging it open with practiced grace.

Minoru straightened his tie, smiled, stood slightly awkward, for he had already learned that innocence, real or seeming, attracts.

He never did finish school, and his mother in the provinces is pleased with the well-paying job he has though she doesn't know what it is. The widow and, after that, the bored wife of a Yamaha executive helped him open his own place. It is very expensive, very popular.

He recently put in a series of ads for new helpers. You too can live a modern life, they said. Easy hours, tips, perks. And, after hours, he gathers these fresh, young, unformed faces about him and imparts the secrets of the craft as handed down to him.

Oharu Kitano

– Oh, no, she was saying: It spoils the line if you wear panties, so we never do. Me, I simply wear a *koshimaki* under this.

She indicated her kimono, a green so dark it was almost black, her sash a pale tan secured with lilac-colored braided cord.

– What color is your *o-koshimaki*? I asked politely, referring to the single sarong-like sheath around her torso, next to her skin.

– Red, she answered, then, explaining: It's traditional. But nowadays the younger entertainers wear anything they like, even white—if you can imagine.

An entertainer, that was how Oharu referred to herself. Not a geisha, though she could probably sing, play the samisen, dance; not a waitress, certainly, though she poured saké and helped with the serving. We were at a table in an elegant Akasaka *ryotei*. It was grand—one entertainer for each guest.

Oharu was older than the rest of them and very handsome. Also very intelligent, I thought. The other girls were laughing and carrying on, covering their giggling mouths with their hands, but she and I were having an interesting conversation.

– I took a bath with Toshiro Mifuné once, I volunteered: He wore BVDs under his armor.

– How interesting, said Oharu: And how anachronistic of him.

Back then, it appeared, samurai wore nothing under their kimono and only a pair of linen shorts under their armor.

– But what about the *fundoshi*? I wanted to know, referring to the traditional loincloth.

Well, the *fundoshi* with tie strings only came in during early Meiji, designed for the new army, for hygenic reasons, she understood. And the old *rokkushaku* not only would have bunched terribly but was far too plebeian. Only porters and runners and fishermen wore it.

– Then the aristocracy wore nothing under their clothes? I asked, pleased to be talking to someone so well informed.

– So it would seem, said Oharu, half smiling: And convenient too it must have been. Court ladies back then still wore those Heian-style layered kimono. You know, with twelve layers. Can you imagine what a bother underwear would be if you wanted to go to the toilet?...

And she gracefully pantomimed the raising of all these kimono skirts and indicated the ease of simply squatting.

How, I wondered, had she come to know so much about this subject? Of course, entertainers traditionally knew what to talk about to amuse or interest the guest. She could probably have spoken equally well on the stock market or the current baseball season.

– Yes, I said: I can see how it would help.

– Particularly with a job like mine where you have to drink all evening, she said with a smile.

The other girls were growing rowdy now, slapping playfully at the men, laughing loudly, accusing them of only thinking about *that*.

And here Oharu and I were having this serious and absorbing conversation about underwear in Japanese history or the lack of it. I was enjoying myself and so was she. There were no laborious innuendos, no flirtation, no coyness. We were simply two adults talking about a subject not much mentioned.

– Did you ever hear why? she asked, pouring me another cup of saké.

– Why the lack of underwear?

– No, why it's now so common, whether it ruins the line or not.

– Drafts? I wondered, thinking of winter.

She smiled: A little discomfort has never discouraged a fashion. No, much worse.

Then she leaned forward, still smiling, and told me about the notorious event of 1937 that had introduced panties into Japan.

There was a fire in the Shirokiya Department Store in Nihombashi and a number of the kimonoed salesgirls had fled to the roof. The fire raged, out of all control, and the only escape was by leaping into the safety nets held out by the firemen far below. The trapped girls, however, refused to jump. All were in kimono. These would certainly open during the fall and the fact that they were wearing nothing under them would become apparent. They would be exposed to the public gaze, and all chose death before dishonor.

– At least that's the story, Oharu concluded: And as a result women all over the country began wearing Western-style panties.

I spoke unthinkingly: What would *you* do if this place caught fire? Expose yourself?

She looked at me, a long level gaze, as though she were seeing me for the first time. It was the look of someone who has mistaken you for someone else and is now politely retreating. The half-smile faded.

Then it curved into brilliance as she leaned forward, slapped my knee, laughed and, in a high voice I was hearing for the first time, said: Why, you silly. We're on the ground floor. If I jumped it would only be into the carp pool!

Confronting me now was the typical would-be geisha who laughed loudly at every sally and would soon be showing the cunning way she could peel a tangerine.

– Foreign women sometimes go around without anything underneath, I said, desperately trying to recover that grave lady who until now had been sitting opposite me. It means, I said recklessly, that they're making a statement.

– Oh, *yada*, she cried, impersonating someone much younger than herself: You awful man. *Etchi!*

This last is the Japanese pronunciation of the English *h* and refers to the word *hentai*, which in the dictionary means "perverted" but in its milder, abbreviated form means only "naughty," with certain overtones. It is also shouted out, as it was here, with laughter or a roguish expression.

I looked at her, hurt.

Had I done something so awful, to be punished like this? Yes, I had.

She had perhaps wanted to step out of her usual role, had wanted to just talk about something, to stop being girlish. She had perhaps thought I was intelligent enough to understand. And I had shown her that I wasn't. Having indicated what I expected of her, she complied. And so the free discourse of two grown-ups, a conversation with no ulterior purpose, an exchange of information, no matter how arcane, all this came to a full stop and we were back where I apparently thought we were supposed to be.

And now she was picking up the saké bottle and holding it out with a simpering smile, saying: We're going to have to drink just lots to catch up with those folks down there.

– I don't want to catch up with them.

– Oh, *yada!*

And that grave, possessed, playful woman who knew how to talk about all sorts of things with detached intelligence—her name was Oharu, family name Kitano, information I later got from the mistress of the *ryotei*—never appeared again.

Taro Furukaki

Shy, plain, wearing an old sweater, speaking with the accent of his private tutor, Oxford perhaps, but sometimes with an invented Texan drawl, perhaps copied from the movies—seeking to amuse, lazy smile, inquisitive eyes. When irritated, speaking Japanese—the flat Tokyo dialect of the Yamanote.

The successfully expatriate Japanese is rarer than the expatriate anyone else. Most of them anxiously await return to the homeland. Some cannot wait—suicides in Queens or Larchmont. Not, however, Taro. He was the kind of Japanese who flourishes abroad—a Foujita who did not paint. And, like most successful expatriates everywhere, he did not have a high opinion of where he came from.

Taro did not speak about it much. When we were together in school he rarely mentioned Japan. Rather, we talked about his enthusiasms. These included Madeleine Grey doing the *Chansons madécasses*, Jane Bathori singing "Le Bestiaire," and Claire Croiza's "Jazz dans la nuit."

These were interests from childhood. They were French because his childhood had been French, though spent in Japan. Father was Francophile, indeed eventually became ambassador to France, and Taro remained loyal to the France of those early years spent in the old Denen-chofu mansion, alone but for the maids. He was loyal to Ravel, Poulenc, Roussel.

Even at school in America he remained loyal. I thought this peculiar because he rarely spoke of his father and, when he did, he did so in Japanese. He did not seem to like him, made fun of the French verse this diplomat wrote and published. I do not know what he would have made of the Order of the Legion of Honor and the First Class Order of the Sacred Treasure that his father eventually received from the two governments. I know he wouldn't have mentioned it unless forced to, and then only in Japanese. He did not, it almost seemed, approve of his father's serious and successful career. The result of this—perhaps the reason for it—was that Taro himself refused, in this sense, to be serious. One of his charms, in fact, was his lack of seriousness.

We both admired the useless and ephemeral. We devised impossible opera seasons comprised of works that had never been begun. His included the Beethoven *Faust*, the Verdi *Lear*, and the Wagner *Life of Buddha*. We also cast Proust as a Warner Brothers film—Swann was Joseph Cotten, Odette was Bette Davis, Charlus was Sydney Greenstreet, and Jupien was, of course, Peter Lorre.

What would Taro do when he got out of school, the complaint of the Furukaki family, was a question that did not concern Taro himself. Something would happen.

Something did. After school he traveled and met the girl he fell in love with, married; the woman had his child. Something else happened, too: Taro's troubles began.

When I met him again in Tokyo I was unaware of the problem and was not told. His father did not mention it, nor did his wife. I was consequently unprepared when, one evening, my wife and I had them over for dinner and Taro refused to say anything. It was strange, a friend suddenly dumb. I tried to talk of what we knew. I even talked about "Jazz dans la nuit." Silence, a straight mouth, unfriendly eyes.

The next day his wife telephoned and explained. He had been seeing a doctor. Taro ought to leave Japan, he'd said, ought to go back abroad. But they couldn't, they hadn't the money. Taro was now working at a job his father had found him at a radio station.

Meetings with him were now serious affairs, or would have been if there had been anyone there. But he was like a house when no one is home. Except for once.

I was at his place. We were playing records, things he had liked. We had just done the Ravel *Don Quixote*. I had bought him, as a present, the new recording of Stravinsky's *Le Rossignol*, an opera he had long wanted to hear.

Taro suddenly stood up, rummaged in the record cabinet, hid the jacket and put on the disc. It was contemporary, for piano and orchestra. What is it? he asked—and these were the first words we had heard from Taro that day.

I listened but couldn't identify it. So I said so. Taro smiled, the first smile we had seen that day, but it was not a nice smile, not Taro's. Then: You—you who know so much. You know all about Stravinsky, right? Well, that was Stravinsky. It was the *Movements for Piano and Orchestra*. Here, look at the jacket. See? I'm not lying. So, you're not so smart. Not so smart at all . . . Then he relapsed into silence.

What had happened? Had I suddenly, somehow, gone over to the other side? Had I become an enemy? Or had the whole world gone over? Was there just Taro left, locked in his childhood, hearing the faint strains of Jane Bathori's songs?

Later, his wife told me that he stopped talking even to her. He stared at the wall, but as though seeing something there. Sometimes he smiled and it was the old Taro again. And he used to hum a tune, though she didn't know what it was. When his family came, however, he hid in the bathroom. The bathroom was America; it was far away. They couldn't come there.

Then one day he left the house. He often did. Took walks. This day he took a walk and the street crossed the railway lines. Taro walked to the crossing just as a train was coming. The train did not stop. Neither did Taro.

The death was listed as an accident. It did not look like a suicide. Such perfect timing, victim and train proceeding at their own rates to their rendezvous, wouldn't seem to have been the work of a suicide. It was simply that, seeing the train, Taro did not stop. But then perhaps he did not see it. He often saw nothing, his wife told me, as though he were looking at a world of his own, or listening to voices she would never hear.

Toru Takemitsu

A postcard—a big blue Yves Klein—said that the chemotherapy seemed to be working and that he thought he could maybe go home at the beginning of the month. I put it down on my desk and remembered.

Small hands cupped over the keys, an index finger stretching to push down the black while the thumb held the white, and softly, as though the secrets of a lock were being probed, the sound of Satie had emerged.

I remember Toru when he was young, back in 1955 or so, playing that old concert grand at the Sogetsu Hall where we met to see new art or look at new films or listen to new music. There was Hiroshi Teshigahara, who was later to make *Woman of the Dunes* for which Toru would do the score, and whose father owned the hall; there was Kuniharu Akiyama who would turn into a fine music critic before dying eventually of stomach cancer; and there was Toru.

We listened while he put the notes together, shaping them as if from clay, holding, warming the tones. Those small-boned works seemed to fit his hands. I could not imagine Liszt—or even Messiaen, whom he was beginning to like—coming from them. Rather, something sparer, more discreet.

He was a student then—small body, large head. We sat around the piano at Sogetsu Hall listening. Satie rolled over the keys like a kitten, and outside the cicadas sang as though summer would last forever.

When we had heard enough the hands would drop from the keyboard and turn themselves into an ocarina. Out of the cupped palms, the thumbs a mouthpiece, came "The Tennessee Waltz." (I remember him years later, at a bar called The Cradle, cradling his fingers and doing his ocarina arrangement of "Red River Valley" to the delight of Francis Coppola. Later still we sat stalled in traffic and he gave me "Don't Get Around Much Anymore.")

Sometimes, on being asked, he would turn again to the piano and play something of his own, his manner diffident and yet assured. I no longer remember what it was, nor do I recall what I felt on first hearing his music. The *Requiem for Strings* was still at the back of his mind and would not appear for several more years. He had yet to take the score of *Jeux* off with him into the mountains to keep him company while he composed *November Steps*.

Up there, besides Debussy, there was the neighbor's music box (it played the "theme" from *Swan Lake*) and the sound of water, the rustle of the wind. All of these went somehow into the score he eventually produced. But they went so deep you can no longer really hear them. The rush of the shakuhachi, the clatter of the biwa, seem to owe nothing to Tchaikovsky, though somehow it is the same landscape, the same steppes. Takemitsu did not like things that floated on the surface. He once listened to another Japanese composer go on and on about the musical possibilities of insect sounds, even that of the common cicada (*semi*). Toru turned to Peter Grilli, sitting next to him, and said: Semi-music.

Now, remembering those small hands on that distant keyboard, I am surprised that such modest movements came to create such large emotions. Now I listen and find I am confronting something vast. In the later works the small has become enormously magnified—a snowflake big as a palace, a sea anemone swaying above us like a mother ship—an expanded natural world, alive, internally coherent, complete in its complexity.

Three decades after the first time, I sat in a concert hall and heard the Takemitsu violin concerto. It has a title, *Far Voices, Calling Far* (Yeats? Joyce?), attractive more for its sound than its sense. The ghost of Satie (*Embryons desséchés, Véritables préludes flasques*) hovers there above the score. The violin climbs, then soars, the orchestra dropping away from the cliff's edge. Then, far below, like the sea, the instruments resurge and, as though the laws of physics had been reinvented for the ear, right themselves to catch as in a net the soaring line. And then silence . . . until, later, "Don't Get Around Much Anymore," done on his hand ocarina, evoking a look of sheer delight on the face of

Richard Brautigan, a face that rarely smiled and finally failed to smile forever.

It is now much later. I turn off the CD of the violin concerto, look at the Klein, and think of Toru in hospital during those last days, rays shooting through his small body, picking at the knot of the illness. And I remember his wake and wondering at how small the box was, then remember his face as he bent over the keyboard, breaking into a smile and nodding in silent satisfaction as the proper combination was found, the levers turned, the door opened.

Mieko Watanabé

I sometimes bought flowers in the shop where she worked, a small shop without much of a selection but conveniently near where I lived. She was a pleasant, open-faced woman in her thirties. Her smile was usually so ready that I was sometimes surprised to see her frowning in the back of the shop when I passed.

As the seasons changed and I bought irises, asters, chrysanthemums, we took to greeting each other as I went by—I on my way to work, she already busy cutting and arranging.

She would look up, scissors in one hand, a long-stemmed flower in the other, and nod, smile, wish me a good morning. But only some of the time.

At other times I would see her there bending over the flowers, would smile, prepare to speak. When I passed, however, she would give me only an empty glance, returning at once to her work. The next time, as I prepared to pass without a word, she might look up, nod, smile, and wish me a very good morning.

What, I wondered, was the reason for this? Had I perhaps done something to make her behave in this way? These typically, guiltily, were the thoughts that first came to mind.

Or did all foreigners truly look alike, as I had often enough been told, and did she only intermittently recognize me? Or, rather, perhaps, was there something the matter with her—some sort of mental trouble where she was only occasionally herself and I, consequently, myself only occasionally to her?

The mystery continued. I could not understand her behavior, and though it derived from a person who had no other part in my life, one whose actions ought to have made no difference to me, I began when alone to think about her, to brood on possible reasons for it.

And, more and more, I began to think that it was somehow my fault, that I was doing something, all unintentionally, that was offending her. When I failed to do this, then she came out, flowers in both hands, smiling as though grateful that I was behaving myself. When she saw, however, that I was doing it again—whatever it was—then she hid her hands in her apron and silently retreated, once again disappointed in me and showing it with a sullen stare or a mere glance of ill will.

Should I ask her to explain, I wondered. But how to go about it? In English one could, I suppose, approach a woman in a flower shop and ask her why she was behaving so strangely. Certainly odder things than this were done in the country I had come from. But I could not imagine doing this in Japan—could not even think how to phrase my hypothetical question. Besides, I was now convinced that I was doing something, innocent though it might be, that in some way merited this response. The one acting strangely was, somehow, myself.

After reaching this conclusion, I now discovered that the flower woman was haunting me. I thought about her before I went to sleep. I found myself thinking of her when I awoke. If she had been consistently friendly or consistently unfriendly, then I would not have spared her a thought.

It was the inconsistency that had snared me. Like fishermen and gamblers, I had become hooked by random circumstance. I never knew what to expect and was always driven to find out. This, I thought, was how they drive rats mad. The unhappy rodent pushes the bar; sometimes it gets a food pellet, sometimes an electric shock: it never knows which to expect. If it did—sated or electrocuted—it would stop pushing the bar.

I could, of course, have crossed the street or taken another route to the morning subway. But I didn't. I even looked forward to the daily encounter at the flower shop. Which would it be today—acknowledgment or rebuttal; food pellet or electric shock?

Then, one fine spring day when I was in an entirely different part of the city, I happened to pass a florist's and, glancing in, I suddenly remembered something I hadn't really noticed before. When the flower woman was friendly she was wearing a green sweater. But when she changed and put on a red sweater she turned unfriendly.

Now what, I wondered, could be the relationship between her sweaters and her attitude toward me? Did she rush and change from red to green or from green to red when she saw me coming down the street? Was she attempting to communicate with me? Don't smile and speak if you see me in red—was that what she was saying?

And, if so, why? I pondered this question. It took on an inordinate importance. I could not look at flowers now without thinking of the baffling woman, smiling, hands full of flowers, or frowning, hands hidden in apron. I was beginning to despair of ever solving the mystery of which I was somehow the cause.

Not long afterward, I was walking again past the flower shop. Aha, she has her red sweater on today. Very well, do not smile, do not speak. Merely cast one cold glance.

As I was casting this one cold glance I saw that she was cutting the stems of some flowers, and that she was having difficulty in doing so, holding the stems with a forearm while she cut with one hand. This was because she only had one hand. The other arm ended at the wrist.

Stopping at the next street corner I stood and thought, remembering her well in her green sweater, both hands full of flowers. She had had two hands then. Had there been an accident, suddenly, recently? Had it happened in a moment of abstraction—perhaps thinking about my strange behavior?

But, no. The stump looked as if it had healed years ago. And then I remembered that on her red-sweater days she usually hid her hands in her apron. There was the answer—she was hiding her stump. But on her green-sweater days—what then? Why was there no stump?

Now actively curious, I asked the tobacco lady. She knew everything else in the neighborhood and would certainly be able to satisfy my curiosity in this.

– Oh, them, she said when I asked: Meiko and Reiko. They have this sick mother. Not surprising, at eighty-something. So they take turns looking after her.

I gazed at her, bereft. The mystery had suddenly collapsed. I no longer had anything to look forward to on my walks to the subway.

Next morning it was Reiko in red. I looked at her stump. Perhaps she had lost her hand in the war. Perhaps we had done it after all and she focused her hatred on me for ruining her life. Hence the dark glances. Meiko, who had not suffered to this extent, was still friendly. But how to find out? If you couldn't ask people why they were behaving strangely toward you, you certainly couldn't ask how they had lost their hand.

Again I had recourse to the tobacco lady.

– Well, just how old do you think they are anyway? That was forty years ago, you know—the war. They weren't even born back then, though we were, you and me. No, all I know is that she was in a car accident.

The final wisps of mystery evaporated. Reiko's sullenness was simply an understandable reaction to her lot. And Meiko's pleasant openness was the result of her having two hands and being healthy. And my self-centered and paranoid suspicions were because I am the kind of person I am and, perhaps consequently, choose to live in this country—an alien among the natives.

Sessué Hayakawa

– No, not Sessué. That's how they did it in Hollywood. I've never liked it. Actually, it's Sesshu—like the famous painter. You know, the old one.

He paused, a large man in a formal kimono with family crest: In point of fact, he went on, Kintaro Hayakawa was the name I was born with ... Kintaro—what a name! He chuckled and raised his glass: That was back in Meiji 19, when I was born. Way back then.

Though we were speaking English, Hayakawa named the year 1886 in the traditional Japanese manner. Since his return to Japan in 1949 he had become very Japanese: kimono, bonsai, Zen as well.

He should have been drinking saké, but whiskey-on-the-rocks, that American invention, was in the process of becoming Japanese, and he was drinking at the old Imperial Hotel which, by that time, was thought of as being very Japanese indeed.

– They're going to tear it down, you know, he said, looking around at the stonework: Going to build some big money-making skyscraper hotel instead. And it's not even fifty years old yet ... I am, though, he added, then laughed again: How old would you say I am?

I knew. He was eighty, but he looked and acted younger. So I wagged my head as though undecided.

– Well, I won't see seventy again, he said. Then: Why, I can remember when the Imperial opened.

That was in 1922, when Hayakawa was so famous in America that he played himself in a film, a matinée idol in something called *Night Life in Hollywood*. But this I did not mention. He did not like talking about those four decades in California.

Yet he had been one of the most successful of the early Hollywood actors. He had gone to America in 1906 and made his debut there in *Typhoon*, a 1914 Ince film; then went on to make some forty more pictures. He became one of the most popular of the early stars: a romantic lead, the first of the exotic foreigners—Valentino came later—to excite American womanhood from the safety of the silver screen.

I had seen some of these pictures. In the earlier ones (DeMille's *The Cheat*, for example) he was a wily Jap, but before long he had become an Oriental William S. Hart, always steely-eyed, brave, strong, different from the others only in that he had Asiatic eyes. He was not playing a Japanese there; he was playing a Japanese playing an American. Perhaps that accounted for his popularity. Perhaps it also accounted for his lack of any interest in that amazing career. Oh, that, he said, when I mentioned it. He did not want to talk about it.

What he did want to discuss was his new career as a Japanese actor. Though he had returned to play yet another foreigner, Jean Valjean, in an expensive local version of *Les Misérables*, he was soon doing Japanese parts: the wartime hero, Tomoyuki Yamashita, and the camp commandant in *The Bridge on the River Kwai*.

Unfortunately, however, this new Japanese career of his was not successful. The post-WWII Japanese audience, unlike the post-WWI American one, did not take to him. It wasn't that it had forgotten about his American success; the problem was that it hadn't. This often happens. Somebody goes abroad, is successful, and finds himself resented at home. One of ours has deserted us.

Was this, I wondered, why Hayakawa was now so assiduously Japanese? Perhaps, but at the same time one knows it is part of a pattern for a person when young to go away, go abroad, and then, later in life, to return, and turn into his father. In this Hayakawa was no different from others. I thought of Tanizaki, of Kawabata, of Yukio Mishima, all of whom had noticeably "returned" to Japan.

– No, I won't see seventy again, he repeated: By the way, did you ever see a certain film of Eizo Tanaka's? It was called *The Kyoya Collar Shop*.

The conversation invariably took this turn. He always wanted to talk about Japanese movies, those made at the very time that he was making his American films. This was, I think, why he invited me out for drinks or dinner—I knew more about Japanese film history than he did.

I said that I hadn't seen it, that perhaps a print no longer existed—

that it was the first of the films in the new realistic mode.

– Yes, he said, 1922—not even remembering that his own *Night Life in Hollywood* was made in the same year.

I, in turn, wanted to hear about those Hollywood days when he drove a gold-plated Pierce Arrow and lost a million dollars one night at the casino in Monte Carlo, and to hear him explain—as he had once done, with traditional modesty—how his enormous social success was due to his having bought a carload of whiskey just before Prohibition. But now he was only interested in what Japanese directors had been up to when he was young and a matinée idol in a distant land.

– I'm sure you've seen *Souls on the Road*, he continued, mentioning another early Japanese film.

I said I had.

– Remarkable film, simply remarkable—a picture well ahead of its time, I think you'll agree.

I agreed, and we talked on into the evening, myself and the once-famous actor, he ignoring his own career, his own past.

And now the Imperial Hotel is gone, though that bar is preserved—after a fashion, stuck into one of the corners of the enormous new glass and steel structure. And Hayakawa is gone as well, though the National Film Center recently acquired a copy of *The Red Lantern* and there he is, intrepid, saving the day again.

Daisetz Suzuki

Given his appearance alone, he would have had no other recourse than to embrace Zen. With his high forehead, his fuzzy eyebrows, his moles, his childlike smile, he looked like one of those acolytes—Jittoku, for example—who in many a scroll and screen laugh and cavort as they sweep the garden or bait the *roshi*. Always in kimono, always the same one, he looked like a young disciple suddenly become a patriarch. Behind the eyes of the attentive priest playfully peered the child.

But, however strong the priestly resemblance, he was a layman. This he would insist upon. He was a teacher but not a *roshi*. He said once that while he knew all about mountain climbing he had never climbed Mt. Sumera. But he did know that one did not climb mountains merely by looking at them. All too many, he said, thought that Zen was a mysticism concerned with visions of the eternal. This was not so.

Dr. Suzuki often defined things by what they were not. His descriptions of Zen were almost entirely negative. The only positive description I ever heard him give was that climbing mountains was hard work. This was said with a glance in my direction.

I had never worked in that sense, and it was, I gathered, understood between us that I never would. Our bond, in that we had one, was that he hadn't either, not if you consider *zazen* meditation as work. Though he had sat often enough and continued to do so from time to time, he awaited no illumination, defining his duty and his own hard work as elsewhere. Specifically this consisted in explaining what Zen was and wasn't—particularly the latter. He was a lay teacher.

Thus, while others sat in the lotus position in the meditation hall, I sat comfortably on the sofa with him. There he talked and I listened, hoping that learning would somehow rub off. In the end he gave me a definite taste for something he knew I could never eat.

This was in 1946 at Engakuji in Kamakura. He was then seventy-six and had established his Zen library across the valley. He also occasionally tended a small vegetable garden which helped feed him. I, a member of the forces then occupying his country, would appear from Tokyo every Sunday with soda crackers, processed cheese, peanut clusters—things that the PX could contrive in the way of offerings to my *sensei.*

Sensei would receive these graciously and then disappear with them into the back of the house. Upon his reappearance I was given a cup of tea and a *koan* riddle, the "answer" to which I was eventually to present. It was always the same cup and always the same *koan*—the one about Nansen's cat.

Then we would talk. Or rather, he would talk and I would listen. It was always about Zen, and I never understood a word. Or rather, it was the words alone I understood. Each word, even each sentence, made sense, but none of the paragraphs did.

Other discourses I had heard were rational enough, but Dr. Suzuki's were something else. The process seemed associative. As I listened I understood that there were modes of thought different from the ones I had always known and considered true. I learned—important discovery—that logic was a creation of the mind and only one of many possibilities.

I got nowhere with my *koan*, of course. Nansen saw two monks quarreling over a cat. He held it up and said if they had an answer the cat would be saved, otherwise not. They could not answer and Nansen cut the cat in two. Later he told another priest about the incident. This priest took off his sandal, put it on his head, and walked out. Nansen then said that if he had been there, he could have saved the cat. It is typical of my disposition that my first and only reaction was concern for the unfortunate feline.

Our conversations went on for a number of Sundays. I had grown used to the train ride, had grown fond of my walk through the towering cryptomeria of the temple, had become addicted to the weekly talks. Then, on one of these Sundays, Dr. Suzuki decided that we should part.

I understood the probable reasons for this but still felt bereft. I had thought I was a disciple. He stood up, a small man with steel-rimmed spectacles and long hairs in his eyebrows, and took a picture from the wall. It was of a seated Kannon, black ink on paper, framed in wicker, an oval picture of great beauty. It was also a genuine Hakuin. He told me to take it with me and live with it for a while.

He did not tell me why, nor for how long—he never talked about things like that. I understood that he was loaning me the Hakuin and that I was eventually to return it. Happily I took it home, put it up on the wall and, as is the way with things, grew used to it, forgot it.

My year of visits was over. I had been going there waiting for something to happen to me, convinced that mere attendance was enough. Here, after all, was Buddhism, Zen at its best—the meditation hall, floorboards gleaming, the smell of incense, the quiet, the stillness. Benefits would accrue if I simply attended.

Dr. Suzuki understood all this, of course. He was well practiced in talking about Zen to those who had no aptitude for it. It was, in a way, a quality he shared with those with whom he talked. He had written about his experience of *kensho*, that first glimpse of enlightenment, but he had never made any claims to a full *satori*.

Then, after half a year or so, I returned one Sunday, carrying the Hakuin. Again we sat. My teacup was there, though Nansen's cat failed to make an appearance.

– You are very much of this world, very much of this flesh, my *sensei* remarked mildly. Then he smiled. That smile was a way of shaking an understanding head at the ways of the world. And before I left he gave me an invitation to a wedding reception.

He himself had been married, to Beatrice Lane, a close collaborator in his work, who died in 1939. They had adopted a child in 1916, Alan Masaru. It was he who was being married.

I looked forward to this simple ceremony, held in the venerable shadows of the cryptomeria, a Shinto priest perhaps imported for the occasion, the sound of the ceremonial *sho*, and the frugal Buddhist repast at its subdued conclusion.

But on presenting myself at Engakuji that evening, great was my surprise. There were kleig lights illuminating the tall stand of trees and sound trucks making the night hideous with their bellowings. And there was the press, held in place by ropes, pushed back against the meditation hall but ready with flashbulbs and magnesium flares.

The bride, it transpired, was a popular singing star, and her recording company had thought that a wedding extravaganza at an ancient Zen temple would do her career no harm. There stood the happy couple, under the great gate (1285), he in striped trousers and waistcoat, she in full Western bridal finery, veil, train. They stood and posed while the flashbulbs popped and the magnesium flared. Then a sound truck bawled out Wagner and the great temple bell (1301, a national treasure) tolled, as the kleig lights under the high branches of the mighty cryptomeria played over the façade of the *shariden* (1290) in close imitation of a Hollywood premiere.

I was, of course, furious. Part of this emotion was sheer territorial imperative. I had thought all this somehow mine, and here it was being invaded by what I had left the West to escape. Another part, however, was simple outrage—that something this venerable should be so demeaned by rank commercialism, by media hype. And yet another was indignant pity for poor Dr. Suzuki and what they were doing to him.

All of these various reactions were quite wasted. It was not a cabal of wicked worldly priests that had arranged this; it was Dr. Suzuki himself. He had gone to get permission from the temple authorities. He had approved the kleig lights and the sound trucks. He had asked that the young couple be photographed under the great gate. This is what they seemed to want, his son and new daughter-in-law.

And why not? I only saw him once on that glittering evening and he was smiling—perhaps shaking an understanding head at the ways of the world. I did not think so then, but I think so now.

The reason is that, long after this, long after his death, I read a posthumous publication of his, an edition of verses composed by one of the *myokonin*. These were lay people, usually of humble origin, often illiterate, who displayed in what they wrote (or said) a profound experiential understanding of the workings of the Amida Buddha.

In the Jodo Shin sect of Buddhism—one far from the subtleties of Zen—these laymen repeated one prayer over and over again, always the same one, giving thanks for Buddha's birth in the Pure Land. And these Buddhist Baptists, as it were, won Dr. Suzuki's unstinting admiration. They had, he said, a position of great importance in Japanese religious history. In these unlettered and simple believers he discovered profound expressions of enlightenment.

Thinking back to the kleig lights and the sound trucks and bride and groom under the great gate, I began to understand. My feelings of outrage and pity, these were merely representative of one way of thinking. The same events could and did produce feelings quite different and equally justified. There were indeed modes of thought different from the ones I had always known and considered true.

Tadanori Yokoo

To remember the 1960s in Tokyo is to remember Tadanori Yokoo, the artist whose style epitomized that era: a hard-edged cartoon line, bright kindergarten colors, and the popular idioms of long before—the frivolity of the early 1920s. Hanafuda playing cards, the Hinomaru and Rising Sun flags, Momotaro's big pink peach; Buster Brown, Betty Boop, Lion Toothpaste, Golden Bat cigarettes. And even further back, the cherry blossoms and *torii* gates of Hiroshige.

What we see—rendered small and intricate like a city viewed through the wrong end of a telescope—is not anything Yokoo ever saw directly for himself. He was not born when Betty Boop adorned the screen. A postwar child, he was still in his early twenties when he began creating the post-atomic Golden Bat. It is through a retrospective telescope that he shows us the wonderful world of prewar Japan, back when Japan still knew what it was and everything was going to be all right.

That it notoriously did not turn out that way gives vibrancy to this early Yokoo world. So innocent, so feckless, and doomed. All these frivolous folk are going to go up in flames.

Yokoo's is a new way of looking at things, both ironic and affectionate. Take Mt. Fuji, for example. The actual mountain had been stared at, painted, talked about, until it had become invisible. Yokoo made it visible again. He did this through that change of focus which distinguished all of his work in the 1960s. His image described not a mountain but an attitude toward a mountain. His small, decorative, ubiquitous Fuji, caricature though it was, did not belittle the mountain. What he caricatured was our preconception of Fuji—sacred, perfect, symbol of Japan, etc. Yokoo's Fuji, an ice-cream sundae of a mountain, suggested a new way of seeing it.

Step back, the artist seems to say. Take a new look through innocent eyes. See things now as you saw them when a child. Yokoo's eye is that of the youngster who sees objects in their purity, before the patina of use, of habit, of maturity has dulled them.

To do so is to question. The 1960s were, in Japan as elsewhere, a searching, questioning, dissident time. From the dull and doctrinaire 1990s, an era which accepts everything as given, the 1960s seem improbable, but it was during this time that thinking Japan questioned just about everything.

To question is to be of two minds—it prefers plurality to the monolithic. Singing star Hibari Misora ("the Shirley Temple of Japan") in tails, the Shinkansen bullet train in a cartouche, and everywhere the trademark mouth—just a mouth, no face, the teeth showing, tongue hanging out. Just how serious is Yokoo being? Is he showing us something because he wants us to admire it? Or is he making fun of it? But, if he is, then why isn't he smiling? Instead, he stares out at us, silently watching as we try to make up our minds.

Let's look at some photos of the artist. He is posing. Well, everyone poses, more or less, when being photographed. But does he know he is posing? Many of us don't. Yet, he must—or must he?

Standing with macho film star Koji Tsuruta, his own T-shirt and leather jacket look like an ironic comment in themselves. Likewise, when cross-dressing chanteuse Akihiro Miwa is making him up as a girl. Sometimes the irony is plain enough: Woody Allen-like and hopeless in an aloha shirt, or as a puritanical kamikaze pilot wearing "I Like Sex" badges, or as a parody of the groom at his own (real) wedding. At other times, however, the irony derives from the contrast of Yokoo's blank, uncommitted scrutiny and the strong, unquestioning image of whomever he is with. With a muscled Yukio Mishima in a loincloth, Yoko is just a black-uniformed high school kid.

Like Mishima, Yokoo is always trying on roles, but unlike him he seems to believe in none of them. The succession of role models, of iconographic crushes, is a long one: from Mishima, Tsuruta, the Beatles, and action star Ken Takakura, right down to Lisa Lyon, female body builder. But with Yokoo the "self" remains fluid. When he "played" himself as the lead in Nagisa Oshima's film, *The Diary of a Shinjuku Thief*, there was no one there; a hole in the screen.

Something of this is due to Yokoo's appearance, his very ordinariness, the unexceptional quality of his face and body. We know what he does, but he does not look as though he does it. Even when someone took a photo of him watering a grave it looked as though he was making a comment on watering graves.

His generic type suddenly appears, however, when he is dressed up in Kabuki costume and makeup. We suddenly recognize him: he is the classical *nimaime*—pleasant, irresolute, accommodating, and curiously featureless. And yet those eyes looking out of that white face are so alive with intelligence. He knows that he looks like some dumb Kabuki type and he is inviting us to share this knowledge, to applaud him, to laugh in his face.

This is irony. Yokoo can never be serious because he seems to know too much ever to "be" anything. He is too busy "becoming" to be "being." In his art, this results in a swing from the hard-line cartoon of 1965 to the soft-line expressionist blur of 1985, with forays into bathing suit and wristwatch design, record jackets, sumo aprons, and posters for fashion folk like Issei Miyake. The core remains fluid.

In this he is unlike those other pop figures, Warhol and Hockney. One never changed and the other changes predictably. Yokoo does, however, share much else with them: the ironic attitude and, at the same time, romantic inclinations. Only in the eye of innocent and untutored youth, say the romantics, can "truth" be perceived. Like some latter-day Rousseau, Yokoo indicates that unspoiled youth alone sees things right. The adult world corrupts because it blurs the youthful vision. This, overwhelmingly, was the message of the 1960s, a time when students threw their books away and took to the streets, when the Japan–U.S. Security Treaty was the big issue, when flower people put blossoms in gun barrels.

Now, in the defeated 1990s, Yokoo persists in showing visible regret for lost innocence. If anything really defines the content of his work, it is an undeniable nostalgia, and this perhaps is what makes him so Japanese. He perfectly mirrors his generation—one for whom history is clearly cut in two: prewar and postwar.

Now, of course, Yokoo is the grand *sensei*. Official, even governmental Japan and its attendant academia not only accept him, they court him. He has lived to see his raunchy nudes used to sell foundation garments, has seen his little Fuji sell ice cream. His iconography has turned into "Tokyo Style" and been put to work promoting the very products it originally challenged.

But Yokoo, in his own way, has remained faithful to himself. The child is still there, fingers grubby, working away at his idea of the world.

Tatsumi Hijikata

The meeting came to order. A group of scholars had gathered to discuss and honor the work of Hijikata, now known as the founder of that important contemporary dance form, Buto. We were also to commemorate the death, which had occurred earlier that winter of 1986.

A noted dance critic was speaking. The audience, mostly students, was listening. I, also on the panel, due to speak later, looked out at those unformed faces and wondered what Hijikata would have thought about this. He had never been much interested in explication.

I remembered him in his early thirties, when he had only some thirty more years to go and was already thinking about death, searching for it, incorporating it into his works.

– See, he once said, gradually collapsing, knees rising to his chest, arms crossing, wrists turning, fingers outspread: It's like dying.

And then the splayed fingers turned outward, reached, growing like roots or tendrils; the head rotated, blind eyes looked up, legs stretched, unfolding from the squat.

This was what it felt like in the far north, in snowy Akita, where Hijikata, son of a peasant, was from. In the long winter you shrank into your body, made it as small as possible to avoid the cold. Then in the spring you reached up for warmth, for the sun. This was what his dance was about.

– Hijikata's artistic vision presents us with alternatives: are these then prehistoric folk, before the benefits of civilization, or are they a postatomic people, after the bombs have returned us all to a primitive state?

The scholar was holding forth. Buto was rapidly becoming a major postwar aesthetic development. I tried to remember if Hijikata himself had ever made such claims for it.

Only once, that I could recall. We had been drinking in a small country inn near the sea. It was late summer. The rice was ripe, reminding him perhaps of northern fields.

– That's where it all comes from, he said: The paddy fields ... You have no idea how tired my parents used to get. They got so tired working in the paddies that they couldn't move. And yet they had to. It hurt to move. And yet they had to because they had to work. No energy, nothing to move with, and yet they moved.

I had already seen something of his work back then: the notorious *Kinjiki* of 1959, where all the movements expressed pain, where everyone seemed to be tied to the stage and straining at his bonds, and where death appeared on the boards.

Pain, exhaustion, death—these were the elements of his dance. But they were not dramatized, they were just there. Not something for a dancer to express; something for a body to show.

And I remembered Hijikata in a Ginza coffee shop—one long since torn down—saying in that occasionally dogmatic way he had: You can't just use the body, you know. It has its own life, you see, a mind of its own.

– And so we can now begin to codify the movements. First there is what we might call the squat. And here we must mention that it so resembles a movement used by Harald Kreutzberg that one wonders if Hijikata *sensei* had not perhaps been in some manner influenced by the German choreographer.

This was the second of the scholars, now just beginning. I was to follow him.

Hijikata's was a northern body, the skin white, the hair black against it. Not the sturdy Japanese peasant body you sometimes see, but the thin farmer's body, all tendon and narrow muscle.

I remembered his squat, and not just from the stage. Back then a lot of Japanese still knew how to do it—it was the normal position for resting by the roadside. Hijikata used to squat down to look at something, to read a passage, to talk.

Pain, exhaustion, squatting. The Japanese body is built close to the earth. Its center of gravity is low. Only Japanese could perform Buto. It has to be low, centered—as though the home of intelligence were not the cranium but the navel.

The navel! I suddenly remembered something else as I sat there looking at those young and unformed faces.

We were at the seaside inn. I was making a film and he had come along to help—no choreography, just a group of children, some fifteen little boys, to be controlled. The plot involved their killing a goat by accident, while playing at war, then holding a funeral for it. They were then meant to forget all about it, to return to being little boys. One of them, however, stays to watch the sea unearth the corpse. The film was called *War Games*.

Among the difficulties was the scene I wanted where the children, wide-eyed with knowledge of death, gradually forget what they have seen. They start to laugh, to play again, to go back to being children having fun on a beach.

And now I remembered how Hijikata, himself so death-filled, did it, that summer day twenty-five years before. Slowly—well out of the range of my camera—he pulled down his shorts so that his navel was exposed. Then, still slowly, he arched his back, stuck out his stomach.

The boys looked up from the mound under which they had buried death, their faces solemn, and saw this strange man with his shorts pulled down and his stomach stuck out. This surprised them but, filled with the importance of the goat's funeral, they did not smile. They looked, then looked away.

And there they are to this day, on film: the boys—now fathers of children like them—look up, sideways, abstracted, then look down again. It is as though the knowledge of death has confused them, as though they cannot detach themselves from it.

Then Hijikata undid the top button. The shorts slipped further. With one finger he pointed at his navel and suddenly smiled, all teeth, a small boy's smile.

The children looked up, then glanced at each other. One of them grinned, because he thought the man funny. He nudged the boy next to him, catching his attention.

In the film the child looks up and, as if thoughts of death were too much for him, he breaks into a smile. A moment later he nudges the boy next to him. He too raises his eyes. He seems to be saying: All right, it's just a dead animal.

Hijikata then began capering about. It was a kind of festival dance, a celebration after the rice planting, after all the back-breaking labor, the exhaustion. And the children recognized something. Two or three swayed, their bodies perhaps responding to his. Two or three laughed, perhaps from the pleasure of remembering other festivals they had seen.

In the film, several start swaying, as though to break whatever binds them to the mound they stand before. Then, suddenly, several more start laughing, as though they have found a way to escape from the fact that death lies at their feet.

The capering Hijikata pointed to the children's navels, one after the other, making a connection, pointing out a resemblance, indicating a natural order. If his was funny, so were theirs.

Soon all the little boys were laughing and pointing at each other, mouths open, eyes half-shut in mirth, and Hijikata still just outside camera range was dancing about, shorts slipping, the spirit of the festival, his navel like a large, comic eye.

In the film, the children begin to laugh and their laughter is infectious. They point at each other, soon laughing so hard that they seem frantic with joy, so strong is their relief at being delivered from death.

From peasant death to peasant life—it is not only pain but release from it that forms Hijikata's art. I see him now, hopping on one foot, then on the other, arms at antic angles, all of this enormous rural energy threading its way through the steps of the festival dance.

– And so we honor here the founder of a new Japanese dance form, Buto. Its beginnings were not without controversy, and indeed many of its earlier elements have now dropped away to offer our dancers and choreographers a new set of movements through which they may express themselves. Here, of course, the influence of Tatsumi Hijikata has been seminal—creating as he did this new vocabulary for purely Japanese expression. Thank you.

He sat down. The polite applause continued for a while, then stopped. The moderator introduced me.

I, still seeing those little boys disappearing down the beach, still seeing Hijikata cavorting alone against that sea, rose to speak.

Utaemon Nakamura

Yatsuhashi appears from behind the artificial cherry blossoms, accompanied by the other *onnagata*—all men as well—acting the part of attendants to the grand *oiran*, and followed by an entourage of young umbrella-holders, clog boys, and little girl apprentices with painted cheeks. High on her stilted sandals she performs that elegant stroll, the *oiran dochu*, the proud procession of the courtesans which opens the Kabuki drama *Kagotsurube*.

It is Utaemon who always plays this faithless *oiran*, grandest of all the old Yoshiwara courtesans. It is he who some two hours hence will be cut down by the sword of the man spurned once too often.

Expressionless, mouth pursed in the *onnagata* pout, a face forever complacent, body a mass of scarlet kimono with a great hanging butterfly sash and a high wig holding chopstick-looking bars of amber, a magnificently cocooned female, almost too slow, too stately to be entirely human, Utaemon places one stilted foot before the other.

And once again the aged Utaemon turns eighteen, as once more to shouts from the waiting throng he steps into the glare of the *hanamichi* runway, stares about with the scorn of the true courtesan, and begins that lofty procession through the Yoshiwara of two hundred years before.

And, in Tokyo at any rate, only Utaemon can do this. Shochiku, the company controlling the Nakamura Kabuki, is quite faithful—unlike Yatsuhashi. It has tacitly decreed that only Utaemon may play this faithless heroine, one of the great *onnagata* roles. No one else for the time being can have this part, not even the younger favorite, Tamasaburo.

This is not, however, the reason why Utaemon appears complacent. *Onnagata* always appear so. It has something to do with the male mouth in repose, also with the Cupid's bow of lip-rouge on which tradition insists. It appears offstage as well.

This is because, as the greatest of *onnagata* have often averred, to fully realize a woman on the stage one must retain all her characteristics off it. Hence perhaps stories of these impersonators wearing women's clothes around the house, using the female side of the public bath, the ladies' convenience, and so on.

Admittedly, some contemporary *onnagata*—Baiko, for example—leave the lady on the stage. They are married, have children, play golf and, at home, look like bank employees. But, says received opinion, the flower of the art is found only in those—and Utaemon is one—for whom the persona is inseparable from the person, who sustain this feminine creation throughout all the phases of masculine life.

Feminine is the proper term. The *onnagata* creates a man's idea of a woman. There is no distortion intended, but still the creation is that of a man, complacent mouth and all. So perhaps it is inaccurate to speak of a persona, to thus suggest that there exists some more authentic alternate. An actor visibly creates himself. We others do the same thing but we are usually not aware of doing so and, in any event, do not do it on the stage. The actor, however, knows what he is about. He consciously constructs himself and it is this fabrication that becomes authentic. Other professionals can recognize and admire it. Like Garbo.

When the Kabuki was making its first New York appearance in the late spring of 1960, she came to City Center every day. Then, one afternoon, she went backstage, determined to meet Utaemon.

When she was finally taken, by Faubion Bowers, to Utaemon's dressing room, Garbo waited while the actor was called. Was it all right if Garbo came in? Who? was the reply, probably incredulous. Then: No, it is not. I am old and not pretty at all. It's better if she sees me all made up. Besides, I'm all sweaty.

This was duly conveyed to Garbo who, straightforward as always, indicated her enthusiasm and regard with: But I want to see his sweat.

Unfortunately, she did not get to see it. Still, once made up, Utaemon did come out and with Bowers's assistance they talked.

Then it was time for *Chushingura* to begin, and Utaemon took his place for the opening scene. The clappers sounded, but just before the curtain began to slide aside, Garbo stepped onto the stage, ran lightly to the dais where Utaemon was sitting, and touched the *onnagata* on the shoulder. Startled, he turned. She waved. He waved back, the *hyoshigi* clapped faster and faster, the curtain was pulled open, and Garbo, at its very fringe, escaped into the wings.

One knows how she felt. Seeing Utaemon, or any *onnagata*, on the stage, one wants to touch him, to make certain perhaps that he is real, for a person contrived with such apparent artifice does seem unreal. And touching conveys, among other things, regard. Garbo, herself her own creation—those great, feeling eyes, the depths of her apparent understanding, the great strength of the woman, barely glimpsed and so often subverted by the whims of love—had contrived a female persona as surely as has Utaemon.

Utaemon's being an *onnagata* has allowed him to adopt a number of mannerisms we might think of as being feminine. Though in many ways his life is that of any artist—always teaching, practicing, seeing patrons and pupils—and though he allows himself a full schedule for masculine pleasure, including an interest in Las Vegas, he is also capable of a prima donna's exhibition of, for example, professional jealousy. His rivalry with Tamasaburo, that younger *onnagata* of whom the media make so much, occasionally surfaces.

He is also capable of displaying the airs of the courtesan he so often impersonates. Yukio Mishima once told me, though with how much truth I do not know, that Utaemon always expected jewels when the younger author had returned from abroad, and that he was particularly delighted with some Mexican fire opals he brought back, a fact that also delighted the grinning Mishima because—something not known to the *onnagata*—they had been dirt cheap.

Utaemon was also capable of pique, as I myself discovered. We were together in New York that spring of 1960 because I was doing the simultaneous (more or less) translation for the local audience, and during this period I had become friendly with the young man who held the umbrella over Yatsuhashi during her opening *oiran dochu* in *Kagotsurube*.

This resulted in my being called to the dressing room, where Utaemon was putting on his makeup for the evening's performance. Smiling, perfectly friendly, patting onto his face the dead white of the *oiran*, painting on those carmine lips, he talked about the weather, about the gratifyingly enthusiastic audiences, and the fact that my attentions were keeping the young man from his proper study and his habitual role in the household. This last was accompanied by the sweetest and most complaisant of smiles, and Utaemon's irresistible little bow, one that combines the winsomeness of an adorable child with the acumen of a woman of the world.

Naturally, I respected these wishes and no longer attempted to show the youth the sights of New York, and all would have been well had I not then been asked, no one else being available, to take Utaemon out shopping.

It turned out that he needed a pair of comfortable shoes to go with the Western suit he thought he ought sometimes to wear in New York and, no, he would not be bringing with him the large stuffed animal, a teddy bear, I believe, that he sometimes carried about.

We set off. Utaemon apparently felt some constraint because of our previous conversation. I felt none, but this was difficult to convey as shoe store after shoe store failed to have anything small enough to fit the *onnagata*'s tiny foot. Was I not, the occasional glance, ever more beady, asked, choosing shops notorious for their large sizes? And was I not doing this to discomfort, to have my revenge for some prior humiliation?

Finally—and I am certain that this was seen as the ultimate insult by the increasingly peevish *onnagata*—a suitable pair was found in the children's department at Macy's. After that my airy greeting of *ohayo gozaimasu* went unanswered for quite a time, and indeed relations which could have been called cordial were never restored.

His pique—understandable, perhaps, but as I say not a quality we usually associate with men, preferring, rightly or wrongly, to call the quality feminine—was yet more proof, if more be needed, of how deep went Utaemon's identification with the part he played.

Yatsuhashi is not all that scornful, all that cold. Indeed, she has a certain regard for the disappointed admirer who cuts her down. He had arrived an uncouth countryman and had pulled himself together through his love for her. If it were not that she had a younger lover whom she really loved, then perhaps she would have let the older man buy her out as he so wanted. Perhaps she would have ended up a comfortable mistress, or the proprietress of her own house, anything but the grandly attired corpse left lying on the stage at the close of *Kagotsurube*.

Utaemon makes us realize this. As we watch, this elegant and artificial creation comes alive, for it is human to have doubts, to realize that one is not, after all, consistent.

Yatsuhashi wavers and Utaemon shows us, by actually wavering, a solitary figure on the darkened stage, a person torn, like us. And yet, the difference.

This difference, we are told, is art.

Tamasaburo Bando

He impersonates that male invention, feminity, and does it so well that only those seams which he wants to show are allowed to be visible. A man imitating a woman imitating a lady. This expert imitation is evident particularly in that weary yet still popular play about Dr. Hanaoka's wife which I went to see him in.

The doctor's mother and spouse are in competition to see who can show the most devotion. Like most Shimpa, it is filled with the stuff of tragedy: lots of cancer, women being gored in the breasts by crazed cows, the doctor's grand experiment where he puts both under anesthesia and the wife goes blind and the mother is consumed with jealousy because she too had wanted in equally drastic fashion to prove her devotion to her doctor son.

Afterward I go to pay my respects. Tamasaburo is in a mauve dressing gown, decolleté. All makeup off, he looks scrubbed, very young.

– I didn't think you'd like Shimpa, he says: Too weepy.

He then tells me something about it, that century-old domestic drama, being careful about its dates and judicious about its qualities. Like many actors Tamasaburo wants to give an impression of seriousness. He wants to talk about ideas, as though to prove that he is capable of them.

All trace of the feminity I saw portrayed on the stage is gone. He is, rather, like an adolescent, still retaining something of the gender freedom of childhood but already concerned with the ways of the adult world; thinking about it, making sense of it.

I spoke of the day's performance and mentioned that his pregnancy was so convincing the audience laughed.

– Well, he said: One has to do something.

I wonder if actors know how dreadful their plays often are. Maybe they are right not to. The audience does, though—laughing during a tragedy, for example. This could easily destroy the supension of belief we are told is necessary for theater to work. Well, maybe, but that is only the case in Western theater. At the Shimpa, disbelief is part of the experience. Nobody goes to see the play, they go to see the actor.

– That's because acting here is all to do with technique, said Tamasaburo: Even when I was little I learned roles as you learn a sport. People come to see me like they go to see a good sumo wrestler or a good baseball pitcher. They watch me perform. Oh, you can see them getting their hankies out, but they're also watching to see how well you do what you do. And you do it well because you know how to do it. You don't have to feel anything. You're not supposed to.

I asked if he didn't feel like a woman when he played a woman.

He laughed. How would I know? he said: I'm not a woman.

Then, remembering that he was the host, he politely asked, since we had been speaking of acting, about my small role in Teshigahara's film, *Rikyu*, which he had heard I was in.

Then, with no transition at all: Was it your first time?

Not unnaturally, I thought he was talking about my acting debut.

– And not very good, I modestly said.

At this he gave a high-pitched laugh. No, no—he had meant, was this my first time at Shimpa.

Straightened out, the conversation continued, but I'd had a glimpse of the charm of a person whose instinctive reaction had been to disarm with laughter. Apparently challenged, he had retreated into that male invention—femininity.

As we went on talking, the intelligent, dedicated man of the theater returned, yet when I rose to leave, there was the lady of the house again—the good hostess seeing off a guest. But then everyone does this: most men everywhere are their fathers at hello and their mothers at goodbye.

We next met at my house. Tamasaburo came bringing boxes of sushi for our supper. All I had to do was make some tea. He was charming, attentive, forthcoming, frank—the kind of guest who knows how to make himself at home without ever forgetting that it isn't his house.

He wanted to talk, and so I learned more about his early life, about a childhood filled with study and little time for play, how he learned to cope with those professional jealousies which began early and never ended, how awful Utaemon is to everyone, not just to him.

As he continued I saw that Tamasaburo was being as honest with himself as he knew how to be. He sat there holding open the doors of his mind, refusing to retreat into accepted opinion, ready answers. This is rare—he is not afraid of upsetting convention, and he has his own standards.

Thus encouraged, I asked something I had sometimes wondered about: when he makes love has he ever done it dressed as an *onnagata*?

Tamasaburo was shocked, putting one hand on the side of his face. Oh, no, this he could never do. When I ask why, he thinks and then says it is because he could never lose himself if he did, that he would always be aware of himself.

– I'm an actor. Even when I was little I made a distinction between who I really was and who I was pretending to me—my role. Some actors purposely confuse them, but I don't.

Then, after more thought: The Kabuki isn't like that. When I am in a role I am aware—intensely aware—of playing a part, not of being that part. Yet being unaware is one of the points of making love, isn't it, surely?

I agree. Losing oneself is a great attraction—and not only through sex.

– When I make love I don't want to know who I am, he says with that shy adolescent smile which has nothing at all feminine about it, but something of the stalwart youth facing up to a fact of life.

Tsutomu Yamazaki

Toyotomi Hideyoshi, warlord, unifier of Japan, advanced upon Gaspar Coelho, Superior of the Jesuit Mission to Japan. This was in 1585, when Coelho was being shown around Osaka Castle.

It was also the Shochiku Film Studio in Ofuna where the great gold assembly room had been recreated. Here the famous actor of stage and screen, Tsutomu Yamazaki, in full kimono, all scarlet and gold, was advancing upon Coelho, in habit and hat, all black, surrounded by his equally black-robed acolytes: Coelho being me, put into the picture as a sign of favor, or perhaps amusement, by director Hiroshi Teshigahara.

The film was *Rikyu*, a historical drama about the conflict between political Hideyoshi and aesthetic Sen no Rikyu, the tea master. The scene in which we were now engaged was meant to show the warlord being political—enlisting the foreign aid of the Jesuits. Just now he had completed a speech welcoming us and hinting that when he had conquered Korea and China we might follow in his steps and make them all Christians. Then he advanced toward me.

Having pondered over my single line—in Portuguese—I had already decided how to interpret my role. Knowing that Hideyoshi was later going to expel the Jesuits, I decided to be as politically canny as he was. It was to be a duel between equals: Gaspar standing up to the warlord. I would be stern and use my single line to lash out with, then retire with dignity, and when shown the gold (next sequence) I would be coldly attentive, nothing more. In front of the mirror I looked sternly at my reflection and delivered my line with a cold smile.

In the great gold assembly room Hideyoshi had gotten out all his foreign presents to impress his guests—that is, the Shochiku prop department had gotten out whatever it could find in the way of regal treasure. There was a Louis XV table and, a bit ahead of its time, a Victorian love seat, together with a Viking helmet, a stuffed polar bear, and lots of Persian carpets.

– Hey, man, said one of my Portuguese acolytes, sitting behind me on the tatami: That polar bear no good. They no got polar bear back then.

– They got polar bear, said the Japanese propman, also in English.

– And the rugs, man, continued my acolyte: They no Persian, they Syrian. They lousy.

The acolytes, chosen for their Latin looks, were actually Iranian, drawn from the large group of otherwise idle men in Tokyo, and they knew all about carpets.

Then Hideyoshi stomped in and at once began his speech. Coelho's interpreter, Luis Frois (the actor Ken Frankel), was supposed to be whispering into my ear the Portuguese equivalent, but since neither of us knew the language, he babbled and I nodded.

Then came my line: A *Coreia e a China não querem a guerra!*—Neither Korea nor China had any desire for war. These were the words I used to lash the barbarian upstart with.

Or would have used, had I been able to get them out. But Yamazaki had advanced on me so suddenly that I forgot the last half. My delivery was consequently less than confident. This was just the rehearsal, however, so I turned to the single real Portuguese on the set and asked if he could simplify my sentence.

– It's pretty simple already, he said, scratching his head: Well, maybe *Coreia e a China querrem pas.*

Again Hideyoshi made his appearance and again delivered his speech. Yamazaki—tragic criminal in Kurosawa's *High and Low*, comic truck driver in Itami's *Tampopo*, Richard III and Oscar Wilde on the stage—is not a big man but he is an imposing one. He is also a master of the techniques of acting, and here I was sitting on the tatami clutching my line and he was advancing on me.

I backed off as best I could, hat wobbling, and tentatively delivered my truncated Portuguese. Then Hideyoshi said that if I wanted anything I could approach him through Rikyu here. This personage bowed and I bowed and my hat fell off. However, it was still just a rehearsal.

– Why does he do that? I whispered to Ken: Come at me like that.

– It's his conception of the role. Notice how he does it?—it's fantastic. You see, an actor has to have a vehicle, and Yamazaki has chosen impatience. That governs every move, and makes his advancing on you necessary. He has to treat you this way. Understand?

– Yes.

– It's just marvelous, what he's doing.

I made no comment.

Now came the first take. Teshigahara and his crew were off to one side, a long shot, the camera then dollying in for a medium shot of the protagonists. There would stand the blustering warlord and there would sit, immobile as a block of stone, the worldly priest, outstaring the warlord with his own steely gaze.

Hiroshi told the camera to start. The set hushed. Yamazaki shouted impatiently and then advanced so swiftly and stood so close that I had to move back (difficult to do when kneeling on tatami), and as I looked up in surprise I knew that a steely gaze was impossible.

And, instantly, like any actor, I knew how to play my part. It all, as they say, came together. I was a pious old fraud—why hadn't I seen that before?

After this scene there was an interval. I was sitting next to Rikyu, played by Rentaro Mikuni. I asked him how I'd looked.

– Fine. The hat is nice.

– No, I meant my acting.

– Oh, he said, then, after some thought: Well, I think that playing the role in a comic fashion is certainly one possibility.

Comic? I hadn't known I was comic. Gaspar Coelho might well have been a pious old fraud but his being comic was far from my newfound interpretation of him. I turned to Ken.

– Actors play off each other, he said: They create right then and there. That's what you and Yamazaki did.

No, I thought, that was what Yamazaki had done.

– Hey, man, you funny, said the Iranian behind me.

We were to take the scene again. I wondered if Hideyoshi had really browbeaten poor Gaspar in that way. If he had, then maybe the Jesuit—peace at any price—had caved in. Maybe his single line was not defiance but defense.

And I thought of Japanese television, where the foreign guest is made a fool of, or makes a fool of himself. I always sternly refused such TV offers whenever they came my way, but here I was in a historical spectacular doing the same thing.

The warlord advanced and I whined my line, then fell timidly back when he moved still closer. This time Yamazaki wanted to shake hands and improvise some dialogue as well. I dropped my rosary and looked up meekly from under my hat.

– Cut, said Teshigahara, who made a thumbs-up sign and gave me a big smile.

– Hey, man, you natural comic, said the Iranian.

I straightened my hat, picked up my rosary, and said savagely: I am not.

But the die was cast, as they said back in 1585, and when everyone moved to the storehouse where all the gold was kept (next set), I tripped over my habit, was struck dumb at all the treasure, raised my hands to heaven, then bent forward greedily to touch. And all without any direction at all. I might not have become Coelho but I had become someone.

Afterward, when my moustache was being removed and my habit folded, I said to Yamazaki as the entire top of his head, samurai pate and all, was being lifted off: *You* did that!

– No, he said: *You* did it. Or, maybe, we did it.

– Is that what acting is like?

– Yes, said this fine actor.

– I thought it was more friendly.

– Nothing personal, said Yamazaki, smiling: Hideyoshi was that kind of person.

– And Coelho, was he what I made of him?

– Maybe, but it doesn't make any difference. The main thing is that he didn't want to become important and that Hideoshi did. He wasn't a warlord. Hideyoshi was. Understand?

I understood.

Sonoko Suzuki

She put up the samisen and took down the *futon*. I was to spend the night. I then remembered seeing my host taking her into a corner, passing something over. Money, as it turned out.

Now she smoothed the sheet and plumped the pillows. Such wifely actions I found inconsistent with her showy kimono, her loud, striped sash, her skewered, piled-up hairdo. They would have seemed even more so if she had been a real geisha.

But she wasn't. She was imitating one—had learned the minimum necessary to enter the guild and escape the anti-prostitution laws: a few tunes on the samisen, a couple of classical songs, and the ability to pose her way through a dance or two.

She was of the recent variety then known as *daruma*-geisha, named after that round-bottomed toy that rolls upright after it has been knocked over, or *makura*-geisha, referring to the pillow she had just given a final kick to.

Earlier, she had given herself geisha-like airs—artificial laughter, hand over mouth, extravagant flattery, an occasional appraising glance, as though trying to guess how much I weighed.

And I, as is my wont, had tried to talk seriously, which sent her into fits of giggles. Then she kept complimenting me on my Japanese whenever I made a mistake. And she wanted unqualified admiration for what her little fingers could do with a tangerine.

Since I had failed to appreciate either her talents or her charms, her manner became cool and, moving to the other side of the table, she started talking about baseball, surmising—accurately—that I would know nothing about it.

At this I grew impatient and sulked. Shortly it became apparent to both of us, if not to our host, that we didn't like each other. Yet now it seemed we were to be yoked together for the night.

We both responded, in our separate ways, with bad grace. She gave the *futon* another kick and I yawned in her face. Then, while I scuffed about the room, she, with no seductive gestures at all, squatted in front of the dressing table and took off her wig, which made her look suddenly small, then wiped off her makeup, which made her look suddenly younger.

This young, pale, sullen girl then removed all her various robes except the final one, lay down on the *futon*, pulled up the coverlet, and closed her eyes.

One knows this happens to foreigners now and again, being taken out to dinner by someone who wants something, and then, after lots of food and saké, ending up in bed with the entertainment. If you're lucky you like each other.

Of course, at this point I could have left. But it would have looked bad, word would have got back to the host of hospitality spurned. And it was late, and I didn't know quite where in the city I was, having paid no attention to the way we had come, and my host had long since driven away.

But *I* could, at least, have left. She couldn't, no matter how much she disliked me. She had been bought, paid for. No matter how she felt she had to go through with it, whatever it was. At least I still had the freedom of refusal. She had no freedom at all.

Not that I felt sorry for her and her lot. She had chosen—like any of us. There was other work she could have found, though the labor might have paid less well. And, as I slowly undressed by the still form in the light of the small *andon* lamp, I found myself wondering how much she had cost.

Typical, that. If it's paid for it's got to be consumed. Like making yourself eat all the food on the plate whether you want it or not, simply because you bought it. And here I was, lying down to a full dinner I neither needed nor wanted, simply because someone had put down the money for it.

Others might have been tempted to turn chummy, to prop themselves on one elbow and listen to the sad story of her life; but not me, because I really did not like her. She was a shallow, artificial, selfish little girl who seemed unhappy with her work. Maybe I ought to show her just who the boss was.

There I went again! So, shaking my head at myself, I propped it on one arm and turned to look at her. She was lying legs together, arms crossed, eyes shut, and with what I fancied was a martyred expression. Waiting, perhaps. Or asleep—her life was doubtless a tiring one.

I turned back and lay staring at the dim ceiling. Strange thing, apathy. My aversion to her erased any sense of difference. I did not think of her as being Japanese, as being different. Indeed, as I knew from experience, that sense of deep difference, that delicious gulf—Japanese vs. foreign— was truly exciting only when you were carnally interested. And now apathy had made us one. We were of a single race, those whose members do not like each other.

Still, I was male. She was female. Perhaps I ought to uphold my sex, as it were. We men are supposed to make the first move. When you are lying down with a woman and don't, it might be construed as impolite.

So I put my hand over one small breast. She did not move. How far, I wondered, would I have to go before my point was made? I opened her kimono and slipped in my hand. The little breast was cold.

As I warmed it I studied her profile. She looked in that soft light like a young bird, eyelids so thin that every movement was visible. Either she was awake, or asleep and dreaming.

Then I saw the little mouth forming an impatient pout as with one hand she removed mine and, at the same time, as if to show me my business, opened her legs.

I lay there, my own legs closed, my hands in my lap, and decided to sleep. But the minutes passed and sleep, naturally enough, did not come. I listened to the steady breathing beside me. Had she really managed to drop off, I wondered, feeling a small kind of fury.

I, of course, failed to fall asleep at all. So, instead, I thought about why I couldn't close my eyes. It was not because I was aroused, I knew; not even that I was repelled, I guessed: merely that she was there, next to me. The fact of her presence.

And the fact of mine. What, I wondered, did she think about me? That I didn't attract was evident, but perhaps in her line of work few did. Did she find me too large, too white, too logical? What could she be thinking?—if she was thinking at all.

I turned again, head on hand, and stared at her in the light of the night lamp. What was going on up there, I asked myself.

Having thus taken an interest in her as a person—not as a Japanese, nor as a whore, nor even as a girl—I found that we eventually came to make quite satisfactory love.

In the morning she glowered and gave me her card. Like its owner, it had rounded corners. Her name was printed on it: Sonoko Suzuki—a very common name.

And over breakfast as the new sun slid across the mats she allowed herself a small smile. It was not, of course, the smile of a woman fulfilled by sexual attention. I don't think that kind of smile even exists, except in bad books and worse films. Nor was it the blowzy smile of the girl who has found a friend—we were not friends and were anxious, once the rice was down, to part.

No, it was the disinterested smile of the craftsman—the carpenter who has turned a tight joint, the potter who has thrown yet another good pot. It was the quietly self-congratulatory smile of the person who has done well and knows it.

What I had not until this moment understood was that Sonoko Suzuki really wanted to be a proper geisha.

Kikuo Kikuyama

Small, fat, wearing thick-lensed glasses, he often lay on the bench in the corridor. For this he was criticized. Lying down like that, they said, taking up room, making a nuisance of himself. The others wanted to occupy the bench themselves because from there one had a clear view of whoever was going into the men's room. And it wasn't as though he even paid proper attention, they complained. He didn't, never once glanced. Just lay there all fat and pale with his eyes closed.

The others used the bench properly, always paid a lot of attention. Did you see that construction worker? one would ask: He was, I'm not lying, *that* big. Stood right beside him when he pissed. *Honto ni oishi so datta no yo*, looked good enough to eat. Well, I scampered right back here and struck a pose, but he walked right past and out.

Kikuyama did nothing like this, merely got in the way. Initially the others used to talk to him: Hi there, mother. You here yesterday? Oh, you weren't? Well, it was *marvelous*—stud students all over the place. I had three of them, I'm telling you—three!

But Kikuyama did not respond properly. He did not laugh or look jealous. He looked at them seriously and said: *Ah, so desu ka?* He was just no fun to talk to.

Nor did he often go and watch the movie. While the others were moving to and fro, staring at the naked giants on the screen, then running out to cruise around the Coke machine in the corner or down the corridor to the gents', he lay on the bench and stared at the ceiling.

Very occasionally he would venture in. Often he would sit next to someone. Just sit. The others were scandalized: And he just sits there! Really, I ask you, what kind of a place does he think this is? I've never once seen him make a proper pass. And if he sits long enough he falls asleep.

But at least it was better for him to doze off inside amid the smackings and slurpings on the sound track than to sprawl on the bench out there in the hallway. That way he caused less trouble.

– And it isn't as though he's just an occasional either, said one: He seems to come here every day. At least, every time I get here he's already around.

Nonetheless, the others gradually got used to Kikuyama's daily presence. He never tried to cut in when someone was cruising a likely trucker, and he never trailed along when a reluctant country youth was dragged off to the ladies'. He was simply there, part of the furniture, something one learned to ignore.

That is, until an equally fat and bossy sister in horn rims and turtleneck took to coming. He knew Kikuyama and called him *sensei*. This title of respect, overheard by the others, piqued curiosity, a curiosity soon satisfied.

– What, you never saw Kikuyama *sensei*? Still, what can you expect from a bunch of low-class *okama-tachi* like you. I suck cock as well as the rest, but there is such a thing as style. You wouldn't know anything about that, of course.

This tough sister—Kuro-chan, Blackie by name—surveyed the assembled few and then patiently, like a kindergarten teacher with backward pupils, explained. Madame Kikuko here was an artist, a star, the most promising of the young hopefuls in the world of *Nihon buyo*, Japanese classical dance.

– Got her black belt yet? asked Midori-chan, Miss Green, the sassiest of the group.

Blackie turned in a flash: You stupid faggot! That's just the way a common little know-nothing like you would talk. You've no understanding or respect for the finer things.

Then, after a short conference with Madame Kikuko and some hunting about in a wallet: *Hora!* Look here!

He flourished a studio polaroid of a beautiful young girl standing poised in a lilac kimono with a spray of wisteria in her hand, her body curved, grace and elegance in the lithe line, her face turned, the black eyes alive with intelligence. It was a pose from the classical dance *Fuji Musume*.

The others, now cowed, oohed their appreciation.

– Oh, she is lovely, murmured Miss Green.

– You bet, snapped Blackie, who then sat down beside Kikuyama and began a discussion of choreographic techniques which soon drove the others away.

They remembered, however. This changed the atmosphere. Though obviously they still went on tracking down the half-reluctant *tobishoku*; though they still said: Oh, what a shame, it was really enormous, I just didn't know what to do, too bad you weren't here (after carefully ascertaining that indeed you weren't); though life continued as usual, there was a difference. This was because they had an artist in their midst.

And a sick one at that. What was the matter—the reason for all this lying on the bench? Well, no one knew. The lungs, perhaps, or the liver, or . . . dared one say it: love.

There was the answer: the lovely Kikuko, doomed to live forever inside the ugly Kikuo, had nonetheless found Him, *anohito*, the true Mr. Right—perhaps a virile laborer, a muscular trucker, or a schoolboy sports star, who had seen beneath the unprepossessing exterior and glimpsed her underlying beauty. And there she sat, enchanted maiden on a rock, daily awaiting his return.

Since all of them were waiting for just this sort of thing, and since all were daily disappointed, it was natural they should find this explanation and welcome it. They took to calling this short, recumbent, unattractive man the Sleeping Beauty and wondering about the chances of Prince Charming's ever reappearing. Not likely, they agreed, but they all found his devotion thrilling.

He blinked his eyes, when he was not asleep, and enjoyed this regard, this new respect. When he arrived, sighing with weariness, the two queens already on their corridor thrones would spring to their feet to allow Madame Kikuko to rest. Later, on their way to and from likely prospects in the mens' room, they would tiptoe past lest they awaken the poor sick girl.

And very ill Kikuyama was. He began coughing, a loud, rattling sound which seemed much too large for that fat little body. Then the gagging. And the spitting. No one he now sat near in the peopled dark stayed long. So he stopped going in to watch the film. He stayed in the corridor.

The story was (details courtesy of Blackie) that, some time ago, he found he could no longer run through *Fuji Musume*, let alone *Dojoji*, and so he gave up going to the *keiko-ba*, the practice room. He then took to coming here instead, to the Shinjuku Basement Meigaza, that other theater of illusion, and here he now lay on the bench, dying.

The others brought him tea, coffee, chocolates, noodles, and he would smile his wan smile and sip or crunch, then once again lie down, pulling his coat over him like a coverlet. At first there had been some smart talk about *Tsubaki Hime*, the Camellia Princess, La Traviata herself. Now, however, such levity was suppressed.

– Does the management know? I once asked them.

– About us faggots? But, of course, how else could this flea-pit make any money?

– No, do they know that he's dying?

– Well, how could they? They never come down here to check up on us. They know better. Actually, he's happy, you know. He thinks that *anohito* is finally going to come back again and he'll be seeing him with his dying glance.

He did not, however, return. Kikuyama, I was told, was finally taken to the hospital. There it was discovered that weeks, months, in the damp basement had finally done him in. Coughing, gagging, the fat little man was carried off.

– And then, said Blackie, who had been there: Then the most marvelous thing happened. We took off his glasses and his face smoothed out and there before us lay Kikuko herself, looking so pretty, so like *Sagi Musume*—one of her favorites, you know—that I would have challenged any man, no matter how straight, not to have fallen right in love with her.

Blackie shed a tear: Oh, if only Kikuko had put all this behind her and devoted herself to her art, she might have become a great performer, a great teacher, even eventually a Living National Treasure, for all I know. But she didn't. She threw it all away . . . for love.

And all day long no one sat on the bench, even though it provided a perfect view of the men's toilet and whoever was standing there and whatever he had and whatever state it was in.

No—the place was, for a time, holy. There, it seemed, hovered the beautiful, smiling, liberated spirit of this fat little man.

Keiko Matsunaga

Balancing my plastic tray—a double hamburger and a small Coke—I looked for a vacant table. There were none. There was, however, a young girl sitting alone at a table for two. I asked permission, which she gave with a nod, and sat, unwrapped my hamburger, opened my book.

She too was reading, an English textbook. Though I had noticed that she was pretty, the book discouraged any attempts at conversation.

Thus occupied, we read, sipped, munched for a time until she looked up at me and asked, in Japanese, what I was reading. I told her, then politely noted that she was studying English.

– Yes, I'm going abroad. To America.

– You'll certainly need it there, I said and waited.

But she did not try out her pronunciation on me. Instead, she said: I'm leaving this spring, so I should study harder than I am.

– You seem to be studying hard.

She smiled—she was very pretty indeed when she smiled: Not really. The fact is I want to leave Japan more than I want to go to America.

Since she was this direct, I too could be. Why, I wanted to know.

She looked at me as though gauging my character, as though trying to determine whether she could trust me. Having, apparently, decided, she said: Trouble with my parents.

She wanted to talk, though not about English, so I asked what kind of trouble.

It all came out at once, the way it sometimes does. She had been in love with a young man of whom her parents disapproved. They disapproved of him because he was of Korean ancestry though, like her, born in Japan. She had left home to go and live with him. But, this being Japan, with pressure from her parents, and his, from their schools, their friends—after a month they had parted. She never saw him again and that was now a whole season ago. So she wanted to leave Japan.

– Is America like that? she wanted to know.

– Yes. But there would be places for you both to go there. You could get married.

– Not here ... Is it true that a girl never forgets her first love?

– They say so. It isn't true only of girls, either. I've never forgotten mine.

She looked at me for a second, then said: I'm not a virgin any more. I loved him that much.

– Did that upset your parents?

– Yes, they're old-fashioned. They think a girl ought to be a virgin when she marries.

All of this had occurred within ten minutes of my sitting at her table. This happens occasionally. One is chosen for sudden confidences. There seems to be a compelling combination of difference and safety. But I had never experienced such revelations so swiftly. I, in turn, became suspicious.

– Going to America will solve no problems. He won't be there.

– I know. But it will solve one problem. I won't be here. You speak the language well but I wonder if you really know Japan. People talking about you, criticizing you, making you live the way everyone else does ... the gossip in this country!

– Yes. I realized long ago that if I were Japanese myself I wouldn't stay here. But I'm not and so none of this affects me. Foreigners are so different that the Japanese don't bother to gossip about them.

– I envy you that. If it were that way with me I wouldn't have to leave. But if I stay I'll have to get married to someone I don't even know, have his child, and then live with him till I die. I don't want that.

– You're brave, I said.

– I'm desperate, she said and smiled again, that lovely smile.

I regarded it with more suspicion. What was she after? Was I supposed to do something, make some kind of offer?

Suspicion is always vulgar, even when merited—like jealousy. I realized that and saw that the oddity of our meeting, our conversation, alone had aroused suspicions. I was no better than her parents.

– Is there anything I can do? I asked to open my thoughts, to rid myself of them.

This, however, made *her* suspicious: Like what? What could you do?

– I don't know. I have friends in America. Introduce you, perhaps, so you wouldn't have to be alone.

– No, I think I want to be alone for a while.

Then, with that pertinence which young girls often have: I'm only telling you this because I don't know you, because you're sympathetic, because I won't see you again.

– Did it hurt? I asked: I've always wondered about that. Does it hurt to lose your virginity? One hears all sorts of stories.

She thought, suspicions oddly laid at rest by my question, then: Yes and no. It hurts, but it's a different kind of pain. Maybe it's like having a child. My mother told me that that hurt but afterward she couldn't remember the . . . well, the quality of the pain.

– Can you remember the quality of the pain?

– Not really. Anyway, it didn't last long.

– Then the pleasure?

– Yes, the pleasure, but that too was different.

There we sat amid our plastic debris, a young Japanese girl and an older foreign man. I was as frank as she was and before long we were telling each other intimate details. But it was all in the spirit of sharing knowledge, as though we were both already quite old, as if we knew that this single conversation was only for itself.

We sat there an hour or more and came to know, if not each other, at least our ideas of our selves. She approved of mine; I approved of hers. The conversation never became oppressive because it never became self-conscious. Neither was in any way investing in the other. Both were aware that it had no continuation.

As I listened, talked, I also saw how my awareness had been dulled by what I had taught myself to believe about the Japanese. None of my many generalizations about the people, necessary enough, I suppose, if I were to live here, would have allowed for this conversation. And it was the same with her: whatever general ideas she may have formed about the character of foreign men were not being upheld by me.

We were two strangers who, because of this, could reach out with a degree of honesty and trust. That she was Japanese, that I was not—slowly these facts and the ideas they habitually trailed after them faded away. We were simply two people talking.

The ending, however, was Japanese. She could not bring herself to simply smile, stand up, say goodbye—a possible "American" conclusion. Instead, on a paper napkin, she wrote her name, address, and telephone number. I responded with mine.

Then, each still holding on to a part of the other, we parted, conventionally enough, with my wishes for her safe and happy journey.

The napkin is here before me, which is why I know her name was Keiko Matsunaga. Somewhere in this vast city, or in some vast city over there, perhaps my name on a paper napkin also exists.

But I will not call her. And she will not call me. This too was understood. We have had our talk. Our next conversation would have been much less interesting because then "we" would have had a future, and when one has that, the present vanishes.

I see her now, existing as she existed then: securely in the present tense.

Hidetada Sato

The new delivery boy at the *nandemoya*, the no-matter-what store, the local emporium, was tall, nineteen or so, with a round face and cheeks as red as the apples grown in the northern province from which he came. His name was Sato, a name as common as apples themselves.

Surrounded by shelves piled with brushes and pots and towels and bottles of detergent, strainers for bean curd, sukiyaki pans, soap flakes, rubber gloves, and no-matter-what, I asked for the single object I couldn't locate, a pumice stone for rubbing the soles of my feet in the bath.

After a protracted search Sato came back with word that they had none.

– You're supposed to have no matter what, I said sternly.

– I'm very sorry, replied apple-cheeked Sato, redder than ever. Newly acquired Tokyo accent forgotten, his apology was in the broadest of Akita dialects.

I smiled, seeing that my heavy little joke had been misunderstood. It doesn't matter, I said, as cordially as this phrase allows. The boy bowed me out, still flushed, still apologizing.

Late that evening, listening to a Mozart quartet, I heard the screech of bike brakes and then a timid thumping on the front gate. It was Sato, still flushed from pumping up the hill. He extended a hand. In it was a small paper-wrapped package. My pumice stone.

– You had it after all, I said and he, nodding, looked past me into the entryway. Realizing that he was curious as to how a foreigner lived, I invited him in for a cup of tea.

He refused and I insisted, as custom demanded. Then he pulled off his boots and stepped up. He was very large. I had not realized just how large until I saw him in the house. Big feet, big hands. But not hulking, too polite for that and—curious in a modern youth—gentle.

Over tea he asked politely: What's that you're playing?

- That's Mozart.
- Ah, Mozart, a composer. It's beautiful.
- K. 590, I added.
- Oh? He leaned forward, concerned, troubled.
- They number Mozart, I explained: He wrote lots. They keep track of it this way.
- Oh, he said, as though relieved, then smiled and shook his head to indicate that it was all beyond him, something from a different world: It's very pretty anyway.

I asked him the price of the pumice stone.
- Oh, no, that's all right.
- No, it isn't all right.

I looked for a price on the paper and noticed that it did not come from his *nandemoya*, but from somewhere in far Shibuya.
- This isn't from your store.
- *Eh*, he replied, a common answer. It means yes, or no, or both, or nothing at all.
- After work you bicycled all the way to Shibuya to get this pumice stone.
- But we ought to have had it, he explained, reddening: You said yourself that we're a store that's supposed to have no matter what.
- That was a joke.

He looked up, cheeks red, surprised. Then slowly he understood, smiled: Ah, he said, a joke. You foreigners are famous for your humor.

He used *yumoru*, there being, typically, no word in Japanese for this famous quality. Then he laughed politely to show he had got the point. After we had savored my pleasantry for a while I again attempted to pay for my pumice stone.
- It cost much less than the cup of tea you gave me, he said.

I understood. It was not for me that he had gone and bought it, it was for the reputation of his store. They had been put to shame. He had atoned. And it was true—pumice stones were indeed very cheap.

Mozart came to an end.
- That was nice, he said.
- Do you like music?
- Yes.

– Who's your favorite composer?

– Hawaiian.

– I see.

– Do you have any Hawaiian?

– No, only classical.

He scratched his head, indicating that *kurasiku* was too difficult for him.

– But you were enjoying the Mozart, I said.

– But it's too difficult to understand, he answered.

– You only discovered it was too difficult when you learned it was *kurasiku*. Before that you were enjoying it.

For the first time he looked straight at me. This was a new idea. It was as if I had awakened him. He laughed with pleasure at the thought. Life was less complicated than he had been led to believe. Here he had been sitting, understanding Mozart.

Still, he had his polite doubts: I wonder, he said. He used a feminine form—*so kashira.*

And I in turn wondered. Was this Akita custom, was he mistaking Tokyo usage, or . . . ?

– Is your father dead? I asked with that directness for which foreigners are also famous.

He closed up instantly, as though my question had been a poking finger. Eyes dropped, smile stopped. Foreigners are like magicians. They deduce. They then disclose. The Japanese deduce things as well, of course, but they never let on.

– Yes, he finally answered: When I was five. (Then, as sometimes happens, he told me something he would not easily tell another Japanese.) He killed himself.

More questions, more answers, and his own short history emerged. Only son of a poor widow who scraped to send her son through middle school. Then, distant relative's introduction, trip to Tokyo, new job, bright lights, excitement. Weekly letter home to mother, monthly day off, vague hopes for the future. Alongside this another story. Father drank, father gambled, father ran around, father finally killed himself, leaving widow and infant behind.

As a consequence, young Sato did not drink, knew nothing of horse-racing or women, and devoted himself to his job; and, a further consequence, he obviously missed his mother, whose feminine *so kashira* I had just heard.

Silence. And a heaviness, as though we had both eaten too much. He was no doubt already regretting his confidences. Why, we had met only that afternoon. The conversation languished as it always does before a departure. Soon he was thanking me for the excellent tea, and giving me a formal bow.

And then, unexpectedly, a warm, country smile appeared. Perhaps Sato felt that besides being indiscreet he had also begun to make a friend. I felt this too and showed it by not mentioning the pumice stone again.

Nevertheless, I saw nothing of him for a time except in passing. Occasionally when I was leaving he would race by on his bike, basket piled with soap flakes, towels, steel wool, detergents. *Konnichiwa*, he would call, speeding on.

Sometimes I also saw him at the bathhouse if I went very late. He sat there solemnly scrubbing his sturdy body. He would smile and say *kombanwa*, but when I got into the water, he got out.

This I quite understood. It is common for a foreigner to be treated to unasked-for confidences. It is also common for him to be avoided because he has been their recipient. The *nandemoya* youth, having indulged himself, at my prodding admittedly, now wished he hadn't. He may have seen it as self-indulgence, always a bad thing in a young, hard-working male.

Then, late one cool evening, I went to the local coffee shop. It was run by a harried, middle-aged woman who always carried a snapping Pomeranian under one arm and who often dropped hair into the cream. Its popularity was due to its being the only coffee shop in the neighborhood.

When I entered, the one table not completely full was that half-occupied by young Sato, shining from his bath. I prepared to leave but he spoke, smiled, indicated the chair opposite. Both of us affirmed that it had been a very long time, the proper way to begin a conversation, then sat in companionable silence until he looked into his coffee.

– There's a hair in it.
– It's hers. She's famous for it.

– It might be the dog's, he said, fishing it out of his cup.

– Too long, wrong color. It's black.

We both examined the hair, now lying on the table. We then talked about various doings in the neighborhood. And what of Mr. Sato? I asked, the third person being polite. He looked at me and touched his nose to ascertain if I was indeed referring to him. This too was polite, as was my gracious nod in reply. Yes, I said, then proceeding to a more intimate level: For example, have you any hobbies yet?

He thought for a time before answering: Guns.

Seeing my surprise—for violence was the last thing I expected from him—he smiled: Not to shoot with, just to collect.

And did he have a large collection?

No, in fact he didn't own a single one, but he was thinking about collecting. It would be a hobby. Like my Mozart. I would have my composer and he would have his guns, he said with no irony, smiling, pleased at the symmetry.

Then, sensing a misunderstanding: Not real guns, you know, just plastic models.

I thought of his father. But he, sitting there, smiling, did not.

It was not until after New Year's that we met again. He appeared late one evening with a gift of fruit—apples from his home province, from far Akita. But he looked serious this time, and when I invited him in he took off his boots at once, no hanging back. He then announced that he wanted to have a *sodan*—a talk, a discussion.

He sat on his cushion and looked at his hands. A *sodan* does not begin immediately. It is prefaced by a silence which can go on for some time as the person needing the discussion apparently turns over in his mind the best way to start it. His bowed head was pregnant with thought but he did not open his mouth.

I went to the kitchen, made tea, peeled several of the apples, cut them, put them in a bowl, brought everything in, and he was still sitting there, steeped in silence. Then finally . . .

– I came to have a *sodan*.

– I see.

– I don't have anyone else to talk to about this.

142

– I see.

– I wanted your advice too because you're a foreigner and know all about things like this.

With that he began, starting so far back and adding so much information that it was some time before I finally understood. To put it simply, he was in love.

He had never thought he would be, but now he felt, now he knew, right here—solemnly thumping his chest with his fist—that this was the real thing. He was deeply in love, would never recover. He spoke with great seriousness. This subdued any levity I might otherwise have shown. I too turned serious.

– But what good news, I said: Being in love is wonderful. It should make you happy, surely.

– It should? He looked at me suspiciously, rubbing his chest.

– Of course. Love is famous for that.

He looked doubtful: Then I wonder if I *am* in love. I'm not happy about it.

More information was forthcoming. He had known the girl from grade school . . . then forgotten all about her . . . but this time, back in Akita for the holidays, he had found her working in the local coffee shop, and she'd been nice to him and taken him to the movies and they'd had a long walk, and she wanted more than anything to get out of Akita and come to Tokyo, and he worked in Tokyo and so they should get married, and she loved him and so he loved her too. Now, what did I think of all this and what should he do?

A Japanese in my position would have been most unhelpful. He would have examined both sides, and just when it seemed he was in favor of one course of action, he would say: But on the other hand . . . In this way all responsibility for further misfortune could be avoided.

But I was not Japanese, which was why the besotted young man had come to me. Here was this awful thing called love, threatening his new Tokyo life. He wanted to be told what to do about it. What to do was clear. He ought to refuse to provide her with an escape route from horrid Akita. But such advice would not, I knew, fit his present mood. He was far too taken with the enormity of it all—being in love. So I mentioned the possibility of not being actually married but of living together for a time in Tokyo.

– Oh, no, he said in alarm: What would the *nandemoya* people think? And besides, what about the children? They'd be illegitimate.

– Well, you needn't have any, not right off at any rate.

– But people in love often do have children.

This raised a delicate matter. I wanted to ascertain just how far this love of theirs had carried them. But how to find out? Sato was still young enough to be prudish.

– Did you have any prior experience? (*Keiken* was, I thought, the proper word to use.)

– Oh, no, I've never been in love before.

– No, I mean, did you and she have any experience? (*Keiken* again, since I could think of no other polite word.)

– No, this is the first time we've ever felt this way.

Keiken was obviously not the word I wanted. How did one say "intimate" in Japanese, with all its genteel and quasi-medical overtones?

– Did you hug each other? I ventured, knowing that *daku* is something used to suggest further intimacies. Perhaps he would follow my drift.

He seemed to. He blushed, then said: Yes. Once. And we kissed too. Once, he added scrupulously.

Here was my opportunity.

– Anything further?

– Standing up in the cold on that beach? And it was snowing too.

– I see.

Satisfied that the love affair had not proceeded too far, I said: So, you'd been seeing her and then one day on the beach you talked and hugged and kissed.

He shook his head: No, it was different. On Sunday she took me to the movies and then we took a walk on the beach and then we hugged and kissed and were in love.

– All in one day.

– In one afternoon.

– Mr. Sato. How do you know you are in love?

– She said so.

– I see.

He looked at me, eyes hopeless, then dropped his head and gazed at the table, the untasted tea. There he sat, undone, a big country boy with large hands.

There is something feminine about boys in love—they seem to become the girls they are in love with. That coffee-shop meeting was easy to imagine. She probably sat there just as he was sitting now: still, consumed with her purpose.

During the days that followed he did not seem to ride his bike as fast, did not scrub himself as thoroughly in the bath, did not wait on the customers with such efficient dispatch. It was as though he were continually preoccupied.

She was writing to him often, he said, and his evenings were filled with writing letters in return. Sometimes he showed hers to me, read them to me. They were not about Sato himself. They were about how awful life in Akita was and what she was going to do in Tokyo after they were married. She had so many things to do that I wondered if he would ever see her, but I said nothing of such thoughts.

– I wonder if she'll approve of your gun collection, was all I allowed myself to say.

He smiled ruefully: She knows about my father. Says it was a dreadful thing to do. Hopes I'll make a better husband than he did.

Even then, I held my tongue. I wish now that I hadn't. I now think that I ought to have told him what I thought. But I said nothing. One of my reasons was my own feelings, my distrust of my own motives for speaking out. Another was that I was beginning to realize how important being in love was to Sato. Not, perhaps, the girl, but certainly the new center this had given his life.

In a few months he had matured. He was now a young man, responsible, no longer a youth. Even his face seemed to have changed, grown leaner. And his gaze was no longer so direct, so innocent. Now it was inward-looking.

And since I was the only person to whom he could speak about this overwhelming event, his visits were frequent. No more listening to Mozart. Even gun talk was brushed aside. I had become the doctor with whom he discussed his ailment. It absorbed him completely.

It did so, doctor saw, because it allowed him to be a person he had not been before. And though this troubled him, he must have welcomed it. At last he had something certain in his changeable life, the rock of his love, standing there, resisting the current.

So, for all these reasons, I made no attempt to treat the patient, simply let him go on, become more and more feverish. Admittedly, though I wished him well, I found these evenings spent singing her praises less and less interesting. No matter how hard I tried to steer him onto other things, like Colts and Winchesters, the conversation would irresistibly settle around Akiko—her name.

Then one night he appeared, white, agitated. He stood in the entryway, a letter in his hand. Briefly, it announced that Akiko was marrying a Mr. Watanabé of her acquaintance who was doing well in an Osaka company, and so she would not, as it turned out, be coming to Tokyo to be Mrs. Sato. She was terribly sorry, but it could not be helped. He was to take care of his health in this unseasonably cool spring weather.

I made him come in and, since it was an unseasonably cool spring evening, gave him a hot toddy. Then, as relieved by her letter as he was upset by it, I told him, among other things, that he was lucky he had discovered her character before marriage, that he was well out of it, that another girl would be much more deserving of him.

All of these sensible observations were rejected and I saw that, despite everything, Sato was still in love—now even more so. He was in love because he needed to be, and now simply listened to my comments, nodding absently. His mind was made up. He was leaving his job, telling no one. He was taking the train to Akita that very evening.

Standing again in the entryway I looked at him—a grown, unhappy man—and wondered at the power of emotion, the strength of need. He tried to smile. He couldn't.

I never saw him again. The rest I heard from the neighbors, all of them scandalized for a week or so. He had gone back to Akita, there'd been some girl there, and who would have thought it, a nice boy, a steady worker, like him.

Anyway, she'd worked in this coffee shop, and he'd gone there, and then . . . but here stories varied. Maybe there was an argument, maybe she'd shouted in front of the other customers. At any rate it was probably after something like that that he went to see his mother—for the last time.

– He killed himself, I said, seeing him before me, thinking of his father: He shot himself.

Well, that they didn't know. Oh, probably killed himself all right. It seems they found him on the beach, in the rain, dead for some time apparently. But shot? No, they didn't think so. He didn't have a gun, you see. The story was that he took a knife from his mother's kitchen and used that. At least that was what people said.

I could learn nothing further. The master of the *nandemoya* refused to answer any more questions. I stood there in front of the store and thought of him: Hidetada Sato, nineteen years old, alone on that cold beach.

Shuji Terayama

Looking at Terayama's stage is like looking into a box. The lid has been removed and one peers down into it, as though from a height. What one sees had been hidden. Now it is disclosed.

There sits the bad mother in her dark corner; there is the son, grop-ing as though blind, trying to escape; there is the androgynous young girl, taunting or helping; and there is the other man—half butler, half elder brother, usually bald.

These creatures live in the depths of the box, an unvarying cast what-ever the name of the play. They are surrounded by—at times half-hidden under—the decor: Taisho-period prints, old Japanese flags, the Victor dog, school uniforms, faded photos, ball gowns, a sword or two; relics of prewar Japan.

A prewar Japan imagined, because Terayama was himself too young to remember any of it. What he remembered was wartime Aomori, the far north, the snow, the family movie theater, a world of black and white where he grew up.

As a child he took the tickets, swept up afterward, and sprinkled water to keep down the dust. His lair was behind the screen, a tangle of canvas flats, old stage kimono, into which he curled and gazed up at the giants, backward, hanging over him as he lay small in the darkness.

We, likewise, gaze now into the miniature, private, magic world that is his theater, where the same drama is endlessly performed. It is an ex-pressionist world, reality seen through other eyes, filtered through another mind, a private mythology. And, as in all expressionist theater, the system is closed; it can also be compulsive, claustrophobic.

Terayama's is a world entirely visual. A deaf man could understand it, but not a blind one. It is theater for the eyes, not for the ears.

To speak with Terayama was to become aware of his gaze. It was the candid stare of a child. The young are all eyes—they have to be. They know nothing, and seeing is their education. Terayama's eyes were like windows behind which he lurked.

Yes, lurked. Though the gaze was direct there was also a sense of constant, guarded assessment. One felt he was rearranging what he saw even as he looked upon it. It is natural that a director of stage and screen be manipulative, but Terayama gave the impression that he was continually manipulating, that there was no time when he wasn't.

Yet the directions that seemed to emanate from him were too private to be other than ambivalent. It was not an order the director was giving but a suggestion. One had to divine for oneself what he really meant, what he actually wanted, uncertain that he even knew himself. One sensed too that he was judging, not for any professional reason—will he do in the part, is he being honest?—but for something more personal: do I like him, does he like me? This he seemed to suggest as he gazed out at you from his secret place, his lair.

Until wasted by illness, Terayama, given to turtleneck sweaters—those emblems of security—had the round face, the pudgy body, large palms, and short fingers of a grown child. And, like a child, he kept intact the wonders of his imagination. These he put on film, on the stage: odd, esoteric, often very beautiful images, variations on his central myth, his own childhood. He took in everything, assigned parts, animated lives. Yet the gaze from those caves in his face remained guarded, vulnerable.

Yes, vulnerable. It was this gaze that killed him. It happened in this fashion: directed outward onto stage or film the gaze is called visual imagination; directed outward onto life itself it is called voyeurism.

That Terayama liked to look was central to his person. He liked to sit in the dark and look at the giant figures, the adults, in their brightly lit space. Everyone knew this. It seemed natural.

Not, however, to the police and, along with them, the journalists and their magazines and newspapers. The law had bothered Terayama before—nudity on the stage forbidden, theater in the streets banned. So had the press, hypocritically scandalized by the directness of Terayama's reconstruction of an amoral childhood which all of us once knew and some of us remember.

Heretofore Terayama had paid little attention, had gone on with his life and his work. Now, however, a common voyeur, caught peeping into privacy—bedroom, bathroom, kitchen?—he was scolded by the law and pilloried by the press.

Not for the first time. But, now, for the last. Before, he had gone abroad with his troupe, or had somehow weathered the local storm. But this one was massive. Everyone now knew—and one can imagine how this phrase must have echoed and rebounded in the mind of a vulnerable man, a man so vulnerable that he had to secretly revisit the scenes of his childhood in this way.

One would have liked it had the artist hit back or, better, paid no heed. He was, after all, in addition to being a well-known director, one of Japan's finest modern poets. But that is not how artists are made. It is their very sensitivity that makes them artists. They cannot be expected to hold their own. And so Terayama became ill—illness, though real, always being a refuge with him.

An old illness, cirrhosis—friend from childhood—had forced him out of university, and now it forced him out of life. This hidden degeneration silently consumed him. The childlike plumpness disappeared, the full cheeks hollowed. Yet the gaze, questioning, rarely answering, remained to the end.

Terayama, child magician, dead at forty-seven. Did no one see the connection between his work and his death? No, no one did. The press, having hounded him, was respectful. Voyeurism was not mentioned in the obituaries.

But that is just where it ought to have been. It was the glorious voyeurism of an artist who had the imagination to will a secret life open to the public, to remove the lid so that, fascinated, we can gaze inside. It was the splendid, single-minded need to truly see, to experience through sight alone, and then reveal the depths within.

Isuzu Yamada

Grand professional of the Japanese stage, every two months or so she appears at one or another of the uptown theaters: sometimes padded and kimonoed in historical roles; more often sleekly neo-traditional—the older geisha, the affluent widow, the knowing mistress of the restaurant.

Great actress of the Japanese screen as well, though now more rarely seen, she was the worldly one in Mizoguchi's *Sisters of the Gion*, the faded geisha in Naruse's *Flowing*, the hopeful widow in Chiba's *Downtown*, the matriarch's daughter in Ichikawa's *Bonchi*, and—well known in the West—"Lady Macbeth" in Kurosawa's *Throne of Blood*.

She is an actress to whom acting is all, to whom getting everything just right is more important than anything else. Perfection is attempted, and often achieved. This she does through her dedication to her craft.

This craft is an unassailable technique. Classically trained, Isuzu Yamada brings to her acting the means of traditional Japanese arts, those forms which make for flawless execution.

In classical dancing and music, in the martial sports, in the No and Kabuki, these forms are the *kata*. In Kendo or Judo the *kata* are training exercises, series of them, practiced until instinctively there. In traditional acting and dance they are a recognized vocabulary of movement and gesture.

Yamada has brought to her appearances a mind formed by this code of learning, of being. To new roles she applies old methods, and the *kata* discipline illuminates her presence both on and off the stage and screen.

One sees it at its most rigorous when Yamada dances, these rote movements once more performing their original magic and turning into a young maiden a woman of considerable years. In her film appearances, even on the tube, one is also aware of the *kata*, though they have been absorbed now to the point of invisibility. One no longer sees them; one feels them.

This art informs everything that Yamada does: the way she turns, the way she lifts her hand, the way she smiles. In classical roles, her admirers say, she is as good as any *onnagata*—high praise indeed.

A knowledge this encompassing means that Yamada always knows precisely what to do and how to do it. When Kurosawa announced a month-long period of full rehearsal before a single frame of *The Lower Depths* was exposed, there was some grumbling among the movie actors. None from Yamada, however. She knew that this was the proper way to achieve the integral performance that Kurosawa desired—indeed, the only way.

As I watch her now, years later, I see an older woman still possessed of this urge to perfection, this need to be continually right. There, the way she turned just now, up there on the stage, that turn, abrupt, right-angled, to indicate disagreement—that was just right. And, an instant later, that single glance, perfectly directed and of just the right duration to let us understand her disappointment at another's failings.

Nothing is allowed to obstruct this urge, as I discovered once when I myself got in the way.

It was long ago when the tube was new, and I was to appear on it with her. It was indeed so new that all TV, apart from films, was live and the gadget was perhaps consequently still regarded as having a degree of artistic potential. At any rate, one was still supposed to behave properly in the studio.

Perhaps the artistic potential was why, already, a famous actress was appearing. I forget why I was. Probably for the novelty I would contribute, foreigners on TV being rarer then than now.

I was writing a book and had gone to interview her. In the course of this and a few further meetings I had become as friendly with her as my knowledge of the language and her inclinations would permit. During our meetings she was perfectly straightforward.

She started in the movies in 1932, and by 1936—when she was nineteen—she was supporting a husband, a child, and her divorced parents. She had to because this was the right way of doing things.

She also talked about *Actress*, a film she made in 1947 with Teinosuke

Kinugasa, which resulted in a highly publicized affair but one, she said, in which she had behaved responsibly. Then there was her political career when she was in the group that led the famous 1948 strike against Toho. Even though this resulted in her being blacklisted by the industry, she congratulated herself on having done the right thing. There was also her marriage (among others) to actor Yoshi Kato, in which she had acquitted herself equally well while it lasted.

Then when she found she could not work because of the blacklisting, she again did the proper thing. She wrote directly to those directors she wanted to work with, Kurosawa included. She effected a great comeback and won all of Japan's major acting awards for two years running, in 1956 and 1957, which indicates that she had indeed done the right thing.

All this was told in language scaled down to something I could understand. In fact, she seemed very soon to realize the modest dimensions of my vocabulary and apparently accommodated herself to them.

Back then my Japanese was much worse than it is now, and while I knew how to say what I wanted, I could do so in only one way—using simple, everyday, colloquial language. Great then was my discomfort when, the red light of the TV camera regarding us, suddenly live on the air, I discovered that I could not understand a word being said because the great actress was addressing me in *keigo*.

This is a polite and refined way of speaking, quite removed from the colloquial, using a vocabulary all of its own, and suitable for formal occasions or when addressing someone thought to deserve such discourse.

Isuzu Yamada's choice of diction was undoubtedly motivated by the former consideration. On an occasion as solemn as an appearance on television, *keigo* was the only possible vehicle. Even if one of us did not understand it. Or perhaps it was not initially apparent that I didn't, no matter how palpable it later became.

This was because—hypnotized by the beady red light, traumatized by being "live on the air," deaf, dumb, naked—I resorted to temporizing measures, such as I still use when I can't understand what is being said to me. Ah, I say, *mochiron* (of course); *watakushi mo so omoimasu* (I think so too); *sono tori* (that's right), etc.

These are all trotted out to hide my inadequacy. And the nature of the language being what it is they nearly always work. Indeed, it is almost impossible to go wrong, however indiscriminately such phrases are used—almost, but not entirely, as I was soon to find out.

Yamada was smiling sweetly, turning an eye of approval on the camera from time to time, and using words like *goran ni naru* for "see" when I only knew *miru*, and *o-kiki ni naru* for "hear" when I only knew *kiku*. And much worse.

Reconstructing the conversation, aided by what *keigo* I now know, it must have gone something like this:

    – And such an elegant, such a skillful Japanese you speak, she said.
    – *Mochiron*, said I.
    – This would seem to indicate a degree of assiduous application.
    – *Watakushi mo so omoimasu.*
    – And perhaps an equal degree of mental aptitude.
    – *Sono tori.*
And so on.

Whether what was occurring was apparent to Yamada or not, it certainly was to the rest of my audience. I imagine people from Hokkaido to Kyushu were rolling on the *tatami* during my part of this nationwide transmission.

Yet it is likely that the great actress did not once realize that I could not understand, and did not once wonder at the oddly static nature of our conversation. At any rate, the steady, serious gaze never wavered, no small smile once flickered in my direction, no irony informed that handsome face. She could not, as a loyal friend or two suggested, have done it on purpose.

The reason is that to have done it on purpose would not at all have been the right way of doing things. And to have acknowledged that this was occurring, had she noticed, would also not have been the right way. And as for using colloquial Japanese, a choice that would have rendered my problem much less acute, well, that too would not have been correct.

Did she detect my muted struggles, did she note that flush of distress which, I am told by those who witnessed it, rendered my performance the more exquisitely amusing? Did she?

Well, that is not a proper question. For, even if she had, she could not have abandoned her mode of expression. She owed it to her public, to her art, to the great new instrument of culture and education on which she was for the first time appearing, to accord it, herself, and me the due amount of formality.

But there was more to it than that. What Isuzu Yamada was doing, something I could actually have watched had I managed to collect myself, was inventing *kata* for television.

Here was this new medium and she was in a way just as lost as I was. Her spectators were no more visible than they were in the movie studio. But there one had time and space and the possibility of correction. Here there was nothing like that. We were "live on the air."

She was thus just as unprepared as I was, but her approach to the problem was much more creative. She started running through available *kata*, as it were. Those who watched told me it was an education just to see the way that the look, the turn of the head, the display of the hands changed as she became increasingly familiar with the medium, as she visibly decided which would be appropriate to the small screen. By the time our fifteen-minute "conversation" was over, the viewers had had a demonstration of a great artist creating before their very eyes. Nothing was allowed to obstruct that creative urge, and in the end she got it all just right.

That quarter of an hour was perhaps historically significant. It may well be that the current *kata* for TV appearances (and they certainly now exist, because people on the tube all act the same way) were born that very night.

I only wish I had paid more attention.

Kon Ichikawa

Bright lights, red carpet, stars, smiling Toho executives—it is a special premiere, Kon Ichikawa's *Happiness*. Director right there at the end of the receiving line. Smiling, greeting, talking—famous cigarette stuck between lips.

– Ed McBain original, he says: Only really this much of a story (holding up a hand, forefinger and thumb almost touching, to indicate how little it was. Fingers then stretch apart). The rest was all us.

Lips expertly juggle cigarette among the syllables. We have been expecting lip cancer for years. No sign of it, however.

– Rest was all us, he says, eyes crinkling in the way they always do. Pantomimes stepping into a pair of overalls, perhaps. That's him getting into the Ed McBain original.

– Great fun to make, this film, he says, beaming.

I have never heard him say otherwise. All films were great fun to make. Great fun to make the cannibal sequences in *Fires on the Plain* too, I imagine. Such fun really that it isn't to be taken all that seriously—filmmaking.

During the obligatory pre-screening speeches the leading actor is unable to say a single word. Part of this is perhaps pose, it being thought smart to be inarticulate in public. But most I think is real, that seeming stupidity which afflicts some actors. In the film itself, however, the same actor is very good, seems to know precisely what he is doing, does it skillfully. Again I see Ichikawa pretending to climb into the overalls.

Since everything is great fun to make, one infers that it isn't all that difficult and that the results aren't all that important. This must reassure actors considerably, I would think, but, just as important, it suggests that this is the way Ichikawa keeps his distance from his work, and himself.

Certainly it explains why he can keep working in a period when other more earnest directors can't. Ichikawa, since he does not have to be serious about it, can take any script he is offered. Then, no matter how bad, he can amuse himself by making it as good as he can. Fun to make that film, he will say of his very worst.

He told me once that the director he most admired, the one he would most like to resemble, was Walt Disney. I thought this was mordant Ichikawa humor until it occurred to me that he meant, literally, what he said. Disney too had great fun making films, he too could climb inside and do everything himself.

Yet there was a period when Ichikawa's films became serious—*Enjo, Kagi, Bonchi*. This was when his wife was doing his scripts. The experience of seeing an Ichikawa film suddenly deepened. One was moved by its beauty, its truth, its sadness. I was very enthusiastic about these films back then. Ichikawa just stared at me, cigarette in mouth, as though he did not know what I was talking about.

Perhaps he didn't. His wife is now gone and others (including a number of film-studio hacks) write his scripts. He takes what is given him, puffing his cigarette, his eyes crinkling.

The film begins. Lots of Ichikawa-type humor involving a cop papa and his motherless kids. Actor very competent—plaintive, amusing, believable. Filled with the that's-too-bad-but-it-can't-be-helped feeling which, even now, is so attractive to Japanese audiences. Let's just get on with life, says the film, and the audience smiles. Applause at the end. Beaming Toho executives, a grinning Ichikawa.

I noticed that the film is, like all Ichikawa's, of a certain temperature. It is cool, not really chilly, not actually cold, but quite cool. People getting into it and moving around in it have not raised its temperature. They all seem to be working in the film from a distance.

I remember Ichikawa getting into his invisible overalls. Moving the film around, moving the actors around, making a cool and pleasant experience of it. Then I remember his earlier films and I wonder who once climbed into Ichikawa and made *him* move around.

Sumiré Watanabé

What to do about the old Yamato; a problem, that. Madame Sumiré gazed around, sucked a tooth. Well over a century and a half, and looking every year of it. Still, the beams were strong. During all those generations the termites had never really settled in. Perhaps something more might be made of this—of sheer tradition. What with all the other older buildings gone from Ginza, what with concrete, steel, glass, and bathroom tile, the novelty of good, expensive wood was growing. Capitalize, perhaps, on that—age, probity, worth.

The place had certainly seen changes. Back in the old days, a famous Edo geisha house, screens by minor master, cakes from Kyoto. Then a suicide, lovesick and indentured maid, so the legend went. No recourse then but to become a restaurant—everything traditional and expensive: eel and turtle, blowfish, shrimps served live. There the Meiji emperor himself appeared, the palace being not that far away. Consequent governmental popularity—part of Pearl Harbor planned within these very walls.

And then decline. Though the place withstood the terrors of war, it could not the horrors of peace. Bombs and conflagrations gave way to higher taxes and the rising price of land. *Tatami, shoji, fusuma*—traditional materials all—now far too dear as demand diminished. No recourse then but to reopen as one of the better hostess bars.

And here was where the fortunes of the old Yamato had become Madame Sumiré's own. Acquired from a second husband praying for peace at any price, it proved a challenge she had overcome. She, after all, knew the business—had met Mr. Watanabé while he was postwar slumming at the ratty Ueno cabaret where she had once worked.

Minor master's screens were sold, partitions were knocked out, *fusuma* junked; holes were cut in ancient walls to hold the air-conditioning; *tatami* banished, giving way to purple wall-to-wall; modern sit-down toilets where the *tokonoma* was; then cocktail bar and floor-length mirrors, box seats and tabourets, cut-glass chandelier for proper mood and red plush drapes which always caught the dust.

And then the girls. More problems there. One trained them, treated them like daughters, then watched each and every one turn bad. How she had encouraged with her nightly talks: Girls, give your all for old Yamato, keep up the spirit, make ours the winning team. And how she had watched them give their all in other, unintended ways, ending up madames themselves at other, rival Ginza bars.

These youngsters, they knew nothing of tradition, of the deference owed an elder, being modest in their proper places, working hard, doing without—virtues all, now all but lost.

Oh, the years of listening to them whine; watching for the wily ones, the ones who cheated on the side; the widows, crying on the customers; the greedy ones who ate the raisin butter. Madame Sumiré sucked her gold tooth and looked about.

Seven o'clock—another night. Soon the old familiars, fewer now, and bringing fewer guests. Business was not going well. The ancient Yamato was sinking, the very beams groaning as in despair. Yet she had tried.

Oh, she had tried. The monkey, so soon dead, unfed, purchased to amuse the guests; all her girls dressed up as nuns, a fad soon past; computer games to attract, she'd hoped, the younger executives.

And then, her greatest folly. Keeping up with things as she invariably did, Madame Sumiré knew of Arab interests. This being so she put in plastic hassocks and glass-topped tables with gilded legs. Purple chiffon, hopefully harem-like, was bunched and candles placed nearby, romantically, despite the risk.

She changed the name to Senichiya, the Thousand and One Nights, spray-painted the front all purple, a favorite color and one she fancied Middle Eastern. She had a star and crescent painted in gold over the bar, imported quantities of arrack to make her new guests feel at home, and redid the facilities: on one door, Sultans; on the other, Women.

Originally she had wanted tiled floors and a purling fountain but, on being advised that the building would then collapse, she made do with plastic *tatami*, lilac-trimmed. This she had thought the Arabs might enjoy but it was her Japanese customers—she had no other—who delighted in the novelty of sliding shod across the mats.

Then, over the new sound system, Bernstein doing *Scheherazade*, night after night, month after month, until the record hissed and one of the girls went funny in the head—and still no Arabs in their quaint burnooses with those cunning water pipes. Why, she'd even gone to the trouble and expense of finding a needy body-builder, stripped and oiled him, twined his violet turban all herself and given him a stage scimitar to shiver with in the neon-flooded entrance.

All for naught. But no one could say that Madame Watanabé—Sumiré to her friends (Violet, a charming name)—lacked punch or fight. No sooner out of one disaster than bravely into yet another.

She'd studied the papers, the financial reports; she knew prosperity when she saw it. Her country on an upward curve and the Dow Jones averages, whatever they were, leaping as though in hot pursuit. The wealth was there for the taking, and despite what the envious said there was nothing better than a pile of cash.

She looked about her domain and her tongue found her tooth. Japan . . . perhaps that, after all, was the answer. Revive the glory of the old Yamato! Yes, put all the *fusuma* back, get new *tatami* for the ones the guests had scuffed, and make them leave their filthy footwear at the door. Make them squat at toilet once again as well.

Ah, there was charm in all this. Practiced eye on public pulse, she could see it now. With foreign novelty so rife, what further titillation than tradition? With things gone this far, old Japan was like a foreign land. A trip to ancient Kyoto was now as exotic as any voyage to London, England, or to Paris, France.

What further novelty than this? And never mind the cost, an investment after all. Enthused, with shining eyes, petite and dumpy Sumiré clasped her hands at her velvet bodice, at the level of her lilac orchid, forgot her incisor, flashed a smile. Sumiré, enterprising yet, would make her money while she still had breath. People always said that things couldn't be helped. How wrong they were. How well she knew. There was always room for hope.

And, outside, the old nameboard hung, almost illegible in the purple glow, and on it—Yamato—the first name for Japan, carved in oak by an artisan long dead, gone for well over a century and a half. Softly the board creaked, slowly swaying in the first night breeze.

Toshio Morikawa

We were talking about the *furosha*, those bums increasingly littering parks and malls and subway passages, propped against the wall or lying on the pavement, sleeping, sometimes drunk, always carrying shopping bags filled with all they own.

They have chosen not to work, not to carry their weight in our society. There is plenty for them to do but, no, they want the easy life of lounging about and foraging in garbage cans. They are simply dropouts. This, at least, is the conventional view.

– Surely, there's plenty of work they could do? I said conventionally.

The youngish man with whom I was talking turned to glance at me. He was a workman, a *tobishoku*, one of those who build tall buildings, walk the high beams in their two-toed rubber *tabi*.

The glance was amused. *Yoku shitte oru da na*, he said: A lot you know about it.

– But these people are dropouts.

– Oh, is that so? he replied, leaning back and crossing his arms over the expanse of bare chest above his woolen bellyband. He seemed to be thinking how best to solve the problem I apparently represented.

– Look, he said finally: There's still work at proper companies, but not at small ones, the kind that use job-brokers. If you want to learn something about it you ought to get out of bed at four in the morning and go watch them lining up for work, hoping they'll be hired for the day—five hundred men lined up for fifty jobs.

He told me you had to look fairly strong, like you could do a day's work, but the trouble was that after a person had been out of a job for a week or two he didn't look too good. So he didn't get picked by the brokers.

And after a month or two of that there wasn't much hope of finding any work at all. That was when you started poking around in garbage cans and drinking anything you could lay your hands on. You didn't wash, your hair got long, your teeth went bad. You stopped caring, you see.

So a person could be a real bum in half a year. But he hadn't dropped out, understand? He hadn't chosen to be a *furosha*. Understand?

I sat, surprised, chastened. One is rarely spoken to this directly and the message is seldom this straight. But then we were not sitting in the polite uptown—we were in the everyday downtown, seated on a bench in Sumida Park, watching the river flow by in the late afternoon of a day in early summer.

After a time he broke the silence by pointing out a bus going over Kototoi Bridge.

– I came to Tokyo on a school trip when I was about fifteen, and we all hung out of the windows looking at this and that. And we went right over that bridge there. I must have looked at this very park. I might have seen this very bench.

He smiled, looked down at his *tabi*: And I sure didn't think I'd be sitting here like this.

– Like this?

– With none of that work that everyone's got so much of if he really wants it. You think otherwise I'd be sitting here in the daytime?

– You're out of a job, then?

– For two days now.

He was from Kyushu, had done a few years in the Self-Defense Forces (which is what Japan calls its postwar army), then taken his separation pay and bought a truck. He and a friend were going into business . . . and, well, he lost the truck—some unexplained misfortune—and began doing highrise construction work.

– But they went and filled up Tokyo. Land is too expensive to build on now unless you're a really big company. But all the big construction companies, they got their own workers now, pay them by the month.

– Then where do you sleep?

– Up to yesterday, a bunkhouse in Sanya.

I knew about Sanya. It was Tokyo's slum, filled with flophouses and often complained about in the papers. *Furosha* sprawled in the streets, drunk or sick or both. Sanya was where the brokers came early some mornings with orders for ten head here and five head there. Newspaper editorials spoke of the area as a blight on the capital.

– And last night it was *aokan*—out in the open, right here in the park. But not tonight. No, tonight I'll be far away.

– Why? Have you found work?

He smiled: No such luck. And you better not be here either, he added.

This was because the police were going to make one of their periodic patrols, here in our park as well as in Asakusa and Ueno. Any vagrants they found would be rounded up and put into vans, then carted off to hospitals. It was for their own good.

I had heard about these, about the welfare centers and the free hospitals for the homeless. One of the official answers to the *furosha* problem was that, with these facilities, there was no problem.

– No problem for them, observed the *tobishoku*: But you just try to stay in one of them. You can get in for a night or two, if you're lucky. Then you're kicked out again for a week or so. There are just too many want in. There's no more room.

– Of course, if you really want a place to stay, permanent, then when they try to shove you into the van you get violent and fight back. That means that you're disturbed and so they pack you off to one of the crazy houses up north. And then you've got a home for good. Just try to get *out* of one of those places.

Smile long gone, he went on to say: You see, if they get rid of everyone, then Sanya will be empty, so they can finally tear it down and build shopping centers or something. And, of course, that would stop the Sanya *senso* too.

I knew something about this as well, the Sanya war, so long-continued now that the papers have stopped reporting about it. This is the endless battle between the gangs and unions.

The gangsters also act as job-brokers. When they find work for a man they then take part of his wage. The labor unions want to remedy this practice, which results in such low pay for the workers. They want job allocation to be fair and they want the worker to have a full day's pay in his pocket. They also hope to organize the men into a real union, able to dictate prices to the bosses. This conflict of interests has led to much violence and a number of killings—most famously a film director making a documentary on the subject. But, I had also heard, the police now had it well under control.

– The police? He laughed: They stand around and watch. They don't want to get involved. Maybe they have orders not to, for all I know.

This, he explained, was because of the landowners, the local merchants, all those who had an interest in cleaning up Sanya; hence, the local politicians as well. They called it a disgrace to have a place like Sanya in this city. What they meant—besides the shame of having people freezing on the streets—was the shame of seeing all that land not being used profitably.

I turned and looked at him more closely. An articulate, dissident laborer is rare.

– And how, I asked, do you know all this? How do you know about the patrol tonight? Surely the cops must keep things like that secret?

– Maybe they tried to. But we were told about it over the loudspeaker when I went to look for work this morning. The truckers announced it just before they drove off. They don't want Sanya destroyed. Good cheap labor like us. Lots of us to choose from.

Then he smiled: Me—I'm off to Yokohama once it gets dark.

– You ought to keep right on going, all the way back to Kyushu.

He nodded: You're right. But when I do, I want to do it properly. I want to go back with a present for my mother, and something for my little nephews. I don't want to just slink back.

– If you wait too long you won't be able to get back at all.

– Yes, he said, nodding again and then, apparently quoting: Fall once into Sanya and there's no climbing out.

Some schoolboys passed, laughing and shouting in the last sunlight.

– That was the best age, wasn't it? I remember that age. I wish I was back there again, he said.

We were silent for a while. I then suggested a meal, though he hadn't asked for one. So we ate chicken pilaf at a local place where the proprietress was visibly disturbed that a common workman with a bare chest should be there, and with a suspicious foreigner at that. She would have been even more upset had she overheard our conversation.

He was telling me about this notorious hospital all the vagrants fought against being sent to. And this wasn't only because of its high mortality rate. It was also apparently because the place was well known for supplying organs to other hospitals: fresh kidneys, eyeballs, hearts—anything you wanted.

This I disbelieved: Come on. That would make too big a stink in the press.

– Well, maybe—if they found out. But, look, people don't care.

We ate in silence for a time, while I picked out the bits of chicken skin and gristle I found. Then with a quick bow he thanked me and said: There, that'll last me till tomorrow morning and I'll be down in Yokohama at the docks. I hear the brokers down there aren't gangsters, at least not all of them.

During the following days as I made my way around Tokyo I found myself looking at the *furosha* on the streets or in the subway passages, and not only downtown but in Ginza, in Shinjuku as well.

On some days there were lots of them, on others none at all. I supposed that the police were moving them out. Certainly attempts were being made to keep them away. I noticed pools of water standing in a corner where the day before several men had been lying down. And wet sand along the corridors where they had sat, to make rest impossible.

Then one night in Ueno, going home, walking along a subway corridor, I saw several of them camped among the colonnades. Some were reading their newspapers, a few were lying down, curled up. But one, drunk or delirious, clothes torn and muddy, was standing by a pillar, pissing.

And coming toward him in their green uniforms were two security guards. The younger saw the old man urinating and rushed forward. Shouting *Hora, kono yaro*—Hey, you stupid bastard—he struck him hard across the back of the head.

The old man, unsteady anyway, fell, sliding in his own piss across the paving. *Kono yaromé*, shouted the young guard, with the other looking on, and kicked the old man's backside as he was trying to get up.

The older guard took his arm to help him, then apparently thought better of it and released the piss-wet coat, and the two of them began cuffing the *furosha* down the corridor.

And I, watching his wet, retreating back, thought of the good-natured, country-faced young worker from Kyushu. Was this what he'd become in a few years? But I would never know. I never expected to see him again.

But I did—in Asakusa. He was striding along in his wide wing trousers and two-toed *tabi*, carrying a small bag and looking as though he was going somewhere.

– *Yo*, he said when he saw me, his smile wide: They didn't pick you up in the park!

– I didn't go. I stayed home.

– Well, you're not the only one with a home now. I got this job. I leave tomorrow morning. Osaka. Good pay. I'll work there for a month and then have enough to get back to Kyushu. I'm going to ride the bullet train. With presents and everything. Here, look.

And he showed me his contract, a precious piece of paper which presumably spelled everything out. I could read none of it except his name—the characters for "forest" and "river."

– Hey, you can read. Yes, Morikawa. What about the given name? No? It's Toshio. Not Toshiro, Toshio.

I congratulated him and then asked how he had happened to get the job. It was pure luck, he said. Some broker he'd never seen before. Said he needed five men but that they'd have to leave Tokyo. Everybody was ready for that, you bet, but there were fifty-some to choose from.

– So what did he do?

Well, the broker had apparently resorted to a *takara*, a lottery, to decide. And Toshio here smiled broadly, remembering: I got lucky.

It seemed that these fifty hopeless adults had stood around and engaged in a primitive elimination game—stone-paper-scissors. This was the *takara*, and the five survivors got the jobs, got the chance to leave Sanya.

Over a *nabé* stew we talked on and on about the bright future and, when that finally ran out, about the dark past. I told him with some indignation what I had witnessed in the Ueno subway passage.

– Well, what do you expect? was his unexpected answer: You can't have these old folks lying around and pissing where people are walking.

– But they were brutal, those two.

– Probably the only way to get him to move. He was probably bombed out of his mind anyway.

166

– Or maybe just out of his mind, I said indignantly.

– Maybe.

Toshio was no longer interested in the fate of the *furosha* now that he was no longer in danger of becoming one. And he was no longer interested in the future of Sanya now that he was no longer condemned to live in it. Instead he wanted to talk about what lay in store for him.

– I've been to Osaka just once, he said: Nice place.

– They have a slum there that's bigger even than Sanya. You watch out.

He laughed, showing his strong teeth, as white as the clean T-shirt he was wearing. Gone was that expanse of tanned skin above the belly-band. Instead, emblazoned on his chest was a picture of the lord of the jungle, with *Lion* under it.

– King of the beasts, I said, and he, seeing where I was looking, opened his half-coat. Under *Lion* was *Dentifrice*.

– Got it from the toothpaste people. Giving them out on the street they were.

After the *nabé* we went somewhere for coffee, for which he paid.

– Got my pride, he said, smiling: And besides, I'm no bum, you know.

He laughed again, then as though remembering: Don't you get too upset about the *furosha*. It's not all that bad, you know. They get taken care of. And if those guards you saw were a little hard on them, well, I guess they probably had to be. Can't really let them get out of hand.

I sipped my coffee and looked at this sincere, intelligent man. No more a rebel, he had returned to the fold, been given a job, a chance to forget the abyss he had glimpsed.

And I was happy to forget it too. How could I understand anything of what those bums were feeling? When I saw some drunk, crazy, dying old laborer I only wondered if he knew what was happening to him.

Nowadays I look more often at the fresh-faced high-school boys up from the country for a day in the capital. From their bus windows they point at the river, point at the park, point at me sitting on a bench in the late summer sun. What, I wonder, will happen to them?

Shintaro Katsu

Katsu, backed up by his entourage, makes a big entrance. He strikes a
Zatoichi pose, hands stretched out, eyeballs turned up until just the
whites show—the blind swordsman himself. Then his eyes slide back into
place, he gives his snorting laugh, and cuffs his sidekicks into the room.

All smiles tonight. Kurosawa has chosen him to play the lead in
Kagemusha. This is a role he very much wants. He wants to be a big
international star, not just a little Japanese one. He has often been to
Las Vegas, so he knows. It is really a big *American* star that he wants to be.

Sitting down, his buddies around him, he keeps the table in stitches.
Las Vegas girl asked him if he liked it French fashion. He had no idea.
She demonstrated. It tickled. He wanted to say so. English inadequate.
So he said: I no like chewing gum.

Buddies collapse, general laughter. Another funny Las Vegas story.
While they were making love she or another asked if he was ready. Given
typical Japanese confusion over *l*'s and *r*'s he heard wrong. I no lady,
he said with indignation: I gentleman. Contingent howls its appreciation, several beat the table with the flat of their hands.

Katsu, small, fat, moustached, funny when he has a good director, looks
around as though surprised at these reactions, then shrugs good-
naturedly: boys will be boys, says the shrug. Parodying an American gang
boss—Okay, okay, fellas, just cool it—he adds in Japanese: And now we're
going to drink to *Kagemusha*, whatever that means (with his impish little grin, a trademark, cute little kid acting tough).

The first day of shooting on the *Kagemusha* set arrived. Katsu, veteran
of dozens of pictures, was ready. So were his cohorts. He even had his
own television crew to capture his performance. This Kurosawa objected
to.

– But I've got to have a record of my daily performance, Katsu is supposed to have said: Otherwise I won't know how I'm doing, how good I am.

Kurosawa apparently informed him that he was the director, *he* would tell his actor how he was doing, how good he was. On further objections from Katsu, Kurosawa pointed out that he was using multiple cameras and that the TV crew would be in the scene.

– Hey, you guys, go hide behind that pillar, the actor is supposed to have yelled, before turning to the director with: There, see? Invisible.

Kurosawa said later: If he was going to be this difficult on the first day of shooting I could just imagine him on the last. Accordingly he said no, the TV crew would have to go. Katsu said no, they would have to stay. Then, depending on which side tells the story, Kurosawa said: You're fired; or Katsu said: I quit.

Another party, another entrance. This one subdued. The entourage is now composed of Toei studio toughs, since Katsu is making yet another gangster film with them. Very subdued now—no Zatoichi imitations. He takes a back table, plays with his chopsticks. The boys hover around him protectively—their wounded leader.

I look at him—fat, funny, and, I now see, lost. He is a little kid all right, but one with what his beloved Americans call authority problems. No, no, he said to the press, being big about the whole thing: He's an artist, you see. Me, I'm just an actor . . . But also at the time just an unruly and disappointed little boy seeing how far he could push papa.

Or maybe it was different. Maybe being a big American star was too much for him. What if he tried as hard as he could and then didn't make it? What then? What if he was a *failure*? Then, maybe better not to try. Maybe just back out.

Or, perhaps, neither. Maybe not much thought involved. Just interested in a good time, just someone trying to do his best. A little laugh, a little drink, a little puff. And a few pals—his own "rat pack" with himself as old brown eyes.

Now Katsu is balancing one chopstick on top of the other. A few of the gang are snickering. He himself is quietly smiling, gray hair glinting handsomely in the subdued light—the kind these places call "lighting." Soon he will give his famous laugh. Maybe even do his Zatoichi imitation.

Hisako Shiraishi

Round face, neat gray bun, hands clutching purse, she looked like any ordinary old woman. And her sighs, her wan smiles, her complaints, these too were those of an ordinary old woman left to herself.

I had noticed her at the vegetable shop, staring at the cabbages, pinching the strawberries, and remarking on the prices. I saw her too at the local variety store—which advertised itself in English, perhaps misunderstanding the term, as the Chic Commode. She was asking for a discount on washing powder because she bought so much.

– I keep a clean house, I heard her say, as though she were being accused of not doing so. And I remember thinking that here was an old lady who did not have anything to keep her occupied. Little did I realize that I was to become that occupation.

She was a neighbor, with rooms directly beneath mine in the twelve-story apartment house (it called itself a "mansion") where we both lived. It was from other neighbors, those on either side, that I learned more about her.

Children, one or two of them, but neglectful they were. This from the piano teacher on my left. Not that she blamed them. Also a husband, long since dead. Probably from having to live with her. This with a snicker from the retired postal worker on my right—at which his wife pinched him and looked disapproving.

Hisako Shiraishi, her name on door and postbox, was not popular. She didn't mean any harm, I was told, but she was a complainer and she tried to take advantage. Apparently she brought "disharmony" into the meetings of the Shuwa Mansion Residents' Association.

– She's always complaining, said the retired postal worker, encountered in the elevator, away from his wife: We just hate to see her at the meetings. The trouble is she's got nothing else to do.

170

So it was that I, quite innocently, volunteered. I began to say good morning to Mrs. Shiraishi. This startled her and she aimed a suspicious eye at me before returning my greetings in a guarded manner. Determined to be pleasant I smiled whenever we met, and held open the lobby door. She would scurry past, then turn to stare accusingly from the safety of the elevator.

Seeing unfriendliness, I ought to have retreated. Instead, I responded as though it were some sort of challenge. I will be nice, I will, I told myself. Whether I was actually concerned about bringing a ray of sunshine into the old woman's life is doubtful. I suppose I simply believed that everyone ought to get along with everybody else. Otherwise I can't explain my presenting myself at her door with a ripe watermelon.

The door opened a crack. A dark eye looked out.

– What do you want? she asked suspiciously.

– I happen to have this watermelon, I said: And I thought you might like it.

– Why? she asked—an instant response, like the snap of a trap.

– Well . . . it's the first of the season, I said, unable to think of another reason.

The door opened a bit wider. She stood there, staring at me. Then: I hope you don't think that this makes up for it.

– Makes up for what?

– It's been terrible, she said, her voice a whine: When you shake out your rugs from your balcony, all that dirt comes right in my windows.

I, feeling absurdly guilty, apologized, promised to take care, and was backing away when a small, strong hand reached out, captured the watermelon, drew it in, and slammed the door. I stood there with that awful prescient feeling that I had done something irremediable.

Sometime afterward I left the city for a week or so, and when I returned—was just through the door—there was a telephone call from her.

– I'm calling to complain. I couldn't get a wink of sleep last week because of the noise you were making. Every night, on and on. I don't know what to do. I must have my sleep, I'm an old lady. It's too cruel.

I said I would come down. She was waiting just behind the door, and pushed it open as soon as I rang. This time she invited me in, as far at least as the entryway. I looked into her neat kitchen and she, seeing this, at once slid shut the sliding door. Then she told me at length what a horrible week she had had.

I guessed what had happened. I had given my friend Fumio the key and told him to use the place if he wanted. He had had friends in. Youngsters all, they had probably made a fair amount of noise. So I apologized to her, bowed, said that it would certainly not happen again, backed out, and decided to talk to Fumio about this.

Yes, they had had a party, until midnight maybe, and one of the girls *was* rather heavy, and, yes, they had danced a bit. But only once, only that Saturday night, certainly not *every* night. What he said, I knew, was true. I also realized that I was beginning to discern the outlines of the vast problem Mrs. Shiraishi would become.

Not for a time, however. Yet even then I noticed that I was actually trying to be quiet in my own apartment. I was trying to walk more lightly, was closing doors more quietly. This I thoroughly resented. It was as though the neurasthenic old woman had come to live with me, as though she were there, in the closet, peering out with dark and beady eye.

Then, quite late one night, a telephone call: I wonder if I could ask you to make a little less noise. It's late. People are trying to sleep—me, for instance. I've not had a wink in the past few days because of all the noise. I need my sleep. I'm an old lady. Do try, please, to walk less heavily. And could you flush your toilet less often? It makes such a noise and it always startles me.

I said I would and the next day went to see my neighbors. How did that old woman get my telephone number, I wondered. Oh, that was easy enough. The Shuwa Mansion Residents' Association would have given it to her. The real problem, continued the retired postal worker, was that she was terrible when she had a grudge. I ought to be careful—just put up with it.

When I told the piano teacher, she expressed a token interest but suggested that, since we did after all have to live here together, perhaps I should be a bit quieter. I stared at her—a woman whose pupils' *Für Elise* I had been enduring daily for some time.

After that there was quiet for a while until one evening a knock came on the door and outside stood a uniformed policeman. He inquired as to my identity and then told me that my downstairs neighbor had lodged a complaint about the racket I was making, had demanded assistance, which was why he was here and just what had I been doing?

I invited him in, showed him my quiet apartment, and told him the history of my relations with Mrs. Shiraishi. He did not seem surprised, merely nodded and said that he would remember this next time she called—if he was on duty, that is. If he wasn't, I might have to explain it to a good many patrolmen before they all understood.

– But this is unfair. I'm doing nothing and she calls the police.

– I know, he said, a young cop, a bit uncomfortable but smiling: Still, Japan's a small country. We all have to get on peacefully together somehow.

When he had left I went downstairs, bearing no gifts this time. The door opened a crack. Inside the eye lurked.

– What do you want? asked that hated, whining voice.

– I want to know why you called the police when I wasn't making any noise.

– You were. You were dancing.

– I was alone.

– I heard dancing.

– I was not dancing.

– That's what you say. But someone was. I heard it. I must have my sleep. I've had no sleep for nights. I'm an old lady. I need my sleep.

– Mrs. Shiraishi! I am going to bring this up at a meeting of the Shuwa Mansion Residents' Association.

– I already have. The meeting was yesterday.

In the morning I went to my neighbors. Neither of them had gone to the meeting, but even if a complaint had been lodged, the husband told me, no one would take it seriously.

– The police do. A cop actually came to my door.

– He was only doing his duty, he explained: Come on, now, this happens to all of us occasionally. We all have to live together peacefully. Japan's a small country. You've just got to learn to put up with it.

– But I'm not guilty, I said, upset, using somewhat dramatic language.

At this point his wife came and pulled him away. Though she whispered, I heard quite plainly what she said: Now you stop—we don't want to get involved.

A short period of peaceful coexistence followed. Then one night, very late, there was a great pounding at my door. I was asleep but I knew who it was. Rushing to the door, barefoot, in shorts, I caught the scurrying Mrs. Shiraishi before she reached the stairs.

– Look, I said, holding on to her, speaking softly, carefully, as though to an upset child, or an excited animal: Look, just come and see for yourself. There is no one here. I am alone. I was asleep. No one was making any noise.

She allowed me to pull her to the door. I turned on the light. She seemed to be searching for signs of a party, but I also saw that curiously greedy look which solitary people have when peering into others' homes.

– They're all on the balcony.

I turned and stared, realizing that she did not believe what she was saying. She merely did not want to be in the wrong.

– Then come over here, I said, crossing the room and opening the balcony door.

She peered into the dark.

– They climbed down.

– Mrs. Shiraishi. This is the eighth floor. There's no way to climb down. You've been hearing things.

– I know what I heard, she said—a round ball of a woman with eyes like knives.

– Look, I replied, seeking to understand what was making her behave in this fashion: This apartment is old. Sometimes I too hear things. They seem to come from just above. But they don't. They're coming from some other apartment. So maybe someone really is having a party and it sounds as if it might be here, but it's not. It's somewhere else.

I was hoping not only to give her some kind of reason for having mistakenly bothered me, but even perhaps to send her out to pound on other doors.

But she stood there in her nightwear, small, compact, her gray hair a helmet: I heard what I heard, she recited, and I know what I know.

In the morning I woke up the head of the Shuwa Mansion Residents' Association and told him what had happened. Clutching his robe about him, shifting on his bare feet, he said: Oh, Mrs. Shiraishi. We know about her.

– Well, if you know about her then can't you stop her banging at doors and waking up members of your association?

It was not until this was said that I realized I had done the same to him, woken him out of a sound sleep to complain. He seemed unaware of this, however:

– The fact is that when we've got a country as crowded as this, one has to learn to get along. Now, I know that Mrs. Shiraishi can be a nuisance. But, even so, the woman has had a pretty hard life. Though it isn't generally known, actually, her husband killed himself.

– I'm not at all surprised.

The head of the residents' association looked at me sadly, as though my attitude was one of the things the matter with this otherwise peaceable world.

– Look, I said, deepening this impression: I can call the police too, you know.

He shook his head: Oh, we wouldn't really want that.

– Well, I didn't really want that old woman banging on my door in the middle of the night either, you know.

Back in my apartment I slammed the door and let my own suspicions have their way. Oh, I knew why this was happening to me. I certainly wouldn't be treated like this if I wasn't foreign. It was because I was a foreigner that this crazy old woman had unleashed her paranoia on me. And it was because I was a foreigner that I was being fobbed off with talk of how tiny Japan was and how we all ought to be living cheerfully together. And this from the man who by rights ought to have been protecting me.

I told the piano teacher as much. She nodded in a sympathetic way, then remarked: But it's true, what he said. Don't you think you could put up with it, a little thing like this?

– A little thing! I cried: That crazy woman pounding on my door in the middle of the night! Is that a little thing?

– But if she thinks you are making all that noise . . . not, of course, that you actually are.

– Look. You live next to me. Have you ever heard any of my wild all-night parties?

– No, I haven't. But you must remember that these apartments have very thin walls and so one can hear a lot. Perhaps it's just the usual every-day noises that she's complaining about.

– Perhaps you're right, I said, now confirmed in my own paranoia: Because I can certainly hear all *yours*!

After that I talked to the retired postal worker:

– And the head of the residents' association will do nothing at all about her. Nothing. She's a menace!

– I know, he said, looking very unhappy: But we're all in the same boat. We've all got to make the best of it.

– Oh? Well, why then do *I* have to make the best of it and *she* doesn't—if indeed I am making all that racket every night?

I knew why, all right: it was because I was foreign and she wasn't; because I was an interloper and she wasn't. This I did not say, perhaps only because I had no opportunity—for at that moment his wife called out (*Anata!*) and with a show of helplessness he closed the door.

I stormed back to my room, and heard the telephone ring. It was, of course, Mrs. Shiraishi. This time, however, she was not complaining. She said, surprisingly: *Naka yoshi ni narimasho*—Let's be friends.

At once I was at her door, anxious indeed to be friends. She stood there, small, round, neat, and invited me into the kitchen. I stared about me, eager to see what kind of lair the monster had.

And there I was introduced to her daughter, a person about my own age, with rimless glasses, cold as ice, staring at me with open belligerence.

– I asked her to come all the way down from Gumma, I was in such a state, no sleep, every night those horrible noises, and she said that if we became friends maybe you would somehow be more quiet and I could get at least a little sleep. Here.

And she put a small glass of plum brandy into my hand.

– All right, Mrs. Shiraishi, I promise not to make any noise and you must promise not to telephone me or call the police or come banging at my door.

– But the noise, the noise.

– Look, Mrs. Shiraishi. There is no noise. It's in your head. You think you hear it.

I turned to her daughter for some kind of understanding. Surely she must know how crazy the old woman was—she was her own child. I met with none, however, merely a cold and rimless stare.

– Oh, I saw Mrs. Watanabé on the street, cried Mrs. Shiraishi: And she said you're getting neurotic, Mrs. Shiraishi, and I said to her yes I certainly was, and why not, me without a wink for weeks because of all the noise going on every night. So as a last resort Mariko here said we should try to become friends.

Despite my earlier eagerness, I did not in fact want to become friends with her or her rimless daughter. I wanted never to see either of them again. And yet I wanted to stop tiptoeing about my own apartment and wincing when I flushed the toilet. I wanted to take back from this old witch the power that I had given her.

Did she herself believe any of this business? I still wonder about that. Perhaps it isn't even a relevant question. She had merely found something, finally, to which to devote her life: me and my noisy ways. Her paranoia had found a perfect object.

And so, I now see, had mine. Mad Mrs. Shiraishi, her chilly child, the piano teacher, the postal worker and his spouse, the head of our ineffectual little organization, even the cop on the beat—all were united in this great plot against me, whose only sin, after all, was that of being a foreigner. This would not have happened to me, was my belief, if I had been Japanese.

As indeed, I realize now, it wouldn't have. For then I would have behaved quite differently. For one thing I would have taken no watermelons to crazed and dangerous neighbors, and even had I done so, I imagine I would then have moved skillfully through the association and among the neighbors until enough social pressure had accumulated to crush the old hag.

As it was, I finally did the thing that Japanese do when they fail. I gave up. When the phone calls began again with tearful pleas for me not to flush my toilet with quite such vehemence, when a new cop appeared and had to be informed, when the postal worker was out whenever I asked, then I did what any ordinary citizen would have done. I moved.

My apartment had become as though haunted. I was creeping silently about in it, sliding doors open and shut ever so carefully, and actually refraining from pulling the chain except when absolutely necessary.

The place is probably haunted still. Whoever was unfortunate enough to move into it probably received visitations from the same old body with her hair in a bun. And if they are fully and successfully Japanese they are probably putting up with it.

For that is the true difference. The problem is not simply whether one is foreign or not, but rather whether one can grin and bear it—whatever "it" is. This is what counts. That foreigners notoriously cannot do so makes the matter seem more fraught with prejudice than it perhaps is.

Now moved elsewhere, with nice quiet neighbors in the apartment below, I sometimes think of Mrs. Shiraishi. Old, alone, with only that cold child to call her own and relations not too good there either, shunted off into an apartment, forgotten—is she not symptomatic, in her way, of these times, of this society?

Well, maybe, but I am not interested in that. Mrs. Shiraishi remains for me a real person, not some representative of her people. A real person who in several and highly uncomfortable ways resembles me. We both cause disharmony. Perhaps that is the real reason why I could not put up with her, why I could not somehow manage to live peacefully with my neighbor in this small country.

Hiroshi Momma

Busy behind his desk, he always had time for the foreigner. Leaning back, he smiled indulgently.

– Well, what is it this time? he wondered, showing his even teeth: More about Ozu?

He knew that I liked the work of this film director and was concerned that it was never shown abroad, though he had told me often enough why it wasn't.

– They wouldn't understand, he had said, smiling: It's just too Japanese for them. You know that all our critics call Ozu the most Japanese of all film directors. So there we are.

This had been stated with such finality that I could think of no reply except: I'm not Japanese and I understand.

He had looked at me as though about to challenge the latter part of the statement, then seemed to think better of it, opting instead to laugh and say: Oh, you. You aren't a real foreigner any more. You've stayed far too long for that. If we tried to judge them all by you we'd be in big trouble.

Big trouble he wanted to avoid. The trouble of having prints subtitled. The trouble of sending them abroad. The trouble of having them fail, as they certainly would. And his position as head of a department in the large motion-picture company that had produced, among many others, the films of Yasujiro Ozu did not permit this sort of failure.

So today, as always, he visibly braced himself when he saw me, and gave me his best smile: More about Ozu?

I nodded. The people at the Berlin Film Festival were interested. Wouldn't the company permit a retrospective?

– But why? he wanted to know: The whole idea is wrong. We'd simply be wasting our time. And money. Making those prints, having them subtitled. And for what?

– For getting Ozu's films known abroad, I repeated. Then, anticipating his next comment: Why can't foreigners understand Ozu's films anyway?

– But I've told you. They're just too Japanese. They haven't been adapted for the foreign market. Look. Foreigners like our sword-fight films, our action dramas. They can make sense of them. They're almost the same as their own pictures except for the swords. And they like that. Exoticism. That's what they like.

– But what about *Rashomon*? What about *Ugetsu*? What about the other films by Kurosawa and Mizoguchi? They were successful.

– Exoticism. That's what foreign audiences want. And Ozu just hasn't got it. His films are realistic. They're about the way we really live. And they're just as slow as life is. Look, films like that would go over nowhere else.

And so it continued during the following weeks; but eventually I had my way and some Ozu films were sent to Berlin—not the full retrospective I had hoped for, but five of the later films, subtitled. I took them there and the reception was intelligent, enthusiastic. And, more to the company's point, the foreign rights were sold.

When I returned I presented myself at his desk and was greeted with the same big smile. I then thanked him for his cooperation and asked if he was satisfied.

– Satisfied?

– Yes, the Ozu films all got excellent reviews, and the foreign rights were sold.

– Oh, yes, I do believe I heard something about that.

– I think that means that they were understood and liked.

– Hey now, wait a minute, not so fast, he said with that laugh of his: Don't you go jumping to any conclusions.

– But, look . . .

– Okay. So a few were sold. Well, good. But I don't think that means anything. You know what they saw, those people? Exoticism. Modern Japan must look pretty weird to people in Berlin, I bet. That's all they saw.

– Did you read the reviews?

– How could I? They're in German.

Yet, despite company skepticism and indifference, the films of Ozu did gradually make their mark abroad. When *Tokyo Story* opened in New York and there was a line at the box office, I visited Momma again, with a newspaper picture of the event.

– Look, he said finally: What do you want?

Forced to examine my motives, I replied: I want you to admit that Ozu's films can be loved and understood abroad.

He stared at me, for once not smiling: Now, how could I do that?

Suddenly, I saw the world through his eyes. It was black and white and divided down the center; they were on one side, we were on the other.

I wondered what made such orthodoxy so necessary; what made its continuation so imperative.

– I'm not saying that *you* don't understand Ozu, if that's what's worrying you, he went on: I *know* you do, because you've been here so long. And that's just fine.

He glared. It wasn't just fine. I ought to have gone back to my own country long, long ago.

– No, he continued: It's the others over there that I'm talking about. Look, be sensible. How could they understand?

How could they, indeed!

– They can understand Ozu, I said, but I don't think they could ever understand you.

He looked at me, surprised, and his smile slowly reappeared. He was pleased at the thought that he personally was a mystery.

– Do you understand me? he asked, the smile broadening, waiting for me to say no, waiting to have his prejudices fully confirmed.

Suddenly, I saw the world through my own eyes. It was all gray, everything sliding about, love and understanding whipping up little waves on its surface. And there I stood, right on the brink. For I had been about to confirm all my own prejudices as well, about to turn into a person who needed an orthodoxy too, who felt its continuation was imperative.

– Yes, I understand you, but I don't approve, I finally said.

His laugh was genuine: And I don't approve of you either.

At this I also laughed.

Then we sat down and had a business talk. I pointed out that if foreigners were prepared to go and see the Ozu films, as they apparently were, then it didn't make any difference if they got the point or not, did it? No, he was the first to admit that, not as long as they actually bought tickets and went to see them. Well, I answered, this is what they were doing, so the company ought to send out more prints, ought to do a catalog, ought to sponsor a major retrospective—as a business venture, mind you. A small initial outlay should bring in considerable returns, I suggested.

And it was not until much later, years later, that I realized how very like an Ozu sequence—both of us busy at his desk—this had all been.

Chishu Ryu

It was 1958 and Chishu Ryu had been asked by *Kinema Jumpo*, the big film magazine, to write something about Yasujiro Ozu, the director, his mentor. *Equinox Flower*, Ozu's latest, was about to open.

But he did not know how to begin. Usually when he talked about Ozu, people said: There you go, off on Ozu again. And it was true, he often talked about him. But how could he talk about himself without mentioning Ozu? It was the director who had formed him, turned him into an actor.

How to begin, that was the problem. And I can imagine him looking puzzled, that boyish pursing of the lips, so like the fifty-two-year-old actor on the screen, so like Ozu.

They had been together almost from the first, director and actor; in fact, he claimed to have appeared in all but two of Ozu's fifty-odd films. And then in 1930, despite his youth and inexperience, Ozu gave him one of the leads in *I Flunked, But...*

Ryu had no idea how to begin there, either. Ozu helped him, gave him something to do, indicated where hands, feet, eyes should be. But he never once told him what the character was like.

– I remember one time, he wrote later, when I was playing the father, the leading role in *There Was a Father* (1942). And there was this difficult scene. And I didn't know how to start. So Ozu told me to stare at the end of my chopsticks, then stare at my hand, and then speak to my child. The simple act of doing these things would convey a certain feeling, an atmosphere. But Ozu never explained what the feeling was. The actions came first. Ozu merely told me what to do and then let me discover how it felt. That can be very difficult. I remember once, in one scene, I tried to follow his precise instructions up to twenty times and each time I failed. So I finally gave up.

Ozu arranged the look of his cast just as he arranged the look of his set. They did what he said, and it usually worked—the Ozu atmosphere being founded on the simple premise that if the outside is all right the inside will take care of itself.

Ryu's outside was perfect. Later on, critics were to say that without him the Ozu atmosphere could not exist. And Ryu was aware at a very early stage that he was the Ozu persona, nothing else.

– I was so awkward, so raw and untrained at the beginning. Ozu showed me everything. He gave me absolute support, as long as I followed his directions.

– Since everyone in the studio knew that I wasn't very good, the whole staff used to take a break when the time came for me to do a big scene. They just walked out and left Ozu and me alone. It was then that we rehearsed, endlessly, he giving me all sorts of advice, showing me just how he wanted it. This went on until somehow I managed to get it right.

– Then at the first screening of the film I would see what I'd done and I was always surprised to find my performance so much better than I'd expected.

Whoever Ryu had been before Ozu, he now became an Ozu character. He felt, he said later, as if he were one of his colors, one of the colors with which he was painting his picture.

– There was this 1936 film called *College Is a Nice Place* and I played a student. In one scene I had to take my new suit to the pawnshop. Then, when I received the money, just two bills, I was to look sorry for what I'd done. I had no idea how to do it. So Ozu told me that when I got the money I should look first at one of the bills, then look at the other, and then look up.

And there it is, up there on the screen—sorrow. In the midst of a comedy we have these poignant few seconds, where the fact that the eyes have looked at the bills at all means surprise or concern or disappointment, and the fact that the actor then looks up implies knowledge, comprehension, and the fact that the two are joined to what we know of the story results in sorrow.

– There was another film, made in 1947, *The Record of a Tenement Gentleman*. I was supposed to be reading someone's palm and was drawing the lines of the hand on a piece of paper, one by one, with brush and ink. Every time I pressed the brush I bent my head forward. Ozu stepped in and stopped me.

– When I saw the film I realized why. My bent head would have ruined the unity of the composition. At the same time, the fact that I did *not* bend my head, as one would normally have done, lent the character a kind of comic charm which is just what Ozu must have wanted. At least that's what we got on the screen when the picture was released.

Then, in 1963, on his own birthday, Ozu died. And shortly after that, on a train returning from Osaka, I happened to meet Ryu again. He was fifty-seven at the time, about the age of the father he had played in *Tokyo Story* some ten years before. We spoke about the dead director.

– Ozu used to tell me, you know—and not just me, told everyone— that Ryu wasn't a very good actor. And that's why I use him, he would say. And it's true. I can't think of myself without thinking of him.

I wonder now if that death seemed like a betrayal. Deaths often do. There is a dreadful sense of being left behind. For who was Ryu now that Ozu was dead?

The bullet train raced on and we sat in silence and thought about Ozu. And, though I said nothing, I wondered about Ryu's future.

But his future was assured. He later appeared in picture after picture and with director after director, and he was always good, a fine actor, and he always played the Ozu character.

I have seen monster-films in which the scientist is the Ozu charac- ter, teen-age singing star films in which the schoolteacher is the Ozu character, lurid murder-mysteries in which the inspector is the Ozu character. Always the same person, whether mad scientist or wily police officer—and always Ryu.

It was 1985 and I had just seen Juzo Itami's comedy, *The Funeral*, and there, playing the Buddhist priest, was Ryu. He mumbled the sutras gorgeously and played with his tassel and averted his eyes when the money appeared, and then extracted a present from the head of the mourning family. It was a perfect performance, one straight out of Ozu— a posthumous Ozu comedy.

Ryu was at the party afterward. He was now about eighty. He had that old man's way of blinking his eyes as though in constant surprise, that blinking which he so brilliantly showed us when he was only in his late forties, in *Tokyo Story*.

Is it because he is eighty that he blinks like a man eighty years old, I wondered, or because he knows from experience that this is how men of eighty should blink?

And there, amid the beer and the orange juice, the strips of dried squid and the peanuts, the posters for the film and, someone having thought to bring it, the picture of Ozu—amid all this I suddenly remembered what the director had told one of his actresses who, baffled, had asked him what she was supposed to be feeling.

His answer was: You are not supposed to feel, you are supposed to do.

And I looked at Ryu, that wonderfully skilled unskillful actor. He was raising his glass. We were drinking to his health. And soon he would begin a little speech. It would be the one he always gives.

– I don't know quite how to begin. When I talk people say, there you go, off on Ozu again. And it's true, I often talk about him. But how could I talk about myself without mentioning Ozu?

Hiroyasu Yano

It was in 1954, on Christmas Day, that Hiroyasu, then a twenty-year-old university student, met the thirty-year-old foreigner in the ancient capital of Kyoto.

They had something in common. The foreigner was studying Japanese and was much interested in the old culture of Japan. Hiroyasu was studying English and was much interested in the new culture of the United States of America, a country from which, it fortunately happened, the foreigner had come.

The day was also an auspicious occasion, fittingly foreign, and seeming to augur well not only for the coming year but for the future of the young Japanese. This is what he attempted to communicate after he had asked the time in English, after accepting the cup of tea at the grand hotel, after ascertaining that their interests seemed to coincide.

Hiroyasu's English had proved inadequate to his needs, but back in Tokyo, where the student's university was located, he saw to it that he and his new friend often met. Yet, though indeed they frequently met during the months that followed, the Japanese's English got no better while the American's Japanese did.

Also, the student learned little of foreign ways, while the foreigner learned more and more about things Japanese. This was because, though their interests were similar, their aims were different. The foreigner, when asked by Hiroyasu, said that he truly wanted to understand life. The Japanese, when asked by the American, said that he truly wanted to become rich.

Out of university—which he quit—Hiroyasu, with the help of some acquaintances he had made in the boxing club, opened an office that sold and rented apartments. From these small beginnings he extended into the lucrative demolition business.

He tore down old dwellings to make way for new. And here he occasionally had to avail himself of the services of some friends in the local gang, friends he had made while still in the rental business. They proved invaluable in evacuating widows or deserted mothers and children so that he could demolish the house. Business prospered.

When the foreigner heard about this, however, he was troubled. Hiroyasu, who had now known him for some years and considered him a close acquaintance, carefully explained that this was business—and, in any event, it was not much different from the way things had been done back in the old Japan of which he was so fond.

The American criticized, but the Japanese naturally went ahead with it. Soon he had made enough to open his own construction company. He now built new apartment houses from the old lumber he removed from homes that had been knocked down. This proved a great saving. Nevertheless he experienced some initial financial difficulties.

Hiroyasu went at once to his foreign acquaintance who, perhaps relieved that his young friend was no longer involved in the business of evicting penniless widows, lent him some money. This helped tide over the new construction-company president, who was soon able to repay the debt.

In the meantime, the foreigner's book on Japan had finally appeared. It did not sell well, but some libraries bought it and this seemed to make the author happy. Hiroyasu, however, simply shook his head at this waste of time and talent. His foreign friend ought to have written a best-seller like *Miyamoto Musashi*. The foreign friend said that *Miyamoto Musashi* was not serious. Perhaps not, said Hiroyasu, but money was.

The years passed, and within a decade Hiroyasu was a success. He owned substantial land in Osaka, where he had set up his company. He also now had money to spend on himself—steak every supper, a nightclub hostess every night.

When the foreigner appeared in Kyoto, Hiroyasu would take him out: always the most expensive beef, and after that the most exclusive nightclub, and after that the costliest of hostesses. The American was appreciative but seemed embarrassed. Hiroyasu said he shouldn't be, that he had helped him when he himself was an impoverished student and again when he was a struggling contractor. Now that he was really rather wealthy, it was only right that he should treat his older friend from time to time.

By 1980 Hiroyasu was really rich. One knew this because he always paid his taxes in the most conscientious fashion, and he was listed in the press as one of the top Kansai taxpayers. In certain sections he owned all the land in sight, as far as the eye could see, he said.

The foreigner, having frittered his time away on history and other scholarly pursuits, had—by way of contrast—very little money. He moved from an apartment into a room, and he came to look forward to his younger friend's Tokyo visits because he could then have a proper meal.

This state of affairs worried Hiroyasu. He saw the poverty and he wanted to relieve it, now that he was in a position to do so. Charity was, of course, out of the question. This one could neither give nor receive. Indeed, though he had been poor, actually much poorer than his foreign friend now was, he had never asked for anything and what little he had borrowed he had paid back, every yen of it.

No, instead he would devise a respectable and scholarly job-opportunity for the impoverished American. So Hiroyasu thought long and hard, sorting through various possibilities, casting about to find a way. And finally he came up with what he thought—and said—was the perfect solution.

The construction-company president had acquired a large tract of land in Uji, near Kyoto, which happened to be adjacent to the Byodo-in, an old building—eleventh-century, in fact—a building, moreover, of which the foreigner had often spoken with enthusiasm.

It looked truly ancient with its pond and its outlying buildings. Hiroyasu had seen it once on a school excursion and had failed to be impressed. Even then old buildings were fit for but a single purpose. But, as he knew full well, it was not important for his project that *he* be impressed; it was enough that his foreign friend was.

His project was simple, direct, impressive. It was, in a word, Byodo-in Land, a recreational park which would tower in authentic Disneyland fashion behind the old buildings that everyone came to see.

There would be a jet coaster and a giant wheel which would be decorated with Heian-period motifs. The pond would be extended so that motorboats, got up to look like Heian pleasure barges, could race by in front of the Byodo-in itself. And there would be the lucrative fast-food concessions to think about—Genjiburgers, perhaps.

Here Hiroyasu, explaining to his friend, paused to smile. The American was to fill the important position of creative manager. He was to have a fine office within view of the beloved building and would think up further ways to make proper use of the existing facilities, turning a profit while exercising his historical bent.

But the American friend was not smiling. He was pale. And it gradually occurred to Hiroyasu that this foreigner did not like the idea, that it seemed to distress him.

This was puzzling, because here, if anywhere, was the opportunity to join their two cultures, the Japanese and the American. This was something that the foreigner apparently had given himself the task—until now fruitlessly—of accomplishing. And here, offered this unheard-of opportunity . . . he did not like it.

It was nearly 1984, the year that would mark the thirtieth anniversary of their meeting, and Hiroyasu had just discovered that he knew nothing about his foreign friend, that he had apparently never understood him and, by the same token, that he himself had perhaps never been understood.

He looked at the American. When they had first met it had been the latter who was rich, with his thick overcoat, and it had been the poor student who had worn only a thin raincoat. And now it was he who was wearing the overcoat.

Hiroyasu was plainly a success. And he had wanted to help his old friend. And this help had been refused. Never would he understand foreigners. They were truly a race apart. And, equally, never would they understand him, or his culture, no matter how hard they tried.

So he sold the land adjacent to the Byodo-in, sold it at a good profit. And he consequently saw less of his friend, saw less because he himself now rarely went to Tokyo, pressure of success keeping him in the home office, and the foreigner perhaps could not afford the fare to Kyoto. Their thirtieth anniversary came and went.

Hiroyasu remembered it. That poor old foreigner had been good to him, had helped him. He, Hiroyasu, really ought somehow to have done something for him. He wished he had. He'd really tried. At the same time, however, he could see now why he hadn't been able to. Hiroyasu saw Japan as it really was and the foreigner, naturally, didn't. That was the reason.

Nagisa Oshima

We had arrived early to discuss what we were going to say. There had been, however, no discussion. Oshima and Nobuhiko Obayashi had both got into the whiskey. Now their tongues were thickening, syllables slurring.

They were supposed to talk about modern cinema from the director's point of view. I was there as a critic, and to lend foreign prestige to the event. It was a panel at a large arts conference and there were now well over five hundred people seated waiting in the auditorium.

I suggested that we ought to be going to the stage. Obayashi rolled his head in agreement but Oshima puckered his lips, eyes closing. He wanted another drink.

– Perhaps, I said, we could put it in the teapot. There's a pot on every conference table, and cups. Then if you feel thirsty everyone will think you're drinking tea.

Oshima smiled broadly, eyes still tight shut, and pounded on the table in approval. Unsteadily a teapot was filled. I offered to carry it onto the stage and place it in front of them. Obayashi gave a courtly bow, his hand a flourish. Oshima curtsied.

I had seen the famous film director drunk many times before. He drank well. Whiskey was a natural element to him, as water is to fish. Though sober enough when working, Oshima found whiskey a relaxation. Yet, no matter how much he drank, no matter how furry the tongue and slurred the delivery, the intelligence remained acute, and critical.

Particularly critical. He is the only person I know who has been consistently so. Usually even the most adamant will eventually compromise, conformity being a dominant urge; and in Japan there is only Oshima who won't.

Himself a radical—one of the University of Kyoto intellectuals—he then turned against the radicals; he also turned against the communists, becoming one of their most severe critics. Working for a large film company, he turned against the company. Writing for a liberal film magazine, he turned against the liberals.

In all this one recognizes a single principle, a noble one, rare anywhere and here all but unheard of: an unwillingness to belong to anything, the strongest disinclination to being a member.

And with this an equally strong conception of what it means to be human. A human being is solitary, and this ought to be respected; he has failings, which call for tolerance; he is distinct, comes in many colors, shapes, and sizes, and all have a reason for being.

Oshima is a humanist, a relativist, a pluralist. All these qualities are rare. Often I have wondered how someone like him even came about. Again, as I followed him down the corridor, holding the teapot, watching him just managing the corner, I wondered at him being Japanese.

That too is relative. However, generalizations are also possible. Oshima's refusal to play the game Japanese-style has resulted in his being able to make less than one film a year, and nowadays more than one only through spending non-Japanese funds. He will not use the old-boy network, though he is plugged in, being ex-University of Kyoto. He will not play the back-scratching game. He will not indulge in quid pro quo, another favorite recreation. And he will say what he thinks regardless of whose toes are stepped upon.

In his work, on television, in the press, he has attacked the rightist, the leftist, the government itself. He has come out strongly in favor of rights for those of Korean ancestry born in Japan but regarded still as aliens. He has criticized the military, the politicians, even the social structure of Japan. He is very brave.

And, just then, very drunk. A slight stumble and we were on the stage, behind the curtain, the sound of a restive audience beyond. Then the curtain rose, the lights came up, and the crowd quieted.

Since we had not decided what to say or how to start, there was silence for a while before Oshima, smiling, began. Perhaps, he said, they came expecting to hear about film, but there are things more important than that. And he went on to talk at some length about learning somehow to say what you mean, to express what you believe.

Then Obayashi started telling a story about catching a fish last week. This interested Oshima, who responded with the story of a lost cuff link that was found in the most unlikely of places. Obayashi then talked about the difference between the sexes, using as example a recent film of his own.

– Oh, the difference between the sexes, cried Oshima, standing, looking straight up, hands at his sides: I made a film about that, but you didn't get to see it here in Japan because of the dirty-minded censors who made my pure film filthy.

Obayashi nodded, filling their teacups to the brim, and Oshima suddenly turned to me: You know a lot about the difference between the sexes. Say something!

I smiled and addressed the audience: You surely don't believe that's tea in the teapot, I hope.

Everyone laughed. The people in the hall laughed from obvious relief. My neighbors' laughter was that of two small boys caught with their hands in the cookie jar. The result was that I did not have to make a statement on the subject.

Oshima, however, did: There are differences, he said, grave differences; in another sense, though, there's no difference at all. Thus it's fine for a man to love a woman, a woman, a man; or a woman a woman or a man a man. I'm now making a picture about a man loving a man, and I'm tired of all the hypocrisy surrounding these topics.

– I'm also weary of the hypocrisy in other things in the world. Look at Japan, he cried: Look at the government. Self-serving, encouraging people to turn into buying machines, keeping them carefully mindless by daily doses of the tube. And all for profit. Look at their city planning, look at the buildings they make. Machines for living, they call them. Hah—hives is what *I* call them. Hives in a desert. That's what they're making now.

The audience had been growing increasingly restive. Both speakers were plainly drunk, and Oshima was shouting, red-faced, and rolling in his chair. Then a small, dapper man stood up.

– Excuse me, *sensei*—

– *Sensei*, roared Oshima: That's a laugh.

– Well, yes, but some of us have come a considerable distance to attend these conferences, and we have a right, I hope, to expect a bit more seriousness and a bit less levity on the part of some of the participants. We ought, I think, to apply ourselves to a more serious discussion.

– Oh, you do, do you? roared Oshima, standing up, large and flushed: Just who do you think you are, coming in here and interrupting this perfectly human conversation we were having?

The dapper man smiled, looked around, gesturing at the maniac on the podium.

– What do *you* do? asked Oshima, quite rudely.

The man smiled apologetically, yet a little triumphantly as well.

– Actually, I'm a member of that profession you were so recently denigrating. I'm an architect. The name—here his voice dropped modestly—is Kurokawa.

Sensation. It was Kisho Kurokawa, the famous architect, designer of many an award-winning building, a particular media favorite. Then, after the excitement, hushed silence. The duel was about to commence. A battle of the titans, sides drawn.

But there was no duel, no sly parrying, no telling thrusts. Oshima simply stumbled to the edge of the stage, bent precariously over it, pointed with one sharp finger and shouted: You ought to be shot!

Another tremor of excitement. Then: It's your kind of people who are destroying this country, your kind with your little boxes who are denying this country its humanity.

Listening to this extraordinary abuse, I thought how very like Oshima it was to say "this country" (*kono kuni*), where anyone else would have said "our country" (*waga kuni*). Even dead drunk and in a fight he remembered the importance of such distinctions.

The architect had perhaps looked forward to an exchange with the drunken film director, one that would reflect favorably upon himself. He had no opportunity. The invective flowed like lava. There was no mistaking it. He stood, ashen-faced, and was buried.

Then Oshima belched loudly and giggled before covering his mouth in a tardy gesture of apology. Taking Obayashi's hand, he proceeded to waltz across the stage. I was invited to join them, and as the three of us glided off the curtain fell.

– More drinks, more drinks, cried Oshima: More teapots. What a good idea of yours that teapot was. (He put his arm around me.) Now, off into the night. Just think. We might even discover the meaning of life. He pinched my cheek and off we went.

Tetsuko Kuroyanagi

Famous—a face known to millions of television viewers, seen nearly nightly throughout the land. A peculiar face, made of small, strong bones, light skin rendered even lighter so that under harsh studio lights it seems almost an abstraction of itself; a small red mouth, always busy with what has been called the fastest delivery in show business; the copper-colored carrottop wig, a trademark; and—in between—the eyes, lustrous, like black grapes on that small, white, triangular plate of a face. A face purposely simplified, a mask.

Memorable—a face lending itself to caricature: made of so little, it takes little to capture it on paper. Whether advertising instant noodles or refrigerators; whether refereeing contests of young popular singers or giving advice to housewives; whether interviewing or appearing in one-woman shows—this face says everything before it even opens its mouth.

It says: Tetsuko, the most popular and admired woman in Japan. Not that the face is in itself admired. What is admired is the real Tetsuko, the person behind the mask, or that part of it she allows to appear on the stage, the screen, the tube.

The television audience knows this person from her talk shows. During these the mouth suddenly shuts, the babble ceases. For as long as the other person, the interviewed, wants to talk, Tetsuko listens. She listens with that rapt attention of the truly interested. It does not matter who the interviewed is. So long as he speaks Tetsuko is silent, regarding him with the gaze of a child, or of certain animals.

Sometimes she talks to help. When the hopelessly inarticulate, profoundly unsure actor Ken Takakura was a guest, she patiently asked questions. Though each was answered with a monosyllable she persevered and the effect was, oddly, as though he were talking. She interpreted each grunt as if it had actually meant something, as well it might have, and out of nothing at all created an eloquent encounter.

This is admirable, and her vast Japanese audience admires it. They also like it when she is emotionally carried away. She often cries when she does Emily's return from the grave in *Our Town*; she is touched and moved by the afflicted, to whose organizations she privately gives sizable amounts of money. Once she had as guest a foreigner, a German, expert in such matters, who showed photos from the extermination camps. While he was smiling—for on television in all countries one is supposed to smile—she became more and more affected and finally broke down.

The audience knows that despite the instant noodles and the pop singers and the fastest delivery in show business, here is a fellow human who can be very funny (her famous imitation of Florence Foster Jenkins singing the Queen of the Night aria, for example) but who also feels deeply—visibly.

You feel that Tetsuko knows about life's miseries, about its tragic side. Part of this feeling is due to the mask itself—it is the face of a tragedienne, lustrous eyes, no nose, proud mouth: a very young Berma in *Phèdre*, the ghost of the princess in the No. But even her gaiety and occasional inconsequentiality seem tinged with sadness. She also allows herself to appear vulnerable, the price she seems to pay for her spontaneity, as fresh, as innocent as that of a child, knowing as we do that the vulnerable get stepped on, that children become adults.

Her fame extracts a price as well. On the street, when out with her, one notices a small crowd gathering around. People stop, stand, stare. The looks are all admiring, but the group grows and Tetsuko, peering through her mascara, says that perhaps we might cross the street or take a taxi.

Fame is dangerous too. Fans are suffocating, in all countries. Few people know where she lives and fewer yet have her home telephone number. If she wants to give it she will do so in the most secretive manner. She hopes you will not think her silly, but actually this number is—lapsing into the Las Vegasese that has now become part of her language—for your eyes only.

She lives alone, in a large apartment near Roppongi, that modern section of town which values what she advertises. It is there that one sees her as herself—and finds that that self is really no different from the one she publicly presents.

The apartment is all white—white on white. The white bed has white sheets and a white coverlet. There is a white piano and an off-white harpsichord. On the bed is a large doll and on the shelves collections of glass animals, paperweights, little things from abroad. There is a large portrait of herself, all in white, in a too large chair. There is also a Marie Laurençin. The eyes are large *prunelles*—this is where Tetsuko's eyes come from.

It is the apartment of a little girl, and that is what she, a mature woman, also is. She makes things in the kitchen like a little girl making cookies. She gleefully tries things out—pickled plums mixed up with *shiso* leaf— then sits back to judge the effect. She is forever running off to go through drawers until she finds whatever it is she wants to show you.

Like a little girl she loves clothes—has never appeared once on her talk shows in the same dress. Her closets are full of them but she seems to have no favorites. Like a child, she likes quantity.

When her best-selling book about Totto-chan appeared, her millions of readers were not surprised at this portrait of Tetsuko in childhood. This is because they saw right through the persona and recognized the child in her, and the child in themselves.

Though nearly fifty she seems nearer fifteen. Her gaiety, her concern are those of an adolescent. If her TV image radiates youth it is because she has remained so young—or, rather, because she has never been anything else.

And, as with most children, there comes a moment when one sees in Tetsuko, sitting there in her white dress on her white chair, a look, not of discontent, but of a kind of uncomplaining wonder. It seems to ask if this is all there is to it, if there is nothing more. It wonders if things could have been different.

Well, yes, is the answer. Things could always have been different, for all of us. Tetsuko, for example, would have made an excellent, serious actress. Earlier, on stage, in films, she made you remember every character she played. I will always remember the innocent, foolish, warm, frivolous wife in *Summer Soldiers*.

Yet this excellence was not enough. Like any child she wanted her gratification right now. Hence, perhaps, TV: instant playback, instant feedback—the perfect medium for kids.

I mention her stage and film roles and she says: Oh, that! Then she drops this inner gaze, opens her eyes wide, and is suddenly the hoyden, the tomboy, or doing her impersonation of the mature woman, a *femme du monde*, all guile and drooping eyelids. We laugh and Tetsuko is reassured.

She finds her maturity in another fashion. Tetsuko wants to be responsible and this she shows in countless admirable ways. She gives much of her money to the afflicted, particularly the deaf. She finances a school and theater for those so disadvantaged. The proceeds of the best-selling *Totto-chan* went to the poor, the needy. She herself went to Africa, taking money to the starving, calling the attention of her country to their plight.

She also wants to be faithful. She never wants to forget anyone she has ever met. She wants to be a completely responsible friend—she keeps up, sends little notes, postcards, remembers birthdays, supports one's ventures; with old loves she has lunch and becomes a sister rather than a lover—doing whatever it takes to stay in there.

In this responsibility, this fidelity, she reminds me of someone. Who could it be? Of course . . . how could one forget: Mother—yours, mine, everyone's.

This grown-up, paradoxical little girl has become everyone's mother. What she wanted most she has become. Though she has no child of her own, we are all of us her children. She gave up a career for us. And yet this look of doubt occasionally remains.

But not for long. Tetsuko adjusts her mask, says something funny, busies herself, then must dress and be off—off to that great, magnifying, loving, and satisfying mirror which has, in its way, created this admirable persona—off to those millions whom she will never see but who see her every night.

Mayumi Oda

The two large silk-screen prints, each perhaps two by three feet, look like Sotatsu's famous panels of the thunder and wind gods. They are supposed to: colors the same, poses reminiscent. But these are goddesses—the wind goddess trails her linen coat, stepping firmly from one cloudlet to the next, long black hair streaming behind her; the thunder deity now wears her drum as a cache-sexe, and above it are her ample, pink-tipped breasts.

Mayumi looks at her two prints; a major reassessment has been made. These female deities are just as strong, just as dominating, as were their male counterparts. *That* is the reassessment.

When she was young Mayumi saw that, like all Japanese, she would have to conform. Like all Japanese girls she also shortly understood that she would be expected to conform more than Japanese boys did. Gone, they may have told her, were the days when a woman was allowed but three roles: obedient daughter, wife, and mother. Yet, as Mayumi grew up, she realized these roles were still all there was.

Men had more choice, a little more. But if a woman was not an obedient daughter, refused to marry, and consequently had no child, then she was a bad woman. It was because of this that most of her friends obediently married.

Mayumi decided not to. She would be an artist. Besides the fact that she was talented (which meant that she cared enough to be skillful), artists did not have to comply to quite the same extent.

She also had a place she could go to. Artists were expected to be international. And from an early age Mayumi had increasingly looked outside to other countries, particularly to America where it seemed, from this distance at any rate, that women had more scope.

She is now working on a new silk screen of Benten, a goddess from the start, the only one Japan has ever officially allowed in from abroad.

She came, perhaps from China, possibly from India, in a *karafune*, a vessel otherwise filled with males. Having assumed Japanese residence, she was given a number of suspicious attributes. Sly, it was said she was, and unfriendly to courting couples, positively dangerous to the happily married—yet all the while lustful herself and something of a threat to young males.

Mayumi's Benten is quite different. She is benign. She sits in her boat and strums her lute. About her happily circle both crane and turtle, auspicious creatures. She is a figure of repose, looking inward on herself. As a goddess should be, she is full, rounded, content.

Mayumi married a man from abroad, John Nathan. As so often happens she saw in him the promise of freedom, life in his country, home of liberty and equality, America. At the same time he perhaps saw in her the promise of security, the warmth and care of Japan. In the event, two children later, it didn't work out—separation, then divorce.

Like the young Benten, she now found herself in a new country. And, since she was a divorced woman, America, not being much different in this regard from Japan, began to disapprove, to gossip. This, however, Mayumi no longer feared or resented. She lived by herself with her children and created her goddesses.

These are all of a single family. They resemble each other. There is a fullness about them, a satisfaction which is never complacent, a natural acceptance and not—its male counterpart—a natural exclusion. These goddesses are thoroughly themselves. Gods, ever fearful of opinion, conceal themselves behind their attributes. Goddesses, magnanimous, do not. They expose themselves freely to the public gaze.

Hers are Japanese. They come from the days long ago when little Mayumi peered into the dim light of the shrine and saw the small, round mirror on that cloud-shaped pedestal.

– I knew it was the sun goddess, she has said: I asked her to help me, though I did not know exactly for what. In return, I promised to be a good girl.

And then, some years later, when she was eleven, her mother took her to an exhibition of Munakata's woodblock prints, where she saw not only Buddha and his ten disciples but also the reclining nymphs, peris, and goddesses of his full-breasted world.

These remained with her, but it was only much later, during her first pregnancy when she had almost despaired of art and had taken to studying Japanese design instead, that they suddenly reappeared.

– I was working in etching, and from the black aquatinted background the goddesses started to emerge. It was like Hesiod's description of the birth of Gaea: there was chaos, vast and dark; then Gaea appeared, the deep-breasted Earth. These newborn goddesses started to play in flowering fields of kimono brocade and swim in oceans of Hokusai waves. My free female figures brought old designs into the present.

They also brought more. They became the personifications of Mayumi herself—who she wanted to be, who she was becoming. And they helped her leave far behind that trinity of dutiful roles: obedient daughter, wife, and mother. For they have no other roles than themselves.

Mayumi stops to make a salad: crisp cucumbers, lettuce, endive, chicory, carrots, celery, anything else she can find in the refrigerator. Her California kitchen is sunny, the windows looking out onto the woods, the hills, and beyond to the open Pacific and, farther still, Japan.

A ship—a modern *karafune*—passes in the hazy distance, and Mayumi pours sunflower oil into a cup. Benten, taped to the wall, is drying, sitting securely on her lotus, looking out over the woods, the hills, over the ocean to Japan and, beyond that, to the lands she came from, long, long ago—Korea, China, Tibet, India.

Toshikatsu Wada

We first met when he was about four, accompanying his father to the public bath.

– Oh, look, he cried, confronted with the sight of a naked foreigner.

– Yes, yes, said his father, embarrassed.

– Papa, look. All white. And hairy.

– Now, you be quiet, Toshikatsu. That's not polite. (This was said with an apologetic smile in my direction.)

A bit chastened, Toshikatsu nonetheless continued: And, Papa, look! Then, pointing: He's a foreigner and still he's got one too!

This resulted in general laughter, in which both the father and I joined. It was thus that I got to know the Wada family. They lived just down the street, and after that they sometimes invited me over.

Toshikatsu always stared. He remembered that first encounter, and was already using it for purposes of his own.

– Papa. Donald-san is bigger down there than you.

– Oh, no, only at times, said Donald-san.

Toshikatsu's mother laughed, and the boy put down his tea to look about and wonder what was funny.

After reaching his own conclusion, he said: Yes, I guess so. My Papa's is probably the best! (He looked surprised at the further merriment.)

Ten years later, in junior high school, he often dropped by to ask questions about English.

– But why is it so difficult?

– Because you don't know anything yet, was Donald's unhelpful reply.

– Japanese is a lot harder.

– Now, how do you know that, Toshikatsu?

– Everybody knows that. It's so hard that half the time even we Japanese don't know what we're saying.

– Look. I'm not Japanese and here we are speaking in Japanese now, and you understand what I say well enough, don't you?

– No, not all the time, he said, warily.

– But most of the time you do, don't you?

– That doesn't count...No—I guess that Japanese must be just about the most difficult language on earth.

And he was visibly pleased that this should be so, that he should have mastered this difficult tongue, should be in possession of, if not the best, the most.

This concern eventually caused him some unease. Since, like most children his age, he was addicted to TV, he was soon troubled that there should be so many bests; and with brand-new products (*shinhatsubai*) hourly even better, the problem of selection became acute.

At first he had importuned his patient mother to buy whatever the box had said was tops. But soon even he saw that if his pleas were heeded there would shortly be no room for the family in the house. After that he became more selective. He remained loyal to Kiddie-Krunch, however, a synthetic breakfast food, because its claims to solitary excellence had been heard so early that they endured.

Otherwise, growing older, he grew more discriminating. As he proceeded through an otherwise painless adolescence he became careful about his clothes, always choosing among the current teen fashions those he thought superior. No transient punk for him, rather the solid, lasting, ivy-league look scaled down: tweed coats, thick-soled brogues, and furry socks. Later, another criterion was added to sheer weight: cost.

– But, Dad, everyone knows that a Mercedes is best, or a Porsche. You get what you pay for. That's the way you get quality. (This argument was occasioned by his father's having finally saved enough to buy a new car.)

– Look, Toshikatsu, said his harrassed parent: Those big cars won't fit on our little streets. And I don't have that kind of money.

– Well, if you don't want the best, said Toshikatsu as though the man were past all hope. After a powder-blue Fair Lady was decided on, however, Toshikatsu acquiesced with some grace.

When in college—the best his father could afford, but not Keio or Waseda, alas: Meiji—he used to come around and speak in awed tones about Columbia, "my" school. He was convinced for some reason that it was better than Meiji.

– If you feel that way you should have tried Tokyo University, I said, naming the institution that was commonly considered the pick of the bunch.

– You've got to start in kindergarten if you're going to get in there, said Toshikatsu: And the old man just doesn't have that kind of money. So here I am at Meiji. And *nobody* goes there.

– Meiji has a large student body. Probably second only to Nihon University.

– Yeah. Well, at least I'm not *there*. Nichidai is the real pits.

All the same, Toshikatsu completed his four-year course, and then took his company entrance exams.

– I took the Sony one. But it's probably no good. I took the Sanyo too and a couple of others, just in case.

– Sanyo is a very good company.

– Not when you compare them. Sony's best. I sure wanted to get into Sony.

– Then you should have worked harder.

Staring ahead, neglecting his coffee, he looked into his future and was dissatisfied because it was only second-best.

Then, after getting his job with Sanyo: You know, I've got these two girl friends and it's about time I got married—

– And you don't know which is best, I said brightly.

– That's just it. How did you know?

– Well, Toshikatsu, you've got to set your goals and then see which one best suits your purposes.

– Yeah, that makes some sense. But how do I know?

– Look. I've known you for a long time, Toshikatsu. You just choose, and the one you've chosen will automatically be the best.

– That sounds a bit wild.

– But that's the way it is. Whether it's prospective wives or colleges or cars or languages or cocks.

– Or what?

– Cocks.

– What's that supposed to mean?

– Don't you remember? I asked. I then reminded him.

– Ugh, that's gross.

– Well, gross or not, that's the way you've always been.

– Okay, okay. But that doesn't help me with the wife problem.

So he married one of them and, sure enough, she turned out to have been the right choice. Then he got himself a car, the best, and a new color TV, the best, and took up golf, both to combat a growing pot and because it was, as everyone knew, the best.

I paid a call and, hoping to please, brought a fifth of Johnnie Walker Black, a beverage that Japan had long agreed was best. I found, however, that it had been surpassed.

– Hey, thanks, said Toshikatsu, polishing a driver: Oh, good old Johnnie Walker Black—then, seriously, confidentially—you know, nowadays, Chivas Regal is considered best.

I saw him less often after that, though occasionally I met him at his parents', his father now gray and petulant, his mother happy and busy with her women's groups.

Toshikatsu's wife was often there too. She was very self-possessed, uncommonly so for someone her age. Perhaps, I thought, it was because she was so pregnant. One hesitated to speak to her, she seemed so preoccupied.

Her husband did not speak to her at all. Whatever they had had to say to each other had been said. They were now united, it would seem, because it suited their purposes to be—for there was this big, important thing: the child.

This was what they talked about. He thought that a boy would be best. She preferred a girl.

– But everyone knows that boys are better, he'd say with an adult laugh.

One of the last times I saw Toshikatsu was at the zoo. He was there with his wife and child. Though he had quite lost the battle with the pot belly he seemed otherwise well.

He held up the child for my admiration. It was so young that I could not even guess its sex.

– Is it a boy or a girl? I wanted to know.

– Can't you tell? Boys never wear pink. It's a girl. Girls are best, you know.

Just then another couple went by with a baby about the same size. Toshikatsu turned to stare, then looked down at his little girl.

– Same age? I asked.

– Seems so. But just look at it. So scrawny. And small for its age too. Doesn't look too lively either. Then: Hey, look at little Noriko here, just waving her arms around. She's strong, and so big, too. Quite a handful she is. She's much the best.

Makiyo Numata

As the landscape unrolled beyond the window, he turned from the passing fields and asked about my childhood. And I, being of my country
and my generation, told him at some length how awful it had been. Then
I asked about his.

Actually, I knew something of it already, and this was so disagreeable
that I expected a tale to quite rival mine. You see, when he was still a
boy the doctors had discovered something, water on the brain perhaps,
some sort of liquid tumor, pressing. A dangerous operation was necessary,
chances of permanent damage were great—a vegetable existence.

During convalescence, a painful one, the doctor ordered rest and
quiet—not simply for the time being, but from now on, throughout his
life. Young Makiyo, however, did not agree. So he began exercising, fur-
tively at first, then more openly as little by little he moved further from
the sick room, further into life. He took up fast walking, jogging, running.

And now at twenty-four, sitting opposite me with the afternoon sun
behind him and the landscape streaming past, he was strong, healthy,
a mainstay of the rugby team, winner of the marathon.

The only reminder of that dangerous operation was the white scar,
from the crown of his head to the back of his neck, which was visible
when he showered. This, and an understanding, a practical intelligence,
beyond his years.

– My childhood? he asked, having heard all about mine: I was lucky.
It was a good one. I had a nice childhood.

And forest following river, field following lake, he told me about it.

Growing up in a small town in Kyushu had been interesting in itself,
and then the circumstances of his family had made possible a number
of experiences he might otherwise not have had.

For example, when he was about six, and his younger brother about
three. His mother was ill and his father had lost all their money by in-

vesting in one of the new religions, and there was never enough to eat. One day his father had taken him and his younger brother off to see the monkeys, which they liked a lot, but he didn't take them home afterward. Instead he left them at a kind of orphanage, run by Catholics; and a large woman came up and said: I am your mother from now on. And his brother had set up a terrible howling.

Life there was hard but interesting. They got enough to eat, but Makiyo sometimes had to protect himself and the three-year-old from the other boys, who were fairly tough.

After six months of this the two of them were sent back home. Makiyo had grown used to the stained-glass windows, the chapel, the prayers, the music, and the bullying, but was happy to return home to his parents. And there something else interesting happened. To help them out he was put to work.

From the age of seven or so he became a newspaper boy. Every morning, whatever the weather, his job began at five-thirty, and he ran through the town delivering the papers, getting back in time for school.

Here, finally, was something he didn't like about his childhood. It was a custom among the schoolchildren to compare what was in their lunch boxes and then exclaim, in envy or derision. Makiyo hated showing anyone his lunch because it was never anything but rice, and the poorest grade at that. There was also the fact that he owned only one pair of trousers, and these were for summer anyway. It wasn't the cold that mattered, though. It was the other kids laughing.

– Still, it was an education. I learned a lot. And I didn't cry any more. We cried a lot back at the orphanage. My brother cried because he was so young, and I cried too, though I couldn't let him see that.

And he smiled in reminiscence, as he continued recounting the wonderful childhood he had had.

– Oh, yes, there was something else. It happened long before the orphanage but I remember it well, though I was only four or so.

After the money and land went to the new religion, Makiyo's mother had no resources left. Already sickly, she had tried hard but now there was no hope. (In fact, she had been too ill to nurse him as a baby, and he was weaned on goat's milk, that being the cheapest available. As he once said ruefully, he had never known his mother's breast.)

Worse still, she had discovered that her husband had another wife, another family, over in Shikoku. And here she had been selling her kimono in order to buy rice. So she gathered her children—four in all, an older brother and sister, Makiyo, his younger brother—and went back to the village where she was born.

There, however, she met with no relief. Her own family shouted at her, called her shameless for leaving her husband like that. And after a few days, worn down by the illness that would later incapacitate her— Parkinson's disease—she made up her mind.

Makiyo remembered that she called her children, all of them quite young, and said: *Kachan umi e iku*—Your mother's going to the sea. This pleased them, the prospect of a walk along the sand with her. So off they set.

In each hand she firmly held those of the two elder children. The youngest she carried on her back. She thus had no way to hold on to Makiyo, who walked along beside them.

He remembered enjoying the walk he was taking with his mother, particularly when it became apparent that they were really going into the sea, though they were all fully dressed. Shortly the water was splashing about Makiyo's ankles, then his knees, his thighs. Then pleasure turned to concern when he saw that his mother, clutching her children, was walking straight out into the ocean, looking only at the distant horizon.

– I didn't know what to do. She wasn't looking at us. She was looking straight ahead and the water was getting deeper with each step. I was still really little, you understand, so that when it was up to her knees, it was already near my chest.

As the water grew deeper, Makiyo decided that something was wrong. So he pulled away from his mother and ran back to the shore, while she continued onward with the other three.

He raced down the beach, found his uncle, explained as best he could, and together they ran back to the bay. Wading out into the sea, his uncle grabbed the children, then shouted at his sister that it was all right for her to kill herself but did she have to kill the kids as well?

– So it was exciting, said Makiyo with a smile.

This was said with no irony at all. The smile held only his pleasure at the memory. It had been a truly exciting time and this Makiyo was acknowledging. There was no resentment of the fact that he had nearly lost his life. And it wasn't simplemindedness that made him act like this. It was simple courage.

Still smiling, he turned to look out of the window again as our journey continued—a grove of trees, a culvert, a distant town hazy in the late afternoon sun.

– Yes, I had a good childhood. And now my father is back from Shikoku, staying with my mother—she's pretty ill now. And all those ten years of running, being a newspaper boy, that made my legs good and strong. So my childhood taught me a lot. I had a good one. I guess I was lucky.

And I looked at this brave twenty-four-year-old sitting there, the landscape unrolling behind him, and I envied him this ability to take an experience and accept it and see what was good in it.

And to refuse that need for a sense of being wronged which so many of us hide behind.

Koichiro Arai

One Sunday I received a telephone call. In country Japanese, the woman said she was Ichiro's mother and wanted to see me.

We met by the bronze dog in Shibuya where everyone meets. I recognized her by her strong, square face—just like her son's. She bowed, saying she had long wanted to meet me to express her appreciation for everything I had done for him. And now she was going to be rude enough to ask for yet another favor. Seated opposite her in a coffee shop, I wondered what it could be, but all she said was that she would like me to visit her house.

In due course, I took the long train ride out to the suburbs of Musashi and was met by a stranger with a car, an uncle, and taken to a small three-room house in the midst of paddy fields. There I found Ichiro's mother dressed in kimono and haori, but no Ichiro.

– Oh, she said, did I forget to mention it? He's in Kyushu right now. At his father's grave. It's been twenty-one years since he died.

While Ichiro was placing flowers on his father's grave, I gave his mother the chrysanthemums I'd brought.

– I haven't seen Ichiro for ages, I said.

– Well, people grow apart, she observed: But I'll always be grateful for what you did for him. She looked at me, and something seemed to bother her: I can see that you're not comfortable, she said, looking me up and down, eyes stopping at my trousers. Tatami ruins pants, she said: You ought to be wearing a kimono. Stand up.

I did so and she took off my coat, then opened a wardrobe, removed a kimono, and held it out for me as though she were my wife. Telling me to take off my trousers, she helped me into it and tied the obi.

– There, she said, arranging the tassles on the haori, while the little white dog chained up in the yard stared at me and began to bark.

– Shut up, she said, then: The tabi. Wifelike, on her knees, she slipped them onto my feet and sat back, appraising me.

– There, she said, isn't that better?

After I said that it was, she announced that she needed my advice. And since I was sitting there dressed as her husband, it only seemed natural that I should listen.

– Again, I want to thank you for all that you did for Ichiro.

It appeared that owing to my influence he had not only stopped smoking and drinking, he had also stopped running after bad girls. She was grateful.

– You set him such a good example I was wondering if, as a mother, I could ask for one more thing. I know I shouldn't, but I will, anyway.

She put down her tea and looked me squarely in the face: My youngest son, Koichiro, is a problem. Oh, he goes to school, is graduating this month as a matter of fact—but he smokes and drinks and runs around with bad people. I was hoping you could maybe take an interest in him.

I looked at her, surprise probably showing.

– No, no. I managed to put him through school myself, so I don't mean money. Nothing like that. I just want him to benefit from your good influence.

I looked hard at her but could detect nothing other than a mother's concern. Still, I decided to refuse, despite the fact that I was sitting there like a packaged parent, dressed up in the bad lad's father's kimono, with his mother pressing in such a wifelike manner. I didn't want to be some young tough's father and was already shaking my head, with every intention of then getting out of her kimono, her house, her life, when she turned and said: Oh, here he is now.

The open shoji held the dark outline of someone haloed by a rim of sunlight. Koichiro—a big, square eighteen, showing the big, scarred knuckles of a karate jock as he bowed on the tatami; raising his head, his thick eyebrows straight, his eyes appraising; then sitting up, solid, Kyushu, serious as a samurai, his mouth a firm line.

Those direct eyes, his mother's, stared at the pale-skinned stranger in his father's clothes. Had his mother told him that his new parent would be calling, I wondered. He regarded me with polite suspicion.

As though we were meeting for a more common form of engagement, Koichiro's mother discreetly went out to make some tea, leaving the young people together to get to know each other.

– Do I look like your father? I asked.

– No, you're American.

– I'm a friend of your brother's.

– I know.

– Your mother wants me to be your new father.

– She does? Then: How about you? He gave me his first smile, the sunlight bright behind him. Square white teeth, creases around his young eyes. Shifting, getting off his knees into an easier position, muscles apparent.

I stared, then swallowed and asked: Would you like me to be that?

– Well, he said, giving that crooked smile I was to know so well: It would be one way out of this place.

His mother came back with the tea.

– Making friends? she asked with that hopeful cheerfulness which gobetweens display. All of a sudden, she was in full obeisance on the mats in front of me: *Yoroshiku onegai ittashimasu*, she said, a phrase used only when making the most serious request.

Feeling embarrassed, I looked at Koichiro and was greeted with the grin of a youngster taking the side of one parent against the other.

His mother soon sat up, self-conscious, pleased, and, turning to the boy, said: It suits him, doesn't it?—Father's kimono. This was followed by a little nod which meant: there, that's fixed now. She then called in the uncle, who took a snapshot or two while the puzzled dog barked.

Koichiro came to call. He had the air of someone appearing on the first day of a new job. I, on my side, felt like a person having his first date. Perhaps out of concern that we might not have enough to talk about, he had brought with him a number of snapshots, all of himself. These he laid out on the table as though playing patience.

There he was at school. School was Takushoku, an institution specializing in traditional sports and right-wing student activities. Here he was in kimono, high geta on his feet, student cap set belligerently on top. Here he was in karate gear, taking a proper stand, fist thrust out. And here, fists again doubled to indicate determination, on the rugby field, knees scabbed, shorts bunched at the crotch.

Having thus modestly displayed himself, he started talking about his future. Koichiro, unlike his older brother, was talkative. He wanted to be a professional sportsman. He was pretty good, he told me, maybe he could coach eventually. Good money in professional sports. Also—perhaps in deference to me—he wanted to learn English.

I said I could help with the latter but I thought his mother probably wanted him to get some steadier profession—maybe an office job with a big company.

– No, no way, said Koichiro. Then: You aren't Japanese so you don't know what it's like.

– What is it like?

– Smiling when you don't want to, agreeing when you disagree, being nice to people you don't like, spending your life in some dumb business.

Maybe he expected me to point out the advantages of a secure salary, to say that you had to find a way somehow to live in society. But I didn't — this really wasn't the life for him. So I said: You're right.

Koichiro turned to me with that bright, inquiring look he had when he was really interested. I felt, absurdly, as though I had made a good impression on my first day at school.

Then, smiling from under those straight eyebrows, he stood up and said: I'm all sweaty from practice. Could I have a bath?

How much did he know, I wondered. His eyes told me nothing. His brother . . . his mother . . . ? No, it was simple: he was a boy in need of a bath. And a bath was in fact ready, just in case I saw an opportunity to suggest one myself. But Koichiro, as I was soon to discover, was ahead of me in most things.

He moved about my room as though he had always lived there, shedding his clothes, finally standing before me with nothing but a slash of sun across him.

– Got a towel?

I obediently went and got one. Then he looked at me and said: Aren't you going to come in too? I'll scrub your back.

He then turned and walked toward the bathroom, the floor shaking slightly under his feet, and I followed.

Little by little Koichiro moved in. His geta were now in my shoe cup-

216

board, his karate gear hung by its strap next to my good gray suit.

He went to practice every day and came back home, as though from a job, knuckles red, to sit on the tatami, do zazen, then after dinner gravely make us a cup of macha, his version of the tea ceremony.

Sometimes he went to Yasukuni Shrine, where the war dead were. He liked it there, he said. It was holy. He thought the Emperor was holy, too. We talked, though we didn't often agree, and slowly areas we didn't talk about spread like mildew.

One such subject was his unwillingness to find a job. Every interview he went to gave him some reason to find the position unattractive. It was like those arranged meetings where the boy always turns the girl down. In addition, he still smoked and drank and, I suspected, continued to frequent the people his mother disapproved of. My influence was not being as beneficial as she had hoped.

– Are these people gangsters? I asked.

– Not really, was all he would say.

Though I learned little about them, I wondered if they weren't learning something about me. There was the matter of money, for example: his allowance, it was called, established to fit the parental role I had unwisely assumed. He would kneel politely in front of me to ask for it.

– But you just got it a few days ago.

On his knees, giving his famous crooked smile, he'd say: But I need it now—next week's. It's not much anyway.

Sometimes the charade of the weekly allowance would be dropped. He would come home, fling off his clothes, wander around naked, say he was going to take a bath but not take one till afterward, then try to touch me for a bit more.

– Look, Koichiro, this isn't going to work. Your mother asked me to look after you, not keep you.

– It's the same thing. You're my father.

– I am not.

– What are you, then? He had an ugly way of thrusting out his lower lip when crossed.

– Does the money go to them? I wondered.

– Who's them? he asked.

And so, day by day, our differences grew. Autumn came, then winter.

He would sit morosely in the pool of warmth seeping from the gas heater. Then, still in his student uniform—a delinquent student—he would fling himself out of the house and leave me sleepless.

One day my trepidation multiplied when he slyly opened his uniform jacket to show me a long, cloth-wrapped object which he had stuck in his belt.

– Know what this is? he asked. It was a knife, plain wooden handle in a wooden sheath, the kind they kill themselves with in samurai movies but larger.

– That's a fish knife, I answered, determined to remain unruffled.

– Kind of. Friend gave it to me. To protect myself.

– Against whom?

– Oh, people.

He took off his pants to look at a scabbed knee, scratched his balls, said he was sleepy.

Unimpressed though I pretended to be, I was now beginning to be frightened. Not so much of Koichiro—who was just a big boy—but rather of his unknown friends and what seemed to be their increasing demands for further funding. My imagination slowly enlarged on it: anonymous phone calls, shattered windows, midnight invasions, blood on the tatami.

One freezing, sunless winter day I called up his mother, told her it wasn't working out, that her youngest was a gangboy. Ah, she said, just as she had feared. And so I was handing him back to her. It sounded like a failed business deal, which in a way it was. Well, no, that wasn't possible, she said. She wouldn't have him in the house.

– But he's your son.

– No, he's ours.

At that point the unwanted child walked in, so I hung up.

Then one snowy February day I threw him out. Not physically; he was much the stronger of us two. No, I took advantage of his manners—made him feel he couldn't stay where he was no longer welcome.

In the hallway, carrying his karate gear, he bowed deeply and thanked me in true gang fashion—as seen in the movies—for having taken care of him. Then he left me alone in the frigid house to dwell on thoughts of snarling phone calls, midnight bangings on the door, sharp samurai knives.

None of this occurred. He did, however, send long, self-justifying letters, all carefully written out in roman letters, the only form of Japanese I can read. But since his prose was formal and he did not know how to transcribe it properly, these letters found me reading things into them. I will tell your people about you. Or, perhaps: I was telling people about him. Or, maybe: people were telling him something about me. The ambiguities worried me, made the unknown darker still. But then the letters stopped coming altogether.

I would lie awake as the nights slowly grew warmer. I would gaze at the square sheet, whitened by the moon, remembering when it had held his naked, sprawled-out, sleeping body.

I missed him, wanted him back, and yet I started at every nocturnal sound in dread that it was him. I had made an important discovery: it is possible to be afraid of what you love.

Ten years later. A telephone call. I recognized the voice immediately, but now with no damp palms, no lifting of the heart.

It had been a long time, he said. It was wrong of him not to have kept in touch but he hoped I was well. The manner was polite, for Koichiro had always been a polite boy. And, though he knew it was impolite to ask, would it be possible to see me? I, also a polite boy, refrained from saying that I no longer had any money for him, but, remembering the knife, suggested a crowded place for us to meet—in front of the Wako windows in the Ginza, a popular rendezvous.

He was right on time. No more keeping me waiting hours while the dinner got cold. Just as the clock had finished chiming he stood there in the winter sun. A blue businessman's suit, white shirt, quiet tie, company badge discreet in one lapel.

Older now, small wrinkles no longer the creases of an adolescent's smile. And something tamed about him. Over our coffee, it all came out, smooth as a school report: he now worked for the Tobacco Monopoly Board, not a bad job, and—smile—he still smoked. The best part, though, was that he was now manager of the company baseball team.

Played Gifu Tobacco Products last week and won. Also, his boss had introduced him to this girl and they had married and as a matter of fact she was expecting their first child even as he spoke.

He sat before me, reformed. Any lingering fears I may have had now shrank, ashamed of themselves, and vanished. Thinking as a parent, I remembered his mother and said that I imagined she was happy.

He nodded. She was, but now she had this high blood pressure. Then, reminded that his other parent sat facing him, he straightened his shoulders and bowed over his coffee.

– Thank you for everything you did for me. I owe you a real debt of gratitude.

– You mean it worked? I straightened you out?

He smiled, as though at his own formality, then said: I mean it.

– I thought I'd failed.

– Well, later I thought a lot about it, our life together. You tried to be good. I was still a kid.

Now he was grown-up, a member of society—and I realized that I had already begun regretting the disappearance of the dangerous youth.

– You were a handful, I said: I was even afraid of you.

– I wanted you to be.

– Was it only money, then?

He looked into his cup, as if embarrassed. Then, apparently deciding to be responsible, he looked at me and said: No, I just wanted more than you gave me. I was disappointed in you. I wanted you to really see, well, all of me.

I remembered the square of moonlight with a body in it, a fine body, but just a body.

– I'd figured it out for myself, he continued. Anyone could have. Except my mother. But I saw it, well, as kind of a beginning. And for you it was the end. That was all there was. So finally I got mad at you. And then I saw you were scared of me. I liked that, and even stole that dumb knife to frighten you more. And you thought I'd joined a gang and I let you think it.

He looked down, then raised his eyes: There's no apologizing for what I did. You ought to have told my mother.

– I did. She didn't want you back.

He smiled and looked at his hands. The knuckles were big—karate.

– You didn't talk with my brother about me?

– Ichiro? No, I didn't.

– Why? He would have straightened me out.

– I was embarrassed, I said. And as I spoke I felt my face redden. Ichiro, so kind, so good, so unexciting.

Koichiro gave me his bright, inquiring glance: I was embarrassed too, he said.

But this talk of embarrassment had now managed to embarrass both of us and soon he was buttoning his blue jacket, becoming as formal as he used to get when he made his cup of ceremonial tea.

– So I just wanted to see you again and tell you how much I appreciate what you did for me.

I knew what he was feeling. He wanted to settle accounts. Not with me—with himself. Then he needn't feel as though he had been ungrateful or bad or misunderstood. And after saying this, he gave a little nod which meant: there, that's fixed now.

– No, no, that's mine, he said, picking up the bill. It was the first time I had seen him pay for something on his own.

– Keep in touch, I said.

Then we stood and looked at each other, this company man and me.

– And let me know about the child.

I had almost offered to be its godfather but decided that this wouldn't be tactful. So I said: Name it after me. That wasn't tactful either but it allowed Koichiro to give me his wonderful smile one last time before he turned away into the Ginza crowds and I saw his shoulders slope like everybody else's.

Noboru Tanaka

An old man came once a week to the Underwear Snack. He came every Sunday at ten in the evening, drank a cup of Nescafé, smoked several Kents, then slipped his cigarettes and lighter back into his kimono sleeve, and was gone by eleven. They called him the old man. The manager of the place said that he was even older than he looked, had a lot of money, wanted to die.

That he wanted to die impressed none of the girls. No one that age would want to live on. That he had money impressed them all at first. Particularly Miki. She sat on his kimonoed lap and wriggled her hips while he, pleased and embarrassed as a boy, was careful to blow his smoke elsewhere. When he rested his old hand on her young rump she lightly slapped his face.

Actually, when one was that old it took a hard slap to make you feel anything, was Miki's opinion. The skin had grown that thick. Still, he was cute.

The other two girls agreed. He was cute as a little boy, always so carefully dressed in his kimono, shaved, hair parted, sitting there so straight, like a big doll, always smiling.

He wanted to die while he's doing it, Miki would say—not that he could, she added. Still, he wanted to have his eyes full of flesh when he finally closed them. Sex, after all, no matter what else you might say about it, was alive. It was, let's face it, the opposite of death. That was why he turned up every week. The others nodded, but one said that he was, well, kind of repulsive too.

Yet he made no demands. Understanding this, the girls made offers. Miki revealed a breast to a gaze greedy as a child's. When he nuzzled her, she laughed and called him her baby, her old, hungry baby.

Little by little his story became known. His life had been ordinary—an ordinary husband, ordinary father. Then his wife had left him or else died, and the children, all grown up, had scattered. And this extraordinary thing had happened to him: he didn't die; instead, he grew older and older. But his distinction was also his calamity. He had no friends, everyone he had known having long since turned to ashes. Also, he became ill. Sometimes he turned pale and put his hand on his carefully tied sash. Cancer—they were certain it was cancer.

Imagine that, the girls would say. He was just like everyone else and then he got old and became a pervert. But, of course, everyone old was kinky. All they could do was finger and lick, and they liked being slapped, as though it made them feel younger. Or worse.

Worse was what they did with each other. Everyone knew that schoolboys messed around. Well, when you were really getting on, it all came back again. One of Miki's boy friends told her that he had once seen two old fogies handling each other in a toilet. He said it disgusted him. It didn't disgust her; it seemed natural that when you got very old you might turn queer again.

Her old man, however, was still interested in women. Yet this interest seemed detached. Never once did the blunt, veined hands stray. A palm on Miki's bottom—that was as far as it went. If it went further it was because she herself had moved his hand.

Since he demanded no attention, he created it. He became over the months a mascot. On Sundays around ten the girls began to wonder if their old man was coming or not. When he had first appeared there was a show of distaste at the idea of doing anything other than tolerating him; but now the girls laughed and dared each other to poke around under that fine kimono. One evening Miki did just that. He smiled throughout it, as though it was he who was tolerating her.

Down there, she later reported, he was just like anyone else, not shriveled away to nothing at all. Admittedly, it hadn't moved, but it had been warm. The other two shook their heads and said they just hoped he wouldn't die in this place, implying that they hoped he would.

Then one night Miki insisted on going home with him. She said it was because of the money, because he might be persuaded to change his will. No one believed her. She was interested in him. They all were.

They all had fathers, living or dead; they respected age, respected anyone who had endured this long. He was a survivor, from war, from earthquake, from history itself. He had experienced what they could only guess at. Every line on his face spoke for itself. Miki said she did it for the money. She didn't.

Later she said it was like lying down with a skeleton. That was what they had done—lain down. She had put his hand on her and he had stroked her. Then he had cried, but he was so dry that no tears came. This had affected her. A good man come to this, she moralized. The others laughed and said that if nothing else happened it was her fault, failing to excite him like that.

Going back with him to his bare little room eventually became a ritual. She always went home with the mascot on Sundays. Side by side they lay until the early morning. Then he slowly made ordinary green tea for her after they had sat up. She received no money. It was restful, she said, companionable too, though they never talked.

He was refined, she said. Younger men want to overcome you; a bit older and they want to be overcome; but when you get that old, just a body next to yours is enough. He asked for so little because that little had become enough. Miki admired him.

At first the other girls asked intimate questions: did he use his mouth down there; did he ever get hard; could he still pee? Later, they came to wonder what he was thinking about, lying there with a girl more than half a century younger than he was. What was he feeling? They decided that he was regretting, not life, for he had already lived, but the loneliness of death.

When he came in, neat, hair parted, put his cigarettes and lighter on the bar, drank his cup of instant coffee, they treated him with deference and, finally, with reverence. At first they had lighted his cigarettes with some disdain. Now they crouched below him to do so. They had changed.

He never changed. From the first day to the last, two whole years of Sundays, he never changed. He smiled, savored his tobacco, his coffee, the usually proffered breast.

He ought to die with dignity, they all thought. He shouldn't be kept alive with tubes and expensive and noisy machines. He should be allowed his own integrity—as a reward for having lived so long, for now behaving so well. None of them ever thought he might kill himself.

But that is what he did. He hanged himself with his fine sash. It was in the newspaper, a small column on a back page. They called him an aged recluse, Noboru Tanaka, age ninety-two, unemployed. And he was not, it turned out, rich at all. Miki thus received nothing. Though she feigned disappointment, it was clear that she had never expected anything.

For a number of Sundays afterward there was much talk of him at the Underwear Snack. Not why he had done it. They thought they knew why—look how old he was, after all. No, they wondered what he had felt, at the very last. Pleasure, relief, gratitude? No one believed it was despair—not in someone as well behaved as he had been.

Then they stopped talking about it. Still, occasionally, even if it were not Sunday, one of them would recall that gentle way he had of blinking, like an infant just awakened, or that small cough, which sounded as if he were clearing his throat to speak, though he rarely spoke.

Hanako Watanabé

Down the subway stairs hurried the tofu man's wife, her face serious, intent. She had perhaps heard the downtown train pull in—bells, shouts, whistles—and was hurrying to make it.

In this station, mine for many years now, there is a long flight of stairs leading to the lower level where the downtown train passes. I, coming from uptown on my way home, had just got out of the car and was walking along the platform when I saw Mrs. Watanabé hurrying down.

Seeing the train about to draw out, she broke into a run. But the doors were closing, the whistle was blown, the train began to move.

Mrs. Watanabé stopped short in front of the closed doors now sliding past and smiled. At a moment when we of the West would have turned our mouths down, she turned hers up. It was not an ironic grimace, common enough, nor was it mock despair for the benefit of those looking on. The smile was innocent and natural enough to seem instinctive.

But what kind of instinct could create this expression of delight, I wondered. And what assumptions must lie behind it? This was not the first such smile I had seen. I saw it daily, on the faces of those apparently pleased to have missed the train. The tofu man's wife was simply the latest in a long line of disappointed grinners.

For surely, I thought, disappointment must be the paramount emotion attending this experience. To then smile was, by my standards, unnatural. What person in his or her proper senses would register pleasure at the prospect of inconvenience?

Well, I reasoned, standing there, pretending to read a poster, it would have to be someone who entertained priorities higher than personal convenience, higher than missing a subway train.

I tried to fit things together. The smile that informed the face of the racing Mrs. Watanabé, and all those other hundreds and thousands I had observed over the years, began to develop only when it seemed obvious that the train would not, after all, be caught. This expression was not then the result of any hope that one might, after all, be on time.

Indeed, as I had seen often enough, if there was time and no uncertainty, the expression was the ordinary, blank subway face, the same the world over. Only when hope was slipping away did the smile blossom.

Confronted with the closed subway doors, the train already in motion, the smile was wide and forbearing, with only a trace of self-consciousness or embarrassment. It was as if the small fact of having missed the subway was already subsumed into the many other uncertainties of life.

Moreover, if Mrs. Watanabé had said anything at that point (I was still pretending to examine the poster and she had not yet seen me), it would probably have been: *Shikata ga nai*—It can't be helped. This comment is heard at least a million times a day on these islands. It is to Japan as "Have a nice day" is to America—something one says without thinking, says even when *shikata ga aru*, when it *can* be helped.

Yet here perhaps, I decided next, lay a clue to these higher priorities. For behind it was the idea (common enough here but revolutionary-sounding where I come from) that acceptance ranks over irritation, that accord is more important than discord, that the positive is more valuable than the negative.

This is to American ears an astonishing assumption. And its reverberations linger on, suggesting thoughts unwelcome: that the communal is more important than the individual, for example. Nevertheless, it is just such notions surely that produced the smile at the foot of the subway stairs.

Still standing there, I tried to imagine the system of social training that was responsible for this phenomenon: whole centuries of it during which all the Mrs. Watanabés and their husbands and children were taught that a display of personal irritation or indignation was not, by and large, socially productive. Rather, as a member of the social body, one ought to uphold its standards. The personal (by definition, often negative) reaction should be subdued, so that the coherent whole could continue in an atmosphere of harmony.

And I also thought how easy to control these generations consequently were, and are. With a populace who believed this, the process of ruling was considerably simplified. Brainwashing, oppression, totalitarianism—

these terms occurred to me, a person really interested only in his *own* atmosphere of harmony, one devoid of any larger social implications.

But I felt sure there were larger implications. It was certainly true that this kind of self-abnegation in the face of personal disappointment can be politically manipulated; it can also result in quite mindless acceptance of a social norm. But there was something else, something of deeper value.

So I turned again to look at Mrs. Watanabé. Though she had long ceased smiling and was staring off into space with that universal subway face, I remembered the form her smile had taken. Yes, it certainly suggested forbearance . . . but also—for want of any better words—a kind of affirmation.

The poster I'd been staring at reminded one not to leave one's umbrella on the subway. This was a pragmatic race, intensely so. It was one that believed in the "rightness" of things, and rejoiced in it. It saw that reality, neither malign nor benign, is all we have; that what *is* exists quite outside the limitations of our personal convenience; and this should be accepted, made much of.

The more I thought about it the more familiar the idea became. I considered the attitude of the haiku master; the attitude of my favorite film director, Ozu. I thought of what the *suiboku* brush-and-ink master puts in and leaves out, and how the true Zen *roshi* approaches the real and instant now. In all these examples that now came flooding to my mind a personal predilection is sacrificed (too strong a term?) in the interests of something else. And that is the appreciation of reality. Not a higher one, merely reality itself; a small celebration of its qualities. It is the attitude of the older Japanese who looks in the mirror, sees one more gray hair, one more wrinkle, and is pleased because things are going as they must. And things going this way are fitting, proper—in a word, good.

I glanced at Mrs. Watanabé waiting for her train. Would she, I wondered—she of the beautiful, indulgent smile—also grin at her wrinkles and gray hairs, affirming the impermanence of life? It seemed unlikely as she stood there rocking slightly in her neat housedress, staring ahead. Yet it didn't seem impossible, for I remembered her expression, common but mysterious, when she realized she would miss her train. I knew that what her smile represented had contributed to and been exploited by centuries of feudal rule; at the same time, I saw in it a token of another scale of values, an affirmation that went far beyond the ordinary concern with positive and negative.

At which point Mrs. Watanabé first noticed my own universal subway face and gave me a friendly smile: *Ara*, is that you, Mr. Donald? Going downtown?

– No, I just got off.

– That was ten minutes ago—just missed it myself. What have you been doing?

– Oh . . . nothing much, just standing around.

– At your age, she said with a smile: Me, I'm off to my sister's for the afternoon. Husband's looking after the shop. And about time, too.

She went on in this fashion until the subway train arrived and she got in. Then I climbed the stairs, still thinking. Whatever its historical associations, I couldn't but approve of that smile of Mrs. Watanabé's, find it admirable in its implications, and envy her its unthinking, assured possession.

H.I.M. Michiko

I stood before her, the Empress of Japan, and congratulated her on her nice new palace. This was all I could think of saying and, adroitly, like a good hostess mindful of her guests, she asked me where I lived. Then, with that distant interest which is apparently common to royalty: Ah, *shitamachi*, old Tokyo. As in the films of Ozu.

– Have you seen many of them? I wondered.

– Well, *Tokyo Story* certainly, she replied, adding that, although they had a screening room in the Imperial Household office, they didn't go there much, so they made do with video cassettes.

It was kind of her to have mentioned Ozu. It showed that she knew why I was there: I had received an official award, and an audience at the palace was one of the perks. Not only would we meet the royals, we would see where they lived.

We were even limousined the long away around, through the Sakashishitamon, so we could see more of the grounds. This I had much wanted to do. After fifty years of looking at them from the public side of the moat, seeing the tops of trees and the roofs of distant buildings, I wanted to see them for myself.

Passing through various checkpoints and the outer gates, which bristled with guards, we were soon inside the inner moat and driving through parklike gardens, then down what looked like a country road on either side of which were further guard boxes, walls, and behind them the virgin forest that lies at the heart of this tract of land. I had heard that rabbits, badgers, and foxes still lived here, in the center of Tokyo.

The cars pulled up in front of what looked like one of the grander wedding halls. This was the new palace, with chamberlains waiting. After a good deal of bowing, we were ushered into a series of rooms, all decorated in a modified imperial style. It was a style set in the Meiji period and hence Victorian, with plush-covered sofas and wainscoting and coffered ceilings. Since the palace was built in 1993 and not 1893, however, there are no sofas and the plush has turned into brocade. Still, the imposing comfort of Windsor is there.

A senior chamberlain introduced himself and with great patience explained how our audience would proceed. He had a piece of paper with circles drawn on it and arrows showing where everyone should stand, how everyone should move. My role was but a modest one. I was second from the right and would simply bob forth and back. The president of the foundation responsible for giving our awards had a more difficult part to play: he was choreographed to move forward, then circle back around the recipients about to be introduced, before coming to a stop on our right.

We all then lined up in another room. This one owed more to Shinto than to Victoria. It was paneled in cedar and had hanging curtains, as in Ise, and though the furniture was Western—blonde wood enclosing gold brocade—it still looked ecclesiastical.

Outside the wide windows stretched the gardens and beyond them the forest. It was like being on a country estate far away from any city, except that over the trees I could see the square-cut top of the Dai-Ichi Building, which half a century before had been the headquarters of the Allied Occupation forces. It was as though General MacArthur were still peering over the hedge.

As the chamberlains bustled about, I was struck by the resemblance of the palace and its staff to a really expensive *ryotei*, a Japanese restaurant which costs so much that absolutely nothing must go wrong. There were the same purposeful scurryings, the same watchful glances. Then someone solemnly announced: They are coming.

We all stood straight and in they walked, the Emperor in a black suit and what looked like a school tie, the Empress in a cream-colored kimono with a matching obi. They took their places in front of us, just as the diagram had indicated, and we looked at each other.

Both of them were half smiling, their expression solicitous, as though they were about to ask us if we felt all right, if we had enough money to get home. Despite their obvious goodwill, however, they were grave—surprisingly so. One did not, of course, expect laughter and tossed heads, but this gravity was so deep that I was reminded of the way people behave at funerals. Gravity can resemble sadness, and that of their imperial majesties certainly did. The graciousness was slightly mournful, like flowers slowly fading. And yet behind all this, I also saw something resembling curiosity and realized that we represented to them not only duty but, perhaps, diversion.

Though I had been anxious not only about what to say but how to say it—my grasp of *keigo* (formal Japanese) being completely insecure—the Emperor, with the air of a man used to coping with such minor problems, put out his hand, thus indicating that the interview should continue in a foreign manner; and, sure enough, he congratulated me in English.

It then being my turn to speak, I asked him if there were any animals in the forest. Yes, he believed so. Some rabbits—yes, as a child he had seen some rabbits.

Properly briefed, he spoke next about films. He was fond of Kurosawa, apparently, and remembered seeing Ozu once when the latter had been given some imperial award. Yes, *Tokyo Story*, he said, with a sort of distant relish.

The Emperor had been going up one half of our line and the Empress coming down the other. Now they met, and with an adroitness one doesn't usually see off a dance floor they pivoted around each other, and she stood before me.

– Yes, *Tokyo Story*, she repeated.

Her husband had looked straight at me in that affable yet detached manner I had noticed before only in the very rich, but her gaze was focused somewhere in front of me and slightly below, as though she were staring at my necktie. Her voice was soft, her English London-accented.

– And I feel, she said, that I ought to—no, *want* to—take an interest in younger directors and find out what they are doing.

I mentioned some recent films. Oh, I wish I could see them, she said, so I promised to send her a few cassettes.

After our little talk, I thought about her life. They were both sequestered here, and besides their duties there must have been little for them to do. Royalty is in this way held captive—displayed and then put back in the box. The temptation to escape must be strong. I remembered the princess in *Roman Holiday* and her escapade; but there had been no escape for Michiko. I remembered pictures of her I had seen when she was young; now she was frail, gracious, tentative, keeping her eyes fixed on my necktie. I resolved to send her all the cassettes I could find.

Later, talking to a chamberlain, I mentioned what I had promised to do and wondered how to do it.

– What a good idea. Just send them to me and I'll make sure she gets them.

He gave me his card and I discovered that the Imperial Palace had an address. It is: Imperial Palace, 1-1 Chiyoda, Chiyoda-ku, Tokyo 100.

Our audience had been scheduled to last thirty minutes and, exactly as arranged, amid gracious smiles and bowing heads, their imperial highnesses glided from the room. Glided—for their gait was also practiced. It was this that made me suddenly aware of a word that had been waiting there during the entire session and now came to mind: ghosts. Quite apart from the otherworldly aspect of all royalty and the sacerdotal roles these particular members of it are obliged to play, I saw a gentleness and sadness which went with a resignation so complete that it was as though life were already over.

After they had left there was a sudden lightness, and we realized we had felt oppressed. There was some laughter, much rubbing of hands, and a chamberlain, having overheard and mistaken my interests, told me all about the badger they had found in the imperial pantry.

As our limousine rolled smoothly over the gravel and out into Tokyo, I wondered whether *Okaeri*, the film I wanted to send first, was such a good choice. It is about this lonely and unhappy wife who develops schizophrenia. I remembered that when the Empress was recently attacked by the scurrilous press (claiming that she keeps the servants up after hours, demands food at night, is bossy), she responded by turning mute —did not speak for weeks.

And back at home again, looking out over the city toward the palace, I wondered whether that soft glint of curiosity had been satisfied or whether we too had disappointed her.

LITERATURE

ABE, Kobo　安部公房
The Box Man　箱男　4-8053-0395-6
The Face of Another　他人の顔　4-8053-0120-1
Inter Ice Age 4　第四間氷期　4-8053-0268-2
Secret Rendezvous　密会　4-8053-0472-3
The Woman in the Dunes　砂の女　4-8053-0207-0

AKUTAGAWA, Ryunosuke　芥川龍之介
Japanese Short Stories　芥川龍之介短編集　4-8053-0464-2
Kappa　河童　0-8048-3251-X
Rashomon and Other Stories　羅生門　0-8048-1457-0

ATODA, Takashi　阿刀田高
The Square Persimmon and Other Stories　四角い柿　0-8048-1644-1

DAZAI, Osamu　太宰治
Crackling Mountain and Other Stories　太宰治短編集　0-8048-3342-7
No Longer Human　人間失格　4-8053-0756-0
The Setting Sun　斜陽　4-8053-0672-6

EDOGAWA, Rampo　江戸川乱歩
Japanese Tales of Mystery & Imagination　乱歩短編集　0-8048-0319-6

ENDO, Shusaku　遠藤周作
Deep River　深い河　0-8048-2013-9
The Final Martyrs　最後の殉教者　4-8053-0625-4
Foreign Studies　留学　0-8048-1626-3
The Golden Country　黄金の国　0-8048-3337-0
A Life of Jesus　イエスの生涯　4-8053-0668-8
Scandal　スキャンダル　0-8048-1558-5
Stained Glass Elegies　短編集　4-8053-0624-6
The Sea and Poison　海と毒薬　4-8053-0330-1
Volcano　火山　4-8053-0664-5
When I Whistle　口笛を吹くとき　4-8053-0627-0
Wonderful Fool　おバカさん　4-8053-0376-X